All of nature dances....

-Sir John Davies, Orchestra

Copyright 2016
The Shakespeare Oxford Fellowship
Designed in Baltimore, MD
Online ISSN: 2157-6793
Print ISSN: 2157-6785

This final 2016 volume VII of *Brief Chronicles*, in keeping with our tradition, was set in **Chaparral Pro**. Our ornament selection continues to be inspired not only by early modern semiotics, but by the generosity of contemporary designers. We've been sneaking in glyphs of **Satanus Humanum Salvator, BD Renaissance, DeiGratia** and **EileenCaps** on the sly — and in this issue, suitably, **Papyrus**. All these, in addition to our original lineup of Rob Anderson's **Flight of the Dragon** Celtic Knot Caps, and T. Olsson's 1993 **Ornament Scrolls,** available for free download from **typOasis,** have finally furnished an inviting opportunity to apply some of the theoretical principles discussed by our more disting- uished con- tributors.

General Editor: **Roger Stritmatter, PhD,** Coppin State University
Managing Editor: **Michael Delahoyde, PhD,** Washington State University

Editorial Board:

Carole Chaski, PhD, Institute for Linguistic Evidence
Ren Draya, PhD, Blackburn College
Sky Gilbert, PhD, University of Guelph, Canada
Geoffrey M. Hodgson, PhD, University of Hertfordshire, United Kingdom
Mike Hyde, PhD, English, Tufts University
Felicia Hardison Londré, PhD, University of Missouri, Kansas City
Donald Ostrowski, PhD, Harvard University
Tom Regnier, JD, LLM, University of Miami School of Law
Don Rubin, Professor, York University
Sarah Smith, PhD, Harvard University
Richard Waugaman, MD, Georgetown University of Medicine and Washington Psychoanalytic Institute

Copy Editor: **Alex McNeil, JD,** Boston College

Contributor Biographies

Elke Brackmann studied English and German at the University of Innsbruck. Being a grammar school teacher in Innsbruck and later Wuppertal for years, she has repeatedly performed Shakespeare plays both with A-level students and younger ones. She embraced the Oxfordian cause in her fifties and, together with Robert Detobel, is working on the project "A Biographical Approach to the Sonnets" for EFL-Students. At present she is also co-chair of the *Neue Shakespeare-Gesellschaft* (www.Shakespeare-today.de), with Hanno Wember.

Robert Detobel is a translator and scholar based in Frankfurt, Germany. He is co-editor (with Dr. Uwe Laugwitz) of the *Neues Shakspeare-speare Journal*, published annually in Germany since 1997. Author of the book, *Wie aus William Shaxsper William Shakespeare wurde* (*How William Shaxsper became William Shakespeare*) (2005), Detobel has appeared in *The Elizabethan Review* and *The Oxfordian*, among other scholarly publications. Together with the late K.C. Ligon, he is co-author of the book *Shakespeare and The Concealed Poet* (2010). This is his third appearance in *Brief Chronicles*.

Kevin Gilvary obtained his BA and MA in Classics and later his MA in Applied Linguistics from the University of Southampton, UK. He has taught at UBC in Vancouver, BC, Canada, at Markham College, Lima, Peru, and for twenty years at Barton Peveril College, Hampshire, UK. He was first alerted to the Authorship Question by inquisitive students and has been a member of the De Vere Society for fifteen years, and recently served as DVS chairman. He has contributed articles to *Great Oxford* (2004) and edited *Dating Shakespeare's Plays* (2010) for which he was awarded the prize of Oxfordian of the Year at a joint SF/SOS meeting in 2011. In 2015 he obtained his doctorate from Brunel University London with the thesis "Shakespearean Biografiction: How modern biographers rely on context, conjecture and inference to construct a life of the nBarnod."

Richard Malim is a retired English lawyer with over twenty-five years interest and study of the Authorship Question. In 2003 he became secretary of the De Vere Society (www.deveresociety), and was the editor of *Great Oxford: Essays on the Life and Work of Edward de Vere, 17th Earl of Oxford (2004)*, a collection of essays to commemorate the 400th anniversary of the death of Oxford. In 2011 he published *The Earl of Oxford and the Making of "Shakespeare": The Literary Life of Edward de Vere in Context,* a book that seeks to contextualize de Vere's life in the context of the history and development of English Literature. The De Vere Society is kind enough to publish an annual cumulative supplement on its website.

Carolyn Morris holds a Bachelor of Science degree in Medical Technology. She has been an Oxfordian since 1989, and for the past five years has studied the satires of the late 1590s, focusing on Joseph Hall's *Virgidemiarum* (1599). In 2013, she published an article in *The Oxfordian*, "Did Joseph Hall and Ben Jonson Identify Oxford as Shakespeare?" She has been a Reader at the Folger Library, The Library of Congress and has interacted with the Huntington Library and the British Library in pursuing this research as an independent scholar.

James A. Warren was a Foreign Service officer with the U.S. Department of State for more than twenty years, during which he served in public diplomacy positions at U.S. embassies and consulates in eight countries, mostly in Asia. Following his career with the State Department he served as Executive Director of the Association for Diplomatic Studies and Training (ADST) and then as Regional Director for Southeast Asia for the Institute of International Education (IIE). In 2013 he received the *Vero Nihil Verius* Award for Distinguished Shakespearean Scholarship from Concordia University (Portland, Oregon) for his accomplishment as the editor of *An Index to Oxfordian Publications*. He is a Fellow with the Center for the Study of the Great Ideas and the Adler-Aquinas Institute.

Richard Waugaman, MD, is a Clinical Professor of Psychiatry at Georgetown University School of Medicine, a Training Analyst Emeritus at the Washington Psychoanalytic Institute, and a recognized expert on multiple personality disorder. He is a regular reader at the Folger Shakespeare Library, and has written extensively on Shakespeare, the psychology of anonymity, and the case for Oxford's authorship of the Shakespearean canon.

Vol. VII (2016) Table of Contents

Articles

Who Wrote the First Biography of Shakespeare? It was not Nicholas Rowe in 1709!
    Kevin Gilvary   1-15

Greed and Generosity in the Shakespearean Question
    Richard M. Waugaman   17-32

An Arrogant Joseph Hall and an Angry Edward de Vere in *Virgidemiarum* [1599]
    Carolyn Morris   33-82

Teaching the Sonnets and de Vere's Biography at School – Opportunities and Risks
    Elke Brackmann and Robert Detobel   83-110

Oxford and *The Arte of English Poesie*
    Richard Malim   111-130

Edward de Vere: Translator of Johan Sturm's *A Ritch Storehouse or Treasurie for Nobilitie and Gentlemen*?
    Richard M. Waugaman   131-146

Engaging Academia: Some Thoughts
    James Warren   147-178

Exchange of Letters between James Warren and John Shahan   179-184

Farewell....and Hello Again.

Nothing better commends a writing to an editor than one that follows the standards established by the journal, including, but not limited to, adherence to the journal's style sheet. A good article, moreover, conducts a *thorough* and *impartial* job of canvassing the relevant scholarship – what has been said before, by others, about the topic being considered. After a judicious summary, it offers something unexpected or novel, raising new points of fact or applying new methods of interpretation to resolve outstanding ambiguities or problems. Still better, the submission that can turn the history of the scholarship on a topic to advantage in an interpretation or a debate will always win against one that is seen to ignore vital sources of possible contradiction or interpretative conflict for fear that these perspectives may fail to support the author's primary contentions. Above all, a good academic article is self-critical – that is, it displays a constant vigilance with respect to the possibility of error and a humility about what is still not known about a topic.[1] Dealing with significant contrary evidence by conspicuous omission does not work in the long run.

That may sound harsh, but at age fifty-eight, after eight issues of *BC*, and nineteen issues of *Shakespeare Matters*, I feel I deserve my chance to say it.

The Oxfordian movement has seen styles come and go over time as different editors have assumed the responsibility of editing the various publications that now are official bibliographical entries in the history of the Shakespeare Underground (a term, for the record, I first used in 1991), as included in James A. Warren's *Index to Oxfordian Publications* (2015) and other authorship bibliographies.

When I joined the Shakespeare Oxford Society in 1991, Morse Johnson was still editing the newsletter on an IBM Selectric typewriter. His issues were full of great heart and vitality. Morse republished old materials that were difficult to find assembled anywhere else but contained much enlightenment, as well as a lively exchange of often very good articles, letters to the editor, and an occasional flight of fiction, by an ever-shifting mosaic of writers. The movement had been recently re-energized by the publication of Charlton Ogburn's *The Mysterious William Shakespeare*, the archival work and publishing of Ruth Loyd Miller, the 1987 Moot Court at American University organized by David Lloyd Kreeger, and major authorship stories in *The Atlantic* and *The New Yorker*. Yet Johnson produced the newsletter on a Selectric, aided, as I recall, by his law firm secretary.

This was in 1991, almost a decade into the microcomputer revolution, which was putting professional desktop publishing tools, of the kind first used by Bill Boyle after he took over the job of editing the newsletter in 1996, into the hands of millions of desktop designers. The succession of the job to Mr. Boyle was controversial, but as much as I admired Morse Johnson and felt grateful for his many years of unreimbursed service to the organization as newsletter editor, I also thought we needed a publication that looked more like the one Boyle produced starting with issue 32:1.

It was quite an issue for a new editor to handle. The volume reported on several controversial events within the Oxfordian community, including the decision of the Shakepseare Oxford Society (SOS) board of trustees to rescind its invitation to Joseph Sobran to speak at the 19th annual SOS conference in Greensboro, NC, on account of objections to some of Sobran's political beliefs that had nothing to do with authorship – just the sort of controversy that can splinter a small vanguard in a literary revolution to smithereens, especially coming on top of a generational transition and threats of financial lawsuits over creatively managed accounting procedures.

By contrast, things seem very sedate and responsible today. The SOS and the Shakespeare Fellowship have merged to become the Shakespeare Oxford Fellowship, which has good membership growth and has embarked, among other great ideas, on a "How I Became an Oxfordian" series on its website, under the general editorship of Bob Meyers, a distinguished Washington, DC, journalist and author of *Like Normal People* (1978), which tells the true story of how his "mentally retarded" brother and girlfriend broke the stigma against marriages among the differently abled. The book made Bob's brother and his wife into romantic heroes for millions of readers, and the Oxfordian series Bob is editing has had the same impact of suddenly turning those weird, otherworldly, "Shakespeare conspiracy theorists" into normal people, with histories, who think about the world, about literature, and about history or biography or psychology or drama, or all of those things, and discuss and write articles about them. In fact, by the last most accurate estimate, in James Warren's *An Index to Oxfordian Publications* (3rd edition, 2015), Oxfordians have written and published more than 6,000 articles, and 300 books or pamphlets over the last 95 years.

I mean, think about it! *6,000* articles, and 300 *books*!

I am proud that *Brief Chronicles* can march in such an equipage, and over the past several years we've been publishing I've greatly enjoyed the opportunity to produce issues in which I take some personal satisfaction, whether from the quality of the contributions or the pleasure of designing the volumes so that each embodies a uniqueness and aesthetic sensitivity to the forms of ideas they contain. Since our first volume in Fall of 2009 we have published, already, 104 articles or reviews, over a space of about seven years. I believe that among these are several – at least – of the most important articles ever written on their respective aspects of the authorship question. Among my favorites are two of the most adventurous, articles that rigorously pursued the "outside the box" topic of the many uses of early modern literary indirection, Robert Debotel and K.C. Ligon's "Francis Meres and the Earl of

Oxford" (2009) and Nina Green's "Eduardus is My Propre Name" (2010), but there are many others that will of course resonate across time and will very likely continue to influence the discourse of early modern authorship for a long time indeed.

Gary Goldstein and I started *Brief Chronicles*, as the Shakespeare Fellowship itself was started, from necessity. In 2009 there was no credible alternative venue for the larger questions of Shakespearean authorship to be treated with the professionalism they deserve; today Chris Pannell and his editors produce an *Oxfordian* that requires no competition or alternative. In that circumstance, it hardly seems a useful employment of the limited resources of our movement to continue to publish two annual journals, each of which depends on submissions from a still-limited pool of researchers prepared to advance authorship studies at their best. Moreover, as SOF President Tom Regnier reminded me in recent conversation, our work is rapidly going mainstream. Every time orthodox authorities try to shut down the discussion (often by changing the channel), others begin to see the problem the Stratfordians are creating for themselves. These scholars are shifting from unexamined opposition to the post-Stratfordian thinking, moving towards endorsing a more open and scholarly debate on authorship. For verification we need look no further than the 2016 issue of the Italian *Journal of Early Modern Studies*, an orthodox academic journal, which includes contributions on authorship by Ros Barber, William Leahy, and Diana Price.[2] More and more, Oxfordians and other authorship skeptics are able to publish their work in mainstream literary journals like *Notes and Queries, Cahiers Élisabéthains,* or *Critical Survey*, among others. Without the responsibility of producing an annual journal, I hope to contribute on a more regular freelance basis for future issues of *The Oxfordian* among other publications.

Setting aside an endeavor involving the large emotional and intellectual investment that has been put into *Brief Chronicles* is not easy. Despite the occasional trials, I believe the series has established a permanent and significant place in the history of authorship studies. Your editor, on the other hand, is increasingly desirous to devote more time to his own writing projects, which include several books and a flotilla of unpublished and sometimes only half-conceived articles, all remaining "murdered in the waste bottom of my chests" from a lack of proper attention. Naturally I am grateful to the trustees of both the SF and the SOF, who entrusted me with the responsibility to lead production of the journal and always graciously overlooked any faults that could not be remedied prior to publication. To each member of our editorial board, many thanks for your good name, your expertise, and your passion. Our many fine contributors movers and shakers have included Gary Goldstein, Michael Delahoyde, Earl Showerman, and Alex McNeil, without whom *Brief Chronicles* could never have existed – and, of course I must thank Lynne Kositsky, who first gave the journal a "local habitation and a name."

Ed

Endnotes

[1] Michael Delahoyde, "On Being Wrong," *Brief Chronicles* V (2014), 1-10.

[2] Tom Regnier, "Price, Barber, and Leahy Counter Stratfordian Myths in Mainstream Journal" Shakespeareoxfordfellowship.org, March 21, 2016.

Who Wrote the first Shakespeare Biography?
It was not Nicholas Rowe in 1709![1]

Kevin Gilvary

Early in every biography of Shakespeare, writers advance two unfounded claims: firstly, that more is known about Shakespeare's life than is commonly realised. The second claim, which I examine here, is that the earliest biography about Shakespeare was written by Nicholas Rowe in 1709. Rowe's apparent biography is an essay entitled *Some Acount of the Life &c. of Mr. William Shakespear* which prefaces his critical edition of Shakespeare's plays. The *Acount* (as it was spelt in the 1709 edition) originally contained about 8,200 words, most of which concern his judgment as to Shakespeare's merit. Only about 1,020 words are biographical (approximately 12% of the total). Alexander Pope reprinted Rowe's essay in 1725 but omitted some small sections amounting to about 1,165 words, none of which refer to Shakespeare's life. It was this Rowe-Pope *Account* (as it was now spelt) which was frequently reprinted for the next 150 years. Despite Pope's cuts, the biographical content of the abridged version is about 1,000 words out of 7,000 (approximately 14%).[2]

In his entry for Shakespeare in the British *Dictionary of National Biography* (1897), Sidney Lee referred to Rowe's *Account* as "a more ambitious memoir than had yet been attempted." E. K. Chambers believes that Rowe made "the first attempt at a systematic biography of the poet." Samuel Schoenbaum states that Rowe made the "first attempt at a connected biography of Shakespeare." Gary Taylor calls it the "first substantial biography of Shakespeare ever published."[3]

These adjectives — ambitious, systematic, connected and substantial — afford far greater authority to Rowe's essay than it actually merits. Such claims, however, continue to be repeated in this century: Michael Dobson calls it a "pioneering biography." Stanley Wells refers to it as the "first formal biography." Peter Ackroyd states that Rowe was Shakespeare's "earliest biographer," while Lois Potter claims that Rowe "compiled the first biography of Shakespeare." Even David Ellis, who is normally dismissive of Shakespearean biographies—he called them bricks without straw—refers to Rowe's *Acount* as "the first real attempt at a biography of Shakespeare."[4]

So, by the sound of things, we should all be studying Rowe's biography of 1709. Yet a modern editor of Rowe's *Acount* comes to a very different view. Samuel Monk prepared his edition in 1948 and said this in his introduction:

> The biographical part of Rowe's *Account* assembled the few facts and most of the traditions still current about Shakespeare a century after his death. It would be easy for any undergraduate to distinguish fact from legend in Rowe's preface; and scholarship since Steevens and Malone has demonstrated the unreliability of most of the local traditions that Betterton reported from Warwickshire.[5]

At this point we need to consult some definitions: the *Merriam-Webster Dictionary* calls a biography "the story of a real person's life written by someone other than that person." The keyword is "story." The *Oxford English Dictionary* similarly defines it as "a connected narrative of a person's life."

How did Rowe's essay come to prominence?

By about the year 1700, the publisher Jacob Tonson had acquired the rights to publish all the plays of Shakespeare. Tonson invited a prominent playwright, Nicholas Rowe, who was enjoying success with plays such as *The Fair Penitent* (1703), to act as editor. Between them, Rowe and Tonson issued an edition of the plays in eight volumes, octavo—a handy format for carrying around in the pocket, rather than the cumbersome format of the folios. Certain useful additions were made to the text: lists of *dramatis personae* for each play, stage directions, act and scene divisions, and illustrations based on contemporary stage performances of the plays. The enterprise was successful: it was immediately reprinted (1709/10), and reissued in 1714 in an even smaller, duodecimo, format,[6] the first volume of which comprised the texts of the first seven comedies in sequence from the Fourth Folio of 1685, preceded by two letters or addresses: a dedication to the Duke of Somerset, Charles Seymour, and a preface entitled *Some Acount of the Life &c. of Mr. William Shakespear*. Most people ignore the "&c" in the title and simply accept the first five words: "*Some Acount of the Life*" amounts to forty pages in octavo format, at twenty-eight lines per page, a little over 8,000 words in total.

The need for some kind of preface offering both a biography and an appreciation was probably required by the publisher. When Tonson published *The works of Mr Abraham Cowley* in 1668, Thomas Sprat had supplied a biography titled

"An Account of the Life and Writings of Abraham Cowley." Similarly, John Dryden wrote a substantial *Life of Plutarch* for his 1683 edition of *Plutarch's Lives*.[7] Whereas Sprat had known Cowley personally and was his literary executor, Dryden was forced to find out about Plutarch's life from various small asides scattered throughout the *Lives* and in other written documents. However, in the case of Shakespeare, there was no contemporary memoir of Shakespeare and (unlike Jonson's texts) there were no explicit comments by the author about himself. So, to discover more about Shakespeare's life Tonson placed advertisements in the *London Gazette* and in the *Daily Courant* in March 1709. He requested materials that may be "serviceable to this Design" and that "it will be a particular Advantage to the Work, and acknowledg'd as a favour by the Gentleman who has Care of this Edition." However, the ads were not very helpful as little or nothing seems to have been forthcoming about Shakespeare's life.[8]

What kind of text is Rowe's *Acount*?

A simple reading clearly shows that Rowe did not attempt to write a continuous narrative of Shakespeare's life. For his prefatory essay, Rowe had little to comment on beyond the works himself. Rowe refers to thirty-three plays from the First Folio as well as *Pericles* and *Venus and Adonis*. He also refers to almost forty named characters in the plays, which demonstrates his great interest in appreciation rather than biography.[9] He mentions Shakespeare's genius six times and also admires his "Fire, Impetuosity, and even beautiful Extravagance" (iii). At the outset, he expresses doubts as to the value of his own or any other literary biography: personal descriptions are offered out of "Respect due to the Memory of Excellent Men," but he dismisses such curiosity as "trifling," adding that only sometimes does knowledge of an author "conduce to the better understanding his Book." Rowe's *Acount* is mostly a critical review of the works (more than seven-eighths of the essay) rather than a biography (less than one-eighth). His purpose is to support Dryden's view of Shakespeare as the "epitome of excellence" (*Of dramatick poesie*, an 1668 essay) against the censure expressed by Thomas Rymer in his *Short View of Tragedy* (1693).

Although he asserted that he had "resolv'd not to enter any Critical Controversie" (xxxiv), Rowe devotes most of his *Account* to answering adverse criticisms: "If he [Rymer] had a Pique against the Man, and wrote on purpose to ruin a Reputation so well establish'd, he has had the Mortification to fail altogether in his Attempt, and to see the World at least as fond of Shakespear as of his Critique" (xvi). He concedes Rymer's point about Shakespeare not following the classical unities in his plays, and accepts the dubious proposition: "It is without Controversie, that he had no knowledge of the Writings of the Antient Poets" (iii).

However, Shakespeare is the poet of nature and to show this Rowe quotes the "All the world's a stage" speech (xxi). He emphasises Shakespeare's poetic abilities: "His Images are indeed ev'ry where so lively, that the Thing he would represent stands full before you, and you possess ev'ry Part of it" (xxii). At the end, Rowe answers some of Jonson's adverse comments (xxxviii-xxxix). Overall, Rowe's *Some Acount of the Life &c of Mr. William Shakespear* is a disjointed collection of critical judgments interspersed with a little biographical material. It does not merit the title of "biography" because it is not a coherent narrative of the life of Shakespeare. It is a commendation or literary puff intended to persuade casual readers to buy the edition. Out of the total 8,000 words only one-eighth of Rowe's original *Acount*, as little as 1,000 words, is concerned with the life, about 12% of the total. Thus we cannot say that Rowe attempted a biography. He wrote a critical appreciation with a few biographical statements, most of which are either wrong or cannot be verified from other sources.

How reliable is the biographical element?

Rowe only mentions one authority, his friend, the actor Thomas Betterton, who was by this time in his seventies and suffering from gout. In line with his own inclination for an aesthetic approach to Shakespeare, Rowe clearly values Betterton for his acting:

> I cannot leave *Hamlet*, without taking notice of the Advantage with which we have seen this Masterpiece of *Shakespear* distinguish itself upon the Stage, by Mr. *Betterton's* fine Performance of that Part. A Man, who though he had no other good Qualities, as he has a great many, must have made his way into the Esteem of all Men of Letters, by this only Excellency.
>
> (1709, xxxiii-xxxiv)

He adds that Betterton had contributed to the biographical record but is not specific:

> I must own a particular Obligation to him, for the most considerable part of the Passages relating to his Life, which I have here transmitted to the Public; his Veneration for the Memory of *Shakespear* having engaged him to make a Journey into *Warwickshire*, on purpose to gather up what Remains he could of a Name for which he had so great a Value.
>
> (1709, xxxiv)

So Rowe is relying on Betterton, who made a special trip to Stratford to find out more about Shakespeare. If he did do so, it is strange that nobody seemed to notice this visit by the leading actor of the Restoration Stage. The Rev. John Ward makes no mention of Betterton (or any other visitor to Stratford) enquiring about Shakespeare in his journal up to 1681. However, there is doubt whether Betterton himself made the journey at all. William

Oldys consulted a member of Betterton's company, John Bowman, who denied that Betterton had ever been to Stratford. Edmond Malone noted:

If Betterton the player did really visit Warwickshire for the sake of collecting anecdotes relative to our author, perhaps he was too easily satisfied for such as fell in his way, without making any rigid search into their authenticity.

(1790 vol. i. pt. ii. 121n)

A little later, Malone expands this note:

Mr. Betterton was born in 1635, and had many opportunities of collecting information relative to Shakespeare, but unfortunately the age in which he lived was not an age of curiosity. Had either he or Dryden or Sir William Davenant taken the trouble to visit our poet's youngest daughter, who lived till 1662, or his grand-daughter, who did not die till 1670, many particulars might have been preserved which are now irrevocably lost.

(1790 vol. i. pt. ii. 154n)

Malone was right to be doubtful. Betterton's friend and biographer, Charles Gildon (1710), did not mention a visit to Stratford, nor does his modern biographer, David Roberts (2010).[10] Overall, Rowe's citation of Betterton as the authority for the Stratford records is not very strong. Nevertheless, somebody was able to provide information about Shakespeare from an inspection of the parish register at the Holy Trinity Church in Stratford.

Malone then evaluated each of Rowe's claims and established which could be accepted (1821, ii. 69). Only a few of Rowe's statements about Shakespeare's life can be verified from contemporary documents:

- He was the Son of Mr. John Shakespear, and was Born at Stratford upon Avon, in Warwickshire, in April 1564.
- William was young when he married a yeoman's daughter.
- Shakespeare dedicated *Venus and Adonis* to the Earl of Southampton.
- His father obtained a coat of arms.
- He Dy'd in the 53d Year of his Age, and was bury'd on the North side of the Chancel, in the Great Church at Stratford, where a Monument, as engrav'd in the Plate, is plac'd in the Wall.
- He had three daughters, two of whom were married. There is a slight error here as Shakespeare fathered two daughters and one son, Hamnet.

Rowe offers the following statements abut Shakespeare's life which have not been verified in any contemporary records:

- He was sent by his father to a "free-school" for some time.
- his father withdrew him due to straitened circumstances.
- He joined "the company," but the top of his Performance was the Ghost in his own Hamlet.
- Shakespear commended an early work of Jonson (xii) to the Company, but Rowe does not state which play, which company or which year.
- Shakespeare's apparent retirement to Stratford is described at length.

Rowe offers the following statements abut Shakespeare's life which have been demonstrated as wrong:

- His father was a "considerable dealer in wool," whereas in fact he was a glover, who may have had small dealings in wool.
- William was caught deer-poaching and punished.
- William wrote a ballad against Sir Thomas Lucy by way of revenge and was forced to leave Stratford.
- He came to the attention of the Queen, who commanded him to portray Falstaff in love, which was "said to be the Occasion of his Writing the *Merry Wives of Windsor*."
- Southampton gave him a gift of £1,000 with a certain scepticism: he would not repeat it but for the fact that "the Story was handed down by Sir *William Davenant*, who was probably very well acquainted with his Affairs."
- Shakespeare composed an epitaph for his neighbour, Mr Coombe, the only acquaintance at Stratford that Rowe mentions. George Steevens noted that the epitaph about John Combe had been published by Richard Braithwaite in 1618 without reference to Shakespeare. Moreover, he noted that two of the lines had previously appeared in 1608 and 1614 (reported by Malone 1790, vol ii. 496-497).

From this analysis we can dismiss claims that Rowe was responsible for the earliest biography of Shakespeare: he merely made some comments about Shakespeare's life, most of which have been proved wrong or at least unverifiable.

I suggest that the following myths or legends, which have not been verifiable according to contemporary documents, constitute Rowe's biogra-fictions regarding Shakespeare:

- He spent his childhood in Stratford, where he attended the local school. There is no evidence as to where Shakespeare spent his childhood or that he ever attended school in Stratford or anywhere else. From his baptism in 1564 until the issuance of his marriage licence in 1582, there is no mention of William Shakespere in the public records. The suggestion by Arthur Gray (1926) that Shakespeare was brought up at an aristocratic household is tenable in the absence of evidence to the contrary.[11]

- He was caught deer-stealing and punished, writing a ballad in revenge against Sir Thomas Lucy. Malone, however, showed that there was no deer park at Charlecote at this time (1790, vol. ii, 145). This myth is sometimes downgraded to rabbit-catching.

- He enjoyed the patronage of the Earl of Southampton. There is no evidence that Southampton ever knew Shakespeare or ever patronised any writer during the reign of Elizabeth. Rowe's description of the patronage enjoyed by Shakespeare from the Queen and from the Earl of Southampton is a thinly disguised appeal for patronage from Queen Anne and the Duke of Somerset.

- He inspired envy in Jonson. Jonson is very dismissive at times about Shakespeare's works, but there is no evidence that Jonson was ever jealous, which is different. The association of envy with Jonson may have arisen from the words of the dedication to the 1623 Folio: "To draw no envy (Shakespeare) on thy name," which expressly refute the accusation of Jonson's envy.

- He retired to Stratford. Rowe seems to be arguing from norms in asserting his retirement "as all Men of good Sense will wish theirs may be." The latest evidence of Shakespeare's home is the testimony in the Belott-Mountjoy case that he "laye in the house" of Mountjoy *c.* 1604. After this, there is no record as to where he lived. A retirement to Stratford in 1611 is difficult to reconcile with his purchase of the Blackfriars Gatehouse in London on 10 March 1613.

Whereas none of these bio-fictions has been confirmed by any contemporary record, they have remained in the standard account of Shakespeare's life and constitute essential elements of the "bio-mythography" of Shakespeare (as noted by Michael Benton).[12]

Dr. Johnson's Unwritten Life of Shakespeare

During the next hundred years after Rowe, there were three great editors of Shakespeare: Samuel Johnson, George Steevens and Edmund Malone. However, these editors were very dismissive of Rowe's *Account* and never referred to it as "biography." Over 150 biographies were published in the eighteenth century, but nobody ever called Rowe's *Account* biography. It was customary for editors (or perhaps for the publishers) to reprint the prefaces of predecessors. It was reprinted in Johnson's edition of 1765, but with little enthusiasm, and only at the end of a string of other prefaces:

> I have likewise borrowed the author's life from Rowe, though not written with much elegance or spirit; it relates however what is now to be known.
>
> (Johnson 1765, i. sig. C8^r).

It is astonishing that Dr. Johnson did not attempt his own Life of Shakespeare. He had been commissioned to prepare an edition of Shakespeare's works by the Tonson family in the 1760s. Whereas Rowe had been a noted dramatist and Pope a noted poet, Johnson was approached as a celebrated essayist and lexicographer. His *Dictionary* of 1755 showed that he had the depth of reading and understanding to explain obscure meanings and expressions. His edition of Shakespeare eventually appeared in 1765. The great doctor was lauded for the brilliant prefatory essay, but the edition produced little new biographically (Murphy 2003, 80-81). It was reprinted in 1766, 1768 and 1771 and the first revised edition appeared in 1773. After his own critical preface (in over seventy unnumbered pages), the prolegomena included the prefaces of Pope, Theobald, Hanmer and Warburton. Only placed after these, i.e., in the least prominent position, did Johnson retain Rowe's preface, somewhat apologetically, as noted above. Finally, he added the text of the anecdote about holding horses but without comment. Johnson might have been tempted to include this anecdote as an example of "diligence and fidelity," praiseworthy qualities which he had discerned in his early life of Drake (1740/1).

Despite gaining fame and fortune from his *Dictionary* and his edition of Shakespeare, Dr. Johnson preferred biography to any other form. In 1750 Dr. Johnson celebrated the writing of biography with a number of precepts that became widely accepted.[13] He defined biography as a mixture of history with romance (i.e., fiction) and moralising: "Biography is, of the various kinds of narrative writing, that which is most eagerly read, and most easily applied to the purposes of life." Johnson himself wrote many biographies, beginning with the *Life of Sir Francis Drake* (published in the *Gentleman's Magazine* 1740/1) and the full-length *Life of Mr Richard Savage* (1744). Later in his career, he returned to biography by writing fifty or so *Prefaces, Biographical and Critical to the Works of the English Poets*, which were soon reprinted as *Lives of the Most Eminent English Poets* in six volumes (1779-81). With this publication, Johnson established literary biography as an important genre.

Few commentators have noted that Johnson, who so promoted the genre of literary biography, never attempted a Life of Shakespeare. He certainly knew the works and quoted from them 17,000 times in his *Dictionary* of 1755. Furthermore, Johnson also came from the English midlands, Stratford being only slightly off the main route from Litchfield to London. Stratford was becoming something of a tourist attraction in the 1760s, mainly due to the success of Johnon's former pupil, David Garrick, as the foremost Shakespearean actor of his age. Indeed, Garrick was planning the Stratford Jubilee from the mid 1760s, which greatly enhanced the popularity of Shakespeare. Moreover, Johnson had previously been commissioned (almost certainly with a cash advance) to write such a life by the literary publisher,

Thomas Coxeter (1689-1747), according to Sir John Hawkins. Regarding criticism made in 1762 about his long-awaited edition of Shakespeare, Hawkins noted:

> [Johnson] confessed he was culpable, and promised from time to time to begin a course of such reading as was necessary to qualify him for the work: this was no more than he had formerly done in an engagement with Coxeter, to whom he had bound himself to write the life of Shakespeare, but he could never be prevailed on to begin it.[14]

Johnson's procrastination over the life of Shakespeare stands in stark contrast to his *Lives of the Poets* in which he gave short literary biography of about fifty other English authors (1779-1781). Johnson gave as his reason for this omission the lack of information about Shakespeare, saying that Rowe's *Account* gave all that was to be known about the life. No doubt, Johnson would have adopted a moralistic tone as he had done in his life of Sir Francis Drake, where he found in the early life signs of future achievement noting that "virtue is the surest foundation of reputation and fortune, and that the first step to greatness is to be honest." In a later paragraph Johnson adds: "Diligence in employment is the most successful introduction to greater enterprises." (*Gentleman's Magazine*, x. 1740, 389). However, in the case of Shakespeare, there were no documented instances of Shakespeare's early virtue or diligence. Dr. Johnson's friend and biographer, James Boswell, reported a lament by Johnson about the loss of personal knowledge on Shakespeare and Dryden:

> How delighted should we have been if thus introduced into the company of Shakespeare and of Dryden, of whom we know scarcely anything but their admirable writings! What pleasure would it have given us to have known their petty habits, their characteristic manners, their modes of composition, and their genuine opinion of preceding writers and of their contemporaries! All these are now irrecoverably lost.

(James Boswell, *Journal of a Tour to the Hebrides*, 1785, 522-523).

Dr. Johnson's inability to write a Life of Shakespeare simply derived from the lack of biographical material, which as he noted, tended to diminish with time:

> History can be formed from permanent monuments and records; but Lives can only be written from personal knowledge, which is growing every day less, and in a short time is lost for ever. What is known can seldom be told; and when it might be told, it is no longer known.

(Johnson *Biographical* 1781, v. 5, 71-72)

This observation seems to have had a profound impact on Boswell's friend Edmond Malone, who was able to find enough material about Dryden for a biography which was published in 1800, but not, as we shall see, for a life of Shakespeare.

What did later eighteenth century authorities think of Rowe?

Johnson's younger contemporaries and assistant editors, George Steevens and Edmond Malone, were equally unimpressed with Rowe's biographical claims. George Steevens stated:

> All that is known with any degree of certainty concerning Shakespeare is – that he was born in Stratford upon Avon, –married and had children there, went to London, where he commenced actor, and wrote poems and plays, – returned to Stratford, made his will, died and was buried.[15]

Edmond Malone lamented the lack of research by previous writers:

> That almost a century should have elapsed, from the time of his death, without a single attempt having been made to discover any circumstance which could throw a light on his private life, or literary career; that, when the attempt was made [by Rowe in 1709], it should have been so; and that for a period of eighty years afterwards, during which this "god of our idolatry" ranked as high among us as any poet ever did in any country, all the editors of his works, and each successive biographer, should have been contented with Mr Rowe's meagre and imperfect narrative.
>
> (Malone, ed. Boswell, 1821 ii. 10-11)

Malone had hoped to be able to write his own Life of Shakespeare, but never achieved this ambition. Like previous editors, Malone included Rowe's *Account of the Life &c.,* in his own edition (1790 i. ii. 102-154) but "endeavoured, in some degree, to supply the defects of Mr. Rowe's short narrative, by adding to it copious annotations" (as reported in 1821, ii. 11n). These notes are printed in a smaller font and are so extensive that some pages have no running text. About half the notes were the result of Malone's own researches, the other half are attributed to other writers, especially Lewis Theobald. Malone further elaborated these comments "for the purpose of demolishing almost every statement [by Rowe] which it contained" (1821, i. xix). Malone's literary executor, James Boswell, Jr., however, offered an apology in the prolegomena: "I have printed the prefaces which have been prefixed to the modern editions of the poet, among which Mr. Rowe's life, as being partly prefatory and partly biographical may be classed." Rowe's *Account* had been repeated so often and its content had become so ingrained in the study of Shakespeare that Boswell conceded: "Notwithstanding its defects in the second point of view, I should not have thought myself justified in omitting it altogether" (1821, i. xix).

Who was the first biographer of Shakespeare?

Nicholas Rowe was the first critical *editor* of the works, but he was not Shakespeare's first "biographer." Neither Johnson, Steevens nor Malone attempted a Life of Shakespeare; nor did any of the other major eighteenth-century Shakespeare scholars, such as Alexander Pope, Lewis Theobald, or Edward Capell. The first biography of Shakespeare did not in fact appear until 1843, over 100 years later than Rowe and almost 300 years after the birth of Shakespeare. Charles Knight included a narrative account of Shakespeare's life as volume VIII of his *Illustrated Edition of Shakespeare's works*. Here is a heavily romanticized passage, needed to establish a turning point in the narrative, but for which there is nothing in the historical records:

> The happy days of Shakespeare's boyhood are nearly over. William Shakespeare no longer looks for that close of day when, in that humble chamber in Henley Street, his father shall hear something of his school progress, and read with him some English book of history or travel.[16]

All this and many other such descriptions were pure imagination as contemporaries noted. Victorian intellectuals were not impressed. One reviewer stated:

> [Charles Knight] the author did not tie himself down to bare facts, but gave free rein to his imagination. As a chronicle of what might have happened to the poet and what he probably did, the people he was likely to have met, etc., this is not surpassed by anything which has been written on the subject. But those who wish to ascertain what we really know of Shakespeare must consult other books.[17]

Whereas Knight eked out his biography with his own conjectures and speculations, John Payne Collier in 1844 resorted to fabricating documents for his 1844 biography, fabrications which were not exposed for another ten years. The use of conjecture, speculation and, yes, even fabrication, in the biography of Shakespeare was thus not established until Victorian times.

Conclusions

Nicholas Rowe did not write a biography of Shakespeare. He wrote an appreciation within which he made some biographical statements. A majority of these comments, however, turn out upon inspection to be unfounded or undocumented. Modern biographers are therefore erroneous in claiming that Rowe was Shakespeare's earliest biographer. They clearly derive this idea from Sidney Lee, who first advanced it in 1897. It was not repeated until Samuel Schoenbaum in *Shakespeare's Lives* in 1970. Since then, almost all biographers of Shakespeare repeat it, presenting their own efforts as coming at the end of a respectable tradition of

Shakespearean biography stretching back to 1709, and not to Knight's biography of 1843, which was not written until almost three hundred years after Shakespeare's birth. For authorship sceptics, it is further interesting to note that the earliest articulated doubt about the authorship of the Shakespeare canon occurs in the 1850s, soon after the first large-scale biographies by Knight and Collier in the 1840s.

Editions Cited

Rowe, Nicholas. *The Works of Mr. William Shakespear in Six Volumes.* 6 vols. London: Jacob Tonson (1709; reprinted 1714).

Pope, Alexander. *The Works of Shakespear,* 6 vols. London: Jacob Tonson (1723-25).

Johnson, Samuel. *The Plays of William Shakespeare*, 8 vols. London: Tonson (1765).

Malone, Edmond, ed.. *The plays and poems: of William Shakespeare.* 10 vols. London: Rivington (1790).

Malone, Edmond (ed. Boswell, James Jr.) *The Plays and Poems of William Shakspeare.* 21 vols. London: Rivington (1821). Third Variorum.

Biographies Cited

Knight, Charles. *William Shakspere: a Biography.* London: C. Knight (volume VIII of *Illustrated Edition of Shakespeare's works,* 1843).

Collier, J. Payne, ed. *The Works of William Shakespeare.* 8 vols. London: Whittaker, 1844.

Lee, Sir Sidney. *A Life of William Shakespeare.* London: Smith, Elder & Co. 1898 (Many subsequent editions: 1899; 1904; 1905; 1908; revised and enlarged 1915).

Endnotes

[1] I would like to thank Professor William Leahy and R.E.M. Jolly for their advice and support in preparing this essay. It is based mainly on Chapter 3 of my thesis, *Shakespearean Biogra-fiction: How modern biographers rely on context, conjecture and inference to construct a life of the Bard*, for which I was awarded a Ph.D. by Brunel University London in July 2015. The essay was presented to the meeting of the Shakespeare Oxford Fellowship, Ashland, Oregon, in September 2015.

[2] Nicholas Rowe's essay can be found in many publications and on many websites, most usefully in *Eighteenth Century Essays on Shakespeare* edited by David Nichol Smith (Glasgow: James MacLehose (1903)), which contains very useful notes.

[3] Sidney Lee (DNB entry 1897; republished as a monograph in 1898, 363; repeated verbatim 1917, 642). Lee's entry to the DNB for Shakespeare amounted to 63,000 words, the longest to date, in line with his cultural significance, not with the level of biographical material available. It was only ever exceeded by the entry for Queen Victoria. E.K. Chambers, *William Shakespeare: a Study of Facts and Problems* (1930, vol i. 12). S. Schoenbaum, *Shakespeare's Lives* (1970), 131. Gary Taylor, *Reinventing Shakespeare: A Cultural History from the Restoration to the Present*. London: Hogarth Press (1989), 74.

[4] Michael Dobson, ed. *The Oxford Companion to Shakespeare* (2001, 423). Stanley Wells, *Shakespeare for all Time* (2002, 200). Peter Ackroyd, *Shakespeare: The Biography* (2005, 476). Lois Potter, *The Life of William Shakespeare: A Critical Biography* (2012, 432). David Ellis, *That Man Shakespeare: Icon of Modern Culture* (Sussex: Helm International, 2005), 37.

[5] Samuel H. Monk, ed. *Nicholas Rowe: Some Account of the Life of William Shakespeare (1709)*. Los Angeles, CA: Augustan Reprint Society (1948), 5.

[6] Andrew Murphy, *Shakespeare in Print: A History and Chronology of Shakespeare Publishing*, CUP (2003) 57-61.

[7] John Dryden, ed., *Plutarch's Lives. Translated from the Greek by several hands. To which is prefixt the Life of Plutarch* (London: Jacob Tonson, 1683).

[8] Schoenbaum, *Shakespeare's Lives* (1970), 129-132.

[9] Rowe mentions the following characters in the plays of Shakespeare: Falstaff, Mistress Quickly, Prince Hal, Ford, Slender, Ann Page, Malvolio, Parolles, Petruchio, Benedick, Beatrice, Rosalind, Thersites, Apemantus, Shylock, Antonio, Bassanio, Portia, Jaques, Caliban, Prospero, Ferdinand, Juno, Ceres, Antony, Cleopatra, Beaufort, Gloucester, Henry VIII, Wolsey, Katherine (of Aragon), Coriolanus, Brutus, Romeo, Juliet, Hamlet, and Macbeth. Rowe also refers to the following unnamed characters: the Pedant, the Ghost of Hamlet's father, fairies, and witches, as well as quoting from various scenes and speeches involving the Queen (Gertrude) or a Maid in Love (Viola).

[10] Charles Gildon, *The Life of Mr. Thomas Betterton, the late eminent tragedian.* London: R. Gosling (1710). David Roberts, *Thomas Betterton: the Greatest Actor of the Restoration Stage.* Cambridge: Cambridge University Press (2010). A text dated 1715 entitled *Some Further Account of the Life &c. of Mr. William Shakespear,* purporting to include reports of Betterton's conversations at Stratford, has been dismissed as a forgery by Holderness, "Some Further Account of the Life &c. of Mr. William Shakespear, with Corrections Made to the First and Second Editions, and with the Supplementation of New Matter Acquir'd from Diligent Researches in the Publick Records, and from Conversations Mr. Betterton had with the people of Stratford-upon-Avon (1715)." *Critical Survey* 21.3, 112-118 (2009).

[11] Arthur Gray, *A chapter in the early life of Shakespeare: Polesworth in Arden* (Cambridge: The University Press, 1926).

[12] Michael Benton, *Literary Biography: An Introduction.* London: John Wile, 2009 (47-66). Establishing the life of a national hero with little or no regard to verifiable facts has been termed "biomythography" by Benton. He notes that these heroes are often literary figures, such as Byron and Dickens, and that biographers continue to exalt their subjects charting their subject's moves from success through celebrity and martyrdom to idolatry. He offers a five-stage paradigm for this process of biomythography:

(i) selection and 'spin' of facts: an early biographer selects and establishes a factual history with his or her own interpretation;

(ii) fact into fiction: the facts become fictionalised through reference to the subject's writings;

(iii) fiction into myth: the fiction becomes mythologised as its characters and landscape become symbols;

(iv) myth into 'Faction': stories with a basis in fact but embellished with invented elements;

(v) demythologising: biographers return to primary sources.

The Shakespeare Authorshiop Question clearly relates to the final stage, demythologizing Shakespeare.

[13] Johnson's principles began to appear in a succession of articles in *The Rambler* 60 (13 Oct. 1750), 28-33, and are reprinted in James L. Clifford, James L., *Biography as an Art: Selected Criticism 1560-1960* (Oxford: at the University Press, 1962), 39-45.

[14] Sir John Hawkins, *The Life of Samuel Johnson, LL.D.* (London: Chambers, 1787), 440. I am indebted to Dr. Paul Tankard of the University of Otago for bringing this allusion to my attention. The criticism in 1762 had been made by Charles Churchill: "He for subscribers baits his hook / and takes your cash, but where's the book?" *The Ghost,* London, i. 800-801.

[15] This note is buried in Malone's commentary to Sonnet 93. The name "STEEVENS" occurs in upper case according to the customary practice at the time of indicating the author of such a note. Edmond Malone, *Supplement to the edition of Shakspeare's plays published in 1778 by Samuel Johnson and George Steevens. In two volumes.* (1780 ii. 653).

[16] Charles Knight, *Life of Shakespere* (1851, 64). Quoted by Julia Thomas, *Shakespeare's Shrine: The Bard's Birthplace and the Invention of Stratford.* University of Pennsyvania (2012, 23).

[17] J. Parker Norris, "The Editors of Shakespeare." *Shakespeariana: a critical and contemporary review of Shakespearian Literature* 5, January 1888, 72-75.

Greed and Generosity in the Shakespearean Question

Richard M. Waugaman[1]

Third Fisherman. Master, I marvel how the fishes live in the sea.

First Fisherman. Why, as men do a-land; the great ones eat up the little ones. I can compare our rich misers to nothing so fitly as to a whale.

Pericles 2.1.69-70

"I know of no country, indeed, where the love of money has taken stronger hold on the affections of men, and where the profounder contempt is expressed for the theory of the permanent equality of property."

Alexis de Tocqueville, *Democracy in America*

Individual and corporate greed, along with growing income inequality, are plaguing the early 21st century in the United States. According to the *Wall Street Journal*, "rising income inequality is weighing on global economic growth and fueling political instability."[2] Mentalization is emerging as a crucial feature of healthy psychological development.[3] But many studies have shown that increased wealth correlates with decreasing empathy for those who have less.[4] The wealthy are at risk of deceiving themselves into thinking they earned everything they possess through their talent and hard work alone, and that birth and luck played no role in their financial success. They tend to regard the poor as lazy and unworthy. And they compare themselves unfavorably to those who have still greater wealth.[5] Giving to others seems to bring deeper satisfaction than keeping more for oneself. Paradoxically, the poorest people in the United States give a higher proportion of their income to charity than do the more prosperous.

Still, greed has its defenders. Ivan Boesky once said, "I think greed is healthy. You can be greedy and still feel good about yourself."[6] This was a few months before he was fined $100 million and sentenced to prison for insider trading. Although some apologists for the wealthy cite misleading statistics in order to deny that there is more income inequality now than there was fifty years ago, economists measure this inequality more objectively with the so-called "Gini coefficient." If incomes were completely identical, this measure would be zero, whereas it would be one if incomes were completely unequal. In the United States in 1960, the Gini coefficient was 0.34; in 2013 it was 0.42 (relatively speaking, a 24% increase in income disparity). Disturbingly, U.S. income inequality is greater than in any other wealthy country. Fifty years ago, the U.S. looked down on Latin America for having a group of very wealthy people, a small middle class, and a large number of poor. We no longer hear that comparison, as the U.S. more and more resembles that once derogated stereotype of Latin American dictatorships that favored the wealthy at the expense of everyone else. Our national identity and democratic values are built on the ideal of equality—that is, equality of opportunity, so anyone willing to study hard in school and work hard at their job can be financially secure. We are now at risk of losing the social cohesiveness that such an ideal facilitated, with only 9% of children born into the poorest fifth of the population ever rising to the top fifth.[7] Three-fourths of those in the wealthiest *quarter* of the population finish college by age twenty-four, but fewer than 10% of those born into the poorest quarter do so.[8]

In understandable reaction against this ever-growing income inequality, socialism has been garnering increased support in the United States. A 2011 survey found that minority groups that have been most harmed by the wealth gap support socialism over capitalism. In a 2012 survey, 39% of all Americans polled expressed a positive opinion of socialism.[9] A 2009 survey of 3,300 U.S. physicians revealed that 42% of them supported a "socialized," single-payer health care system.[10]

In this era of growing economic disparities, what could be more timely than an exploration of greed, viewed psychoanalytically? I will offer some suggestions as to what we might learn about this topic through the life and literary work of Edward de Vere, 17th Earl of Oxford (1550-1604), who wrote under the pen name "William Shake-speare," as well as under other pseudonyms (such as "Ignoto"). Given that he was a high ranking member of the nobility when feudal class distinctions were being challenged by the rising merchant class, it is remarkable that he suffered less from greed than did many of his contemporaries, including William Shakspere of Stratford, who is still thought by many to be the author of the literary works that have so little in common with what we know about him. Thus, another necessary psychoanalytic aspect of this chapter must be some exploration of the individual and group psychology that helps us understand this monumental authorship misattribution.

For more than 150 years now, reasonable challenges to the traditional authorship theory have been met with avoidance on the part of Shakespeare scholars, or with ad hominem attacks on those who present evidence that contradicts the traditional theory. Instead, we are told repeatedly that only snobs who cannot stand the literary genius of the commoner from Stratford, and those given to "conspiracy theories," would dare to defy the authority of the Shakespeare experts as to his identity. Since those experts begin from the unquestioned premise that the traditional attribution is unequivocally correct, they unconsciously select from the mass of ambiguous but relevant evidence only those data that fit with their preconceptions, while they ignore, minimize, or ridicule inconsistent evidence and those who present it.[11] Further, there is a striking pattern of what seems to be unconscious projection of every one of the weaknesses of their own thinking onto authorship skeptics (e.g., faulty evaluation of evidence; biases from preconceptions; circular thinking; problems with the lifespan of the alleged author; elitism; and excessive emotional attachment to one's theory).

Another approach, that is more consistent with the ideals of science and of objective literary scholarship, is to consider every theory a hypothesis, open to possible disproof. Starting by assuming that one's conclusion is infallibly correct guarantees that one will reason deductively from axiomatic assumptions. Stratfordians (who believe that Shakspere of Stratford was the author) demonstrate this fallacy repeatedly when they write about the authorship question. They assume, for example, that Shakspere attended the local grammar school in Stratford, in the absence of any surviving records that might document his attendance. Even more basically, they assume he was highly literate, in the complete absence of any objective evidence that he knew how to read; or to write; or even to sign his name. The illiteracy of most English commoners in his day, including his parents and his children, instead suggests that he may not have been able to read the works of Shakepeare, much less to write them. There is no shame in that.

In fact, a more objective appraisal of the authorship question suggests that Edward de Vere wrote the plays of "Shakespeare" because this was the best way to shape public opinion, in a day when the many people who could not read could still enjoy—and be influenced by—the public theater. Plays remain even today a collective literary experience that harkens back to Homeric and other ancient epics being recited aloud to a group of people. Queen Elizabeth may have provided financial support to de Vere with the understanding that his plays would help legitimize her rule and that of her Tudor predecessors. His history plays would be more effective as propaganda if they were widely thought to be written by a commoner from Stratford.

Initially, it was assumed that Shakespeare had "little Latin and less Greek," as Ben Jonson wrote in the 1623 First Folio collection of Shakespeare's plays. Scholars' flawed assumptions about what works Shakespeare may have read in other languages therefore narrowed our awareness of his actual literary sources. More recent evidence suggests, however, that Shakespeare the author read works in Latin, Greek, French, and Italian that had not yet been translated into English. For example, an entire scene of *Henry V* is written in French, including some bawdy puns. Shakspere of Stratford's coat of arms, finally granted in 1596 after several earlier refusals, has the motto "non sans droit," ostensibly French for "not without right." Many Shakespeare scholars agree that this motto is ridiculed in Ben Jonson's comedy *Every Man Out of his Humor* as "not without mustard."[12] Intriguingly, post-Stratfordian scholars (who question the traditional authorship theory) speculate that the illiterate

Shakspere misunderstood the words "non, sans droit" (i.e., "no, he has no right" [to a coat of arms]) on his initially rejected application for a coat of arms. There are even characters in Shakespeare's plays, such as Christopher Sly in *The Taming of the Shrew*, and the clown Costard in *Love's Labors Lost*,[13] who seem to be caricatures of Shakspere.

Shakespeare scholars often maintain that no one challenged the traditional authorship theory until the mid-19th century. That is not so, however. For example, Thomas Vicars referred in 1628 to "that famous poet who takes his name from shaking and spear" ["celebrem illum poeta qui a quassatione et hasta nomen habet"].[14] This circumlocution sounds very odd if the poet to which he referred were Shakspere. The other poets that Vicars lists are referred to by their actual names. So Vicars's unusual allusion to Shakespeare is more consistent with "Shake-spear" being a pen name, especially since hyphenated last names in Elizabethan literature (including those in many Shakespeare plays) were usually assumed names.

The documentary evidence from Shakespeare's own day proves that de Vere was known as an excellent author of comedies and courtly poems, who preferred to write anonymously. But it offers no proof whatsoever that Shakspere was an author. However, there is ample evidence that Shakspere of Stratford was a notoriously greedy and unscrupulous businessman. Business success required numeracy, but not literacy. Shakspere was a moneylender, and he may have become involved with the London theater by lending money to those who staged plays there. His father John's application for a coat of arms in the late 1560s was rejected because of the father's violation of laws concerning usury, and for illegal activity in his wool trade. In 1598, when food was in short supply, William Shakspere was accused of illegally hoarding more than three tons of malt.[15] In 1600, he sued a man in London for repayment of a debt of £7. In 1604, he sued another man for a debt of little more than £1; in 1608, a third man for £6. These suits help document his occupation as a moneylender, whereas there is no unequivocal documentation that he was a writer.

Shakspere's unsavory side received widespread publicity in 2013, when scholars from Britain's Aberystwyth University made international news by reporting evidence that, "There was another side to Shakespeare [sic] besides the brilliant playwright—as a ruthless businessman who did all he could to avoid taxes, maximise profits at others' expense and exploit the vulnerable...."[16]

It has emerged that, over a fifteen-year period, Stratford's Shakspere repeatedly bought grain to hoard and resell at inflated prices. He was fined for this, as well as threatened with jail for tax evasion. Trying to put the best face on this disappointing information about a man who is still regarded by many as a major cultural icon, the researchers claimed that he was just trying to feed his family. However, we should ask ourselves: if we did not assume that Shakspere wrote the works of Shakespeare, does this sound like the author of these beloved works?

When this story was in the news in 2013, one commentator praised Shakspere's business acumen, for buying grain when prices were low, and holding out for the highest possible prices. If we wish to judge Shakspere solely by such standards of greedy business practices, we can praise him. But it further weakens his claim to authorship of the literary works that consistently honor generosity, and condemn greed.

You may be wondering why you have never heard about this documentary evidence of Shakspere's business career. Perhaps because it makes it seem less likely that he had time to write the works of Shakespeare. Shakespeare experts have systematically ignored all evidence inconsistent with their authorship theory, while turning their speculations into ostensible "facts." At his death, Shakspere left an estate of some £2,000. Writers were paid little; Ben Jonson earned a total of about £200 from *all* of his writing. Fellow theater investors left much smaller estates than did Shakspere (except those whose wives were wealthy in their own right). There are records of payments to other playwrights, but none to Shakespeare.[17]

What evidence do we have of de Vere's personal generosity or greed? In Sidney Lee's 1899 biography of de Vere, written some twenty years before de Vere was first proposed as author of Shakespeare's works, Lee wrote of de Vere as an adolescent, "While manifesting a natural taste for music and literature, the youth developed a waywardness of temper which led him into every form of extravagance."[18] When he was older, Lee said, "Oxford's continued extravagance involved him in pecuniary difficulties....[He] seemed to take delight in selling every acre of his land at ruinously low prices.... Oxford had squandered some part of his fortune upon men of letters whose bohemian mode of life attracted him."

Lee could be sharply critical of de Vere's many personal failings, but he did acknowledge de Vere's generosity and artistic talents—for music, the theater, and literature. Lee wrote,

> Oxford—despite his violent and perverse temper [that included a homicidal streak], his eccentric taste in dress, and his reckless waste of his substance—evinced a genuine interest in music, and wrote verse of much lyric beauty. Puttenham and Meres reckon him among "the best for comedy" in his day; but, although he was a patron of a company of players [i.e., actors], no specimens of his dramatic productions survive. A sufficient number of his poems is extant, however, to corroborate Webbe's comment that he was the best of the courtier-poets in the early years of Elizabeth's reign.

Some leading Elizabethan authors such as John Lyly and Anthony Munday served as de Vere's literary secretaries. One book that Munday translated became a source for Shakespeare's *The Winter's Tale*. In the 1580s, de Vere's home was at Fisher's Folly in London, where he welcomed still other writers, such as Robert Greene and Barnabe Riche. A 1598 account reported that the Queen "hath lodged there [i.e., at Fisher's Folly]."[19]

Thirty-three books were dedicated to de Vere during his lifetime, "an unusually large proportion of which were literary."[20] Thirteen of Shakespeare's plays are set in Italy (aside from the history plays, only one play is set in England). So it is noteworthy that "a large share of [de Vere's] patronage was extended in particular to literary works with an Italian flavor" (Dunn, 3). It is likely that this reflects not only his financial generosity to fellow writers, but also his encouragement of their work. In another act of generosity and patronage, de Vere gave the lease of his Battails Hall estate in Essex to the famous composer William Byrd, around 1573. (More about Byrd below.)

Every single Shakespeare play contains music or refers to music. Many figures of speech in Shakespeare use musical terms—always correctly. Christopher Wilson wrote that "nearly every composer, since Shakespeare's time had been inspired, directly or indirectly, by our poet."[21] The Elizabethan composer John Farmer said de Vere's musical talents rivaled those of professional musicians. Farmer dedicated two published collections of music to de Vere, in 1591 and in 1599. By 1599, de Vere's precarious finances made it unlikely he could have offered much financial reward as a patron. Nonetheless, Farmer wrote an extraordinary dedication to de Vere that year. It is worth quoting at some length, since it helps us understand de Vere's contemporary reputation as a generous, leading patron of literature and music:

> There is a canker worm that breedeth in many minds, feeding only upon forgetfulness, and bringing forth no birth but ingratitude. To show that I have not been bitten with that monster (for worms prove monsters in this age, which yet never any Painter could counterfeit to express the ugliness, nor any Poet describe to decipher the height of their illness) I have presumed to tender these Madrigals only as remembrances of my service and witnesses of your Lordship's liberal hand [i.e., de Vere's financial generosity to Farmer], by which I have so long lived, and from your Honorable mind that so much have loved all liberal Sciences.[22]

De Vere's annotated Geneva Bible is another crucial window into his mind. One of my favorite Biblical stories (2 Samuel 12:1-14) about telling truth to power is when the prophet Nathan wants to confront King David with his evildoing. He does this so subtly that David falls into his trap, ordering the execution of the disguised "rich man" with many sheep, who stole the one "little sheep" the "poor" man owned. When David ordered that the rich man "shall surely die" (verse 5), Nathan replied "Thou art the man" (verse 7)—the story was an allegory about David seizing the beautiful Bathsheba to satisfy his lust, and having her husband Uriah killed in battle. De Vere marked several phrases in verses 9, 10, and 11 in this chapter, which describe David's sin and how he would be punished.

De Vere annotated only one verse in the entire Gospel of Mark. It was chapter 10, verse 21, which states, "And Jesus beheld him [the rich man], and loved him, and said unto him, one thing is lacking unto thee, go and sell all that thou hast, and give to the poor, and thou shalt have treasure in heaven, and come, follow me, and take up the cross." As a "rich man" himself, it is understandable that de Vere would have special interest in this well-known story. De Vere also marked Matthew 19:21, a paraphrase of that verse in Mark. A printed marginal note next to this verse in Matthew, however, reassures the wealthy that Jesus was "not generally commanding all to do the like."[23] De Vere did not literally follow Jesus's advice, but his interest in Mark 10:21, out of that entire Gospel, shows that he was acutely aware of the spiritual hazards of being excessively attached to wealth. And he did indeed act charitably as a literary patron.

As King Lear is about to seek shelter in Mad Tom's hovel during the storm of Act III, he has an epiphany about his previous neglect of the poor. His words may be inspired partly by Mark 10:21 and Matthew 19:21, the verses that so interested de Vere: "Poor naked wretches, wheresoe'er you are,/ That bide the pelting of this pitiless storm…O, I have ta'en/ Too little care of this! Take physic,[24] pomp,/ Expose thyself to feel what wretches feel,/ That thou mayst shake the superflux[25] to them,/ And show the heavens more just" (III.iv.28-36). Later, Lear literally disrobes, exposing himself indeed. However, despite his effort to feel what Mad Tom feels, Lear is still trapped in his own subjectivity, as he assumes Mad Tom surely must have also been betrayed by *his* three daughters to be brought to his (feigned) madness: "nothing could have subdu'd nature/ To such a lowness but his unkind daughters" (III.iv.70-71).

De Vere showed special interest in biblical passages that dealt with usury, the poor, and the giving of alms.[26] For example, Matthew 6:1-4 deals with the correct way to give alms, and each of these four verse numbers is marked in his Bible. These verses exhort the righteous to give alms in secret—"That thine alms may be in secret, and thy Father that seeth in secret, he will reward thee openly" (Matthew 6:4). Did de Vere interpret these verses as encouraging him to remain anonymous with his literary gifts to mankind? Perhaps.

Another source of information about de Vere is his letters. We might note his eighteen uses of various forms of the word "fortune" in his letters—including "misfortune," "unfortunate," etc. In his 1603 letter to his wife's brother Robert Cecil about Queen Elizabeth's death, he crossed out the word "fortune" because he had already used it so many times earlier in the letter; he signed this letter "your unfortunate brother-in-law." In de Vere's day, the word "fortune" usually meant luck—good or bad. The OED's first example of its use in the modern sense of fortune as wealth is in Edmund Spenser's 1590 *The Fairy Queen*.[27] But de Vere was himself already using the word in that modern sense in his letters. I suspect he used the word so many times in his letter about the Queen's death because he worried what impact her death would have on his luck—*and* on his economic status. After all, she had been paying him an unprecedented pension of £1,000 per year since 1586.

De Vere's personality had all the contradictions of a Shakespearean character. His attitude toward money is but one example. He could be generous to a fault. As noted earlier, Sidney Lee tells us that "Oxford had squandered some part of his fortune upon men of letters whose bohemian mode of life attracted him," like Prince Hal in the Boar's Head Tavern (in *Henry IV, Part II*). Since his adolescence, he spent lavishly on his clothing. He showed no regard for the impact on his finances of his fourteen-month trip to the Continent when he was 25 and 26. He was successful in his appeal to the Queen for his generous pension, but he was apparently unsuccessful in his many bids for other royal favors that would have been profitable to him. He showed poor judgment in his investments in risky ventures, such as Martin

Frobisher's expedition to the New World.

De Vere had good reason to consider himself to be a repeated victim of the greed of other people. De Vere's repeated suits to the Queen for financial assistance were fully justified, once one considers her role in causing his financial ruin. Nina Green, in an important article, concludes that "It was the Queen's mismanagement of de Vere's wardship and the stranglehold which she held over his finances during his entire lifetime which led inevitably to his financial ruin" (60). De Vere's father John died when de Vere was only twelve. Green builds a plausible case that John de Vere may have been murdered at the behest of Robert Dudley (who later became Earl of Leicester).[28] Dudley was Queen Elizabeth's favorite, and possibly her lover. He profited financially from the death of de Vere's father, after the Queen assigned the management and income of much of de Vere's land to him.

The Court of Wards was set up to "protect" and educate noble children who lost their fathers. But it allowed the nearly unrestrained financial exploitation of these children. Always struggling with her own financial problems, Queen Elizabeth was creative in rewarding her favorites by granting them royal commercial monopolies—or awarding them guardianship of a wealthy "orphan." This is precisely what happened to de Vere when he was twelve and his father died. Green has shown how badly de Vere was harmed financially by the wardship system—he owed £11,000 to the Court of Wards when he attained his majority. This unscrupulous system is the veiled target of Shakespeare's first long poem, the 1593 *Venus and Adonis*, according to the Stratfordian scholar Patrick M. Murphy.[29] But, as early as 1576, de Vere wrote to his father-in-law, Lord Burghley (who was formerly his guardian after his father died), "I understand the greatness of my debt and [the] *greediness* of my creditors grows so dishonorable to me" that he asked that some of his lands be sold to pay them, "to stop my creditors' exclamations[30] (or rather defamations I may call them)" (quoted in Green, 59; emphasis added).

The celebrated physician and humanitarian Paul Farmer has helped popularize a folk saying from Haiti—the poorest country in the Western Hemisphere—that God gives mankind all it needs, but He leaves it up to us to share our resources fairly.[31] Greed corrupts this moral obligation of those who have more to share with those who have less. Greed typically refers to the inordinate desire for wealth, in contrast with excessive ambition, which craves inordinate power, as do many of Shakespeare's characters. Shakespeare's contemporary Ben Jonson wrote the comedy *The Alchemist*, considered to be one of his best plays, as a satire on greed. Shakespeare did not write such a play himself. His plays are full of ambition and its casualties. When asked about the topic of greed in Shakespeare, many people first think of his unforgettable Falstaff, and of Shylock. It is true that Falstaff is an unscrupulous glutton, but one does not think of financial greed as his central characteristic. Gluttony is one of the seven deadly sins, and greed is another.

I come now to Shylock's play, *The Merchant of Venice*. Its character Antonio displays the sort of reckless generosity toward his friend Bassanio that Lee described in de Vere "squandering" some of his fortune on fellow writers. In fact, this play has special significance to the theory that de Vere wrote the works of Shakespeare.

Thomas Looney, whose 1920 book[32] persuaded Freud of de Vere's likely authorship, explained that it was his experience teaching this play in a secondary school year after year that made him realize how implausible the traditional authorship theory was:

> This long continued familiarity with the contents of one play [*The Merchant of Venice*] induced a peculiar sense of intimacy with the mind and disposition of its author and his outlook upon life. The personality which seemed to run through the pages of the drama I felt to be altogether out of relationship with what was taught of the reputed author and the ascertained facts of his career....This particular play...bespoke a writer who knew Italy at first hand and was touched with the life and spirit of the country. Again the play suggested an author with no great respect for money and business methods, but rather one to whom material possessions would be in the nature of an encumbrance. (2)

Looney recognized some of the psychological factors that create such strong belief in Shakspere of Stratford, and that might interfere with an objective evaluation of his competing authorship theory. For example, "The force of a conviction is frequently due as much to the manner in which the evidence presents itself, as to the intrinsic value of the evidence" (4). Thus, when one starts with unshakeable faith in the traditional theory, one will overemphasize those facts which seem to support it, and downplay facts that are inconsistent with it.

The Stratfordian authorship theory leads to the false assumption that Shakespeare did not know any Jews in England, which in turn promotes the misreading of the play as exploiting bigoted stereotypes of Jews. In reality, de Vere had many opportunities to become acquainted with Jews during the several months he lived in Venice, in 1576.

Charlton Ogburn, Jr., who is largely responsible for revival of interest in Looney's authorship theory since the 1980s, uses *The Merchant of Venice* to illustrate Shakespeare's firsthand knowledge of Italy:

> Hugh R. Trevor-Roper writes that Shakespeare's "knowledge of Italy was extraordinary. An English scholar who lived in Venice has found his visual topographic exactitude in *The Merchant of Venice* incredible in one who had never been there." Dr. Ernesto Grillo in his *Shakespeare and Italy*...says of *The Merchant* that "the topography is so precise and accurate that it must convince even the most superficial reader that the poet visited the country" (302).[33]

Shylock has stimulated more books than has the play in which he is found.[34] As Thomas Wheeler observed, "The dark shadow of the Holocaust falls about *The Merchant*... and makes it... impossible to regard [Shylock] as a comic villain" (xi). In contrast with the protagonist of Christopher Marlowe's earlier play, *The Jew of Malta*, Shylock demonstrates far more complexity. He is not as purely a villain as is Marlowe's Barabas. Wheeler quotes A.D. Moody, who saw *The Merchant of Venice* as "a disturbing play in which tensions between two different standards [of Belmont and of Venice] are never resolved....[The final act] reveals the hypocrisy and superficiality of the Christians, who have triumphed by ignoring the spirit of mercy and conforming to the letter of the law" (xi). J. M. Murry wrote in 1936, "Antonio and his friends ...do not realize... that their morality is essentially no finer than Shylock's" (49).[35] Norman Rabkin, in a wonderful 1972 essay on the play, wrote, "At every point at which we want simplicity we get complexity. Some signals point to coherence.... But just as many create discomfort, point to centrifugality..." (121, in Wheeler, 1991).

What about Shylock's ostensible greed? There are few plays of Shakespeare that are as controversial as this one, due to its ostensible antisemitism. What is often overlooked, though, is that Shakespeare uses the blatant antisemitism in this play not to express his own bigotry, but to hold a mirror up to the audience, to help us see it in ourselves; to help us understand the dynamics underlying antisemitism, not to promote it.

Further, he does so precisely to help us see how Christians project their own disavowed greed onto Jews. The actor Al Pacino refused offers to play the role of Shylock, until he changed his mind about the play's ostensible antisemitism. He then gave a wonderful performance in Michael Radford's 2004 film version.

Antonio self-righteously boasts that he never lends money at interest. In the Middle Ages, Christians were not allowed to charge interest, so Jews filled the void and served as moneylenders. It was a 1545 law under Henry VIII that made it legal to charge interest in England. When this play was written, the maximum legal interest rate in England was 10%; only charging more interest than that was condemned as usury.

Portia's many fortune-hunting suitors, and Antonio's pursuit of great wealth through foreign trade, are but some of the instances of gentile greed depicted in the play. In many productions, Shylock is made sympathetic by end of the play, just as Malvolio is in *Twelfth Night*. We recoil at our own vicarious cruelty toward these victims, however much we scorned them earlier in the plays. It is just these sequences of contrasting emotions that Shakespeare exploits with genius.

In his play *Timon of Athens*, de Vere offers a plausible self-portrait of his own charity run amok. Timon gives away so much of his wealth that he ruins himself financially. Like Timon, de Vere ignored his servants' attempts to warn him of his financial recklessness before it was too late. It was the unrestrained greed of Timon's "friends" that ruined him, as they exploited his generosity by demanding more and more expensive gifts from him.

People sometimes ask, "What difference does it make who wrote Shakespeare?" This is usually a not-so-veiled defense of the traditional authorship theory. But, however rhetorical its intent, this question has many serious answers. One has to do with the possibility that our conception of the Shakespeare canon is far too narrow—that the author wrote many not yet identified works, in addition to the known plays and poems. Among other things, identifying these other works gives us a more realistic picture of the gradual development of his peerless creative skill. He was writing and translating poetry since his adolescence. His well-known plays and poems are the product of his mature years (though some "Shakespeare" plays were probably revisions of much earlier "anonymous" plays that he wrote when he was younger).

In Act III of *Henry VIII*, the corrupt Cardinal Wolsey makes a fatal parapraxis. In giving the King some official documents to read, he inadvertently includes a secret inventory of his vast, stolen wealth. It is as though his unconscious wish to flaunt his riches before the King gets the better of his conflicting wish to conceal his crimes. Alternatively, his superego may be unconsciously arranging for appropriate punishment for his astonishing greed.

Reading this shocking inventory, the King exclaims, "What piles of wealth he hath accumulated/ To his own portion!" (III.ii.7-8). After the King asks if anyone has seen Wolsey, the Duke of Norfolk finishes his reply with the words, "In most strange postures/ We have seen him *set himself*" (III.ii.117-118). De Vere's biblical annotations shed light on those last two words. Although these two words may seem trivial, de Vere was extraordinarily verbal, perhaps with a photographic memory for everything he read. The phrase "set himself" does not occur in the Geneva Old or New Testament. But it is found in 2 Esdras, in the Apocrypha. De Vere underlined many entire verses of chapters 8 and 9 of 2 Esdras. Chapter 8 proclaims that "There be many created, but few shall be saved" (verse 3). All the words of verse 6 were underlined by de Vere. The verse says, "O Lord, if thou suffer not thy servant, that we may entreat Thee, that thou mayst give seed to our heart, and prepare our understanding, that there may come fruit of it, whereby every one which is corrupt, may live, who [other than God] can *set himself* for man?" [36] In fact, in keeping with this verse, the exposure of Wolsey's corruption leads to his contrition.

De Vere underlined the words "The plowmen that till the ground" in 2 Esdras 15:13. He also drew a pointing hand in the margin next to these words. This was the only time he drew a "manicule" in the margin, other than in his Whole Book of Psalms (bound with his Bible).[37] Verse 13 in its entirety says, "*The plowmen that till the ground* shall mourn: for their seeds shall fail through the blasting and hail, and by a horrible star" (emphasis added). The emphasized words are strikingly similar to the first words of de Vere's commendatory poem at the beginning of the 1573 English translation of *Cardanus Comfort*, whose publication de Vere arranged.[38] Here are the poem's first four lines (emphasis added):

> *The labouring man, that tills the fertile soil*,
> And reaps the harvest fruit, hath not indeed
> The gain but pain, and if for all his toil
> He gets the straw, the lord [i.e., the master] will have the seed.

Clearly, the first line of the poem paraphrases the first words of the verse— the very words de Vere underlined. And the first verse of the poem generally parallels the content of the verse. These close parallels, by the way, help refute Shakespeare scholars who have tried to claim that a later owner of de Vere's Bible underlined verses that reminded him or her of Shakespeare's works (typical of Stratfordian circular thinking at its worst). More significantly, de Vere's poem echoes the biblical concern with injustice. The biblical verse reassures the righteous that God will punish iniquity; de Vere's poem describes in detail the injustices caused by class and economic differences.[39] Similarly, some of Shakespeare's sonnets echo the laments of psalms he marked in his *Whole Book of Psalms*, while omitting the reassurance that follows in those psalms.

In doing research for this chapter, I came across lyrics that were set to music by the composer William Byrd. As you will recall, Byrd was on such good terms with de Vere that de Vere gave him the lease of one of his estates. It is known that Byrd set some of de Vere's poems to music (e.g., "If Women Could Be Fair and Never Fond"). There are probably more as yet unattributed de Vere poems among Byrd's song lyrics.[40] In Byrd's 1588 collection, *Psalms, Sonnets, and Songs of Sadness and Piety*, the first secular poem begins, "I joy not in earthly bliss,/ I force not Croesus' wealth a straw...."[41] A few lines later are words that may capture de Vere's sentiments about excessive wealth: "I scorn no poor, nor fear no rich;/ I feel not want, nor have too much."[42] The poem's final phrase is "I find/ No wealth is like the quiet mind."

In conclusion, a study of greed and generosity in the works of Shakespeare supports the theory Freud endorsed that these works were probably written by Edward de Vere, Earl of Oxford. De Vere followed a consistent pattern in writing words in his Geneva Bible. He wrote them only in the left and right margins, and they were all key words in passages that interested him. With only one exception: it is the word "*continue*," written *above* a verse whose number is underlined. This is in the Apocrypha, in a book that is known to be an important source for Shakespeare's works. Ecclesiasticus 11:21 exhorts the righteous, "Marvel not at the works of sinners, but trust in the Lord, and abide in thy labor: for it is an easy thing in the sight of the Lord suddenly to make a poor man rich." De Vere may have found in this verse inspiration to "continue" with his anonymous literary labors, in the assurance that God would see them and would one day reward him—in his heavenly and literary afterlife, if not while he lived.

[Editor's note: This article was originally published in Salman Akhtar, ed., *Greed: Developmental, Cultural, and Clinical Realms* (Karnac Books, 2015)]

Endnotes

[1] For the full text of most of Dr. Waugaman's sixty publications on Shakespeare and on the psychology of pseudonymity, see his Georgetown Faculty website, http://explore.georgetown.edu/people/waugamar/

[2] March 13, 2014, online article by Ian Talley, "IMF Escalates Focus on Income Inequality," retrieved March 13, 2014.

[3] See Peter Fonagy, "On Tolerating Mental States: Theory of Mind in Borderline Personality," *Bulletin of the Anna Freud Centre*, 12:91-115 (1989).

[4] Daniel Goleman, "Rich People Just Care Less." *New York Times*, October 5, 2013.

[5] One thinks of the owners of the two largest private yachts in the world, who seem anxious that the other one will build a yacht larger than theirs. See "Ruling the Waves: The £390 Million, 590 Foot Super-Yacht that has Knocked Roman Abramovich's Eclipse Off the Top Spot." *Mail Online*, August 14, 2013.

[6] Commencement address at University of California's School of Business Administration, May 18, 1986.

[7] "A Memo to Obama." *The Economist*, March 1, 2014, 25.

[8] Suzane Mettler, "College, the Great Unlever." *New York Times*, March 1, 2014.

[9] *The Nation*, December 16, 2013, "Socialist in Seattle," 4.

[10] Danny McCormick et al., "U.S. Physicians' Views of Financing Options to Expand Health Insurance Coverage: A National Survey," *Journal of General Internal Medicine* 24:526-531 (2009).

[11] Paul Edmondson and Stanley Wells (eds.) attempted to prove that the traditional theory is beyond dispute in their 2013 book *Shakespeare Beyond Doubt*, which I reviewed in the *Journal of the American Psychoanalytic Association* 62(1):180-186 (2014).

[12] The buffoon Sogliardo (Shakspere?) has paid £30 for his coat of arms, and has chosen this motto. He explains that the crest of his coat of arms shows "a boar without a head." A boar was the de Vere family's heraldic animal. Another

character replies, "I commend the herald's wit, he has deciphered him well: a swine without a head, without brain, wit, anything indeed, ramping to gentility" (III.i).

[13] In *The Taming of the Shrew*, a Lord (de Vere?) finds the drunken beggar Sly passed out in front of a tavern where he refused to pay his bill, and plays an elaborate practical joke on Sly, having the Lord's servants treat Sly as if he himself was a "mighty lord." Costard is called "that unlettered small-knowing soul" (I.i.251). Costard uses the word "remuneration" nine of the twelve times it occurs in Shakespeare's works.

[14] In *Cheiragogia Manuductio ad Artem Rhetoricam* (London: Augustini Matthews, 3d ed., 70). See Fred Schurink, "An Unnoticed Early Reference to Shakespeare." *Notes & Queries* 53(1):72-75 (2006). One wonders if this early allusion to Shakespeare remained "unnoticed" until 2006 because it might cast doubt on the traditional authorship theory.

[15] In *Coriolanus*, a citizen protests that the wealthy patricians "ne'er cared for us yet: suffer us to famish, and their store-houses crammed with grain" (I.i.80-81).

[16] Quoting Jayne Archer, a researcher in Renaissance literature at Aberystwyth. In online *Telegraph*, March 31, 2013 (accessed February 27, 2014).

[17] For details on Shakspere's business career and financial success, see Anthony Pointon, *The Man Who Was Never Shakespeare*, Tunbridge Wells, UK: Parapress (2011).

[18] In online *Dictionary of National Biography*, retrieved March 8, 2014.

[19] Charlton Ogburn, Jr., *The Mysterious William Shakespeare: The Myth and the Reality*. McLean, VA: EPM Publications, 671.

[20] Jonnie Lea Dunn, *The Literary Patronage of Edward de Vere*, Master's Thesis, University of Texas at Arlington (1999). Dunn speculates about why scholars of Elizabethan literature have not dealt with this fact: "It is ...likely that, because of his being put forward as a candidate for authorship of the Shakespeare plays, some scholars feel called upon to savage his reputation and overlook his patronage rather than assess its scope and influence" (2).

[21] In *Shakesepare and Music*, London: The Stage (1922).

[22] *The First Set of English Madrigals*. London: William Barley (1599), 1.

[23] Although de Vere underlined some of the printed marginal notes, he did not underline those adjoining Matthew 19:21.

[24] Medical treatment.

[25] An excess amount of something—in this case, wealth—but also playing on the excess rain of the storm.

[26] "Almes" is the largest of all the words that de Vere wrote in the margins of his Geneva Bible.

[27] Spenser wrote a dedicatory poem to de Vere in this book; and "Ignoto" (de Vere) contributed a commendatory poem to it as well.

[28] "The Fall of the House of Oxford." *Brief Chronicles: An Interdisciplinary Journal of Authorship Studies* 1:41-95 (2009).

[29] "Wriothesley's Resistance: Wardship Practices and Ovidian Narratives in Shakespeare's Venus and Adonis." In Philip C. Kolin (ed.), *Venus and Adonis: Critical Essays*. London: Routledge (1997).

[30] This use of "exclamation" meaning a "loud complaint" was used only *once* in the 436 books printed in 1576 that are digitized in Early English Books Online [EEBO] database, but the OED records that it was used in that sense in Shakespeare's *Henry VIII* (I.2.59). This is but one small example of the striking verbal parallels between the writings of de Vere and those of "Shakespeare." Not surprising, if de Vere wrote those works.

[31] In Haitian Creole, "Bondye bay, men li pa konn separe."

[32] *"Shakespeare" Identified in Edward de Vere, the Seventeenth Earl of Oxford*. London: Cecil Palmer (1920).

[33] *The Mysterious William Shakespeare: The Myth and the Reality*. McLean, VA: EPM Publications (1984).

[34] Thomas Wheeler, ed., *The Merchant of Venice: Critical Essays*. New York: Garland (1991), ix.0.

[35] In Wheeler, 1991.

[36] I.e., to cause one's affections to center upon man (OED 37.a.).

[37] Further, he drew a vertical dotted line next to this verse, leaving little doubt as to his strong interest in its message.

[38] And whose translation may be his own, knowing his pattern of publishing anonymously, and of attributing his own works to others.

[39] Roger Stritmatter connected the same de Vere poem with another passage from the same chapter of 2 Esdras—verses 33-38, in his "The Biblical Origin of Edward de Vere's Dedicatory Poem in Cardan's *Comforte*." *The Oxfordian* 1:53-63 (1998).

[40] This surmise is consistent with Thomas Nashe's dedication of his 1593 *Strange News* "To the most copious Carminist of our time," thought by some as an allusion to de Vere. "Carmen" is Latin for "poem or song"; "Carminare" means "making verses or songs"; "carminist" thus seems to refer de Vere writing

[41] That latter phrase means "I attach no importance to Croesus's wealth." The same expression is used in Shakespeare's *The Rape of Lucrece*: "*I force not* argument *a straw*" (line 1021). Once again, we see an uncommon usage that makes authorship by the same writer more plausible.

[42] The next line, "The court and cart I [neither] like nor loath," brings up a central antithesis of 1589 *The Arte of English Poesie*, an important book I have attributed to de Vere. Although the poem is sometimes attributed to Edward Dyer, it is found in many manuscript collections along with poems of de Vere. Bear in mind that his authorship sometimes had to be hidden due to the so-called "stigma of print" for noblemen such as the Earl of Oxford.

An Arrogant Joseph Hall...

and an Angry Edward de Vere

....in *Virgidemiarum*, 1599

Carolyn Morris

A noteworthy literary event occurred in December 1599 with the publication of *Virgidemiarum*,[1] a compilation of two earlier books of satires: *Toothlesse Satyrs* (March 1597) and *Byting Satyres* (March 1598). Only six months earlier, it prominently sat atop the list of works to be collected and burned in the Bishops' Ban of 1 June 1599. The author was identified by name: "*Satyres termed Hall's satyres viz. Virgidemiarum or his toothles or bitinge satyres*."[2] It should have been destroyed, as had the satires and epigrams of other authors, yet there it was in December, newly printed and available to the public with the notation, "Corrected and amended with some Additions. By I. H."[3]

Before the Bishops' Ban, the books had been printed as anonymous works, but now they were known to be by Joseph Hall, a 24-year-old fellow of Emmanuel College Cambridge, an academic star of the Loyal Puritan faction, those who gave their support to Queen Elizabeth, but who wanted the Church of England to be more pure. With the publication of *Virgidemiarum,* there was no more anonymity; Hall would have to own what he wrote.

Why the work was allowed to be published after it had been banned with such notoriety remains unanswered. A second document, issued by the bishops only three days later on 4 June, listed *Virgidemiarum* and one other publication, *Caltha Poetarum* (1599) by Thomas Cutwode (also known as Tailboys Dymoke) to be "staid," or not burned. "Willobies *Adviso* to be Called in," of uncertain authorship (1594), was added to the list to be burned.[4] There were two main reasons for the Bishops' Ban: lasciviousness and, more importantly, satirical personal attacks on highly placed people that came too close to exposing them. Allowing *Virgidemiarum* to be published may have been a veiled threat to those people. From an opposite point of view, it may have been a way to embarrass Loyal Puritans by identifying one of their own as the author of a lascivious work.

The Latin title, *Virgidemiarum*, means a small bundle of rods to be used for scourging, with the sense of Hall's satires as the rods. Hall describes *Tooth-lesse Satyrs* as "gentle Satyres, pend so easily," with relatively gentle scourging. He says of *Byting Satyres*, "I write in crabbed oake-tree rinde, search they that meane the secret meaning finde."[5] He's going to be much rougher and he wants to be clear that his satires contain covert meanings.

Hall deals in general with perceived vices of the age; he deals specifically with persons hidden under Latin or allegorical names, often using numerous names and characters for one person, or combining two or more people into one character. He breaks apart people and events and puts them back together into an abstract, but recognizable, form to those with inside knowledge. His aim was to be obscure, and this obscurity gave him the credible deniability that every writer of satire needed to protect himself from charges of libel or exposure.

This article is composed of excerpts from the whole of *Virgidemiarum* that, I propose, concern Edward de Vere and reveal the deeply hidden story that he is William Shakespeare. The approach is to be conceptually simple and to follow a single thread of a larger, intricate tapestry. It is an analysis of Hall's words and focuses on those satires that concern de Vere. It is Hall who drives the story that evolves, one which contains a surprisingly vivid portrayal of de Vere, although from a Puritan point of view. My analysis looks to what Hall has said, but I also seek his hidden meaning as well as his apparent one. Evidence that Hall is writing about de Vere grows stronger as the satires progress and build upon each other; they tell of other scandals in his life, not only of the "baseness" of his participation in the public stage as William Shakespeare. I have chosen not to include some allusions to de Vere because they are too general or obscure. One concerns a mature, lusty courtier with auburn locks whose wig is blown off by a gusty wind and it's revealed that he is bald underneath. A "yonker" (a dignified gallant) picks up the wig from a deep ditch.[6] I think that allusion is to de Vere as the lusty coutier and to William Shakspere of Stratford as the yonker. Another satire concerns a poor, rustic gallant named Ruffio, a "fayre yonker" (a dignified gallant) who struts around London in the latest foppish fashions, walks the aisles of St. Paul's and is compared to a "Shak-forke."[7] I think that is another allusion to William Shakspere, who is ironically called a "Shak-forke" instead of a Shake-speare. I have omitted a few concise allusions, i.e., "I loath… *Labeos* poems or base *Lolios* pride.…"[8] There are likely other allusions that I have not recognized.[9]

One can see a progression in the satires, starting late in Book 1 and continuing into Book 2, with a scourging of de Vere for writing lewdly in *Venus and Adonis*. It leads to a harsher, more personal scourging in Book 4, which contains five satires in a row that concern him, and then Book 6 contains the ultimate recantation of all the scourging that has preceded it. *Virgidemiarum* is an exceptional source for information about de Vere. It calls for much more study than this essay provides.

The text for the excerpts is from the 1599 edition with its use of italics and capitalization and it uses the corrections and additions listed at the end of the book, as by "I.H." The letter *u* has been changed to *v* where appropriate, e.g., "love" instead of "loue," "ever" instead of "euer." The interpretations of Hall's text which follow each excerpt are mine. Portions of the work presented below first appeared, in slightly different form, in "Did Joseph Hall and Ben Jonson Identify Oxford as Shakespeare?" *The Oxfordian* vol. 15 (2013).

TOOTH-LESSE SATYRS: The first three Books (March 1597)

Hall did not use mottos for his satires in the first three Books. The subtitles quoted are those supplied in 1825 to help identify the content.[10] They refer to the apparent meaning of the satire, not to the hidden meaning.

HIS DEFIANCE TO ENVY: A poem prefixed to the satires

Nay: let the prouder Pines of Ida feare
The sudden fires of heaven: and decline
Their yeelding tops, that dar'd the skies whilere.
(1-3)

From the first lines, Hall says what he intends to do. The proudest people in Queen Elizabeth's court, the highest Pines, need to fear Envy and the attacks of the gods. Hall defies Envy because, he later implies with false modesty, he isn't important enough and his poetry isn't good enough. He presents himself as the instrument of Nemesis, the goddess who chastises the proud. He wants those with great pride to bow their heads and repent.

Edward de Vere was England's preeminent earl, the 17th Earl of Oxford. John Aubrey says, quoting King Charles I, "The three ancientist familes in Europe were the Veres in England, Earls of Oxford…Fitz-Geralds in Ireland…and Momorancy in France."[11] De Vere was known for great pride about his ancient heritage.[12] He was closely associated with Queen Elizabeth from the age of twelve, when he became her ward upon his father's death in 1562, and came to live in the home of William Cecil, her chief councilor and Secretary of State.[13]

The influence of *Virgidemiarum* on other writers can be shown in that many of them imitated the use of a prefatory poem or prose: John Marston, *To Detraction* in *The Scourge of Villainie* (1599); Thomas Middleton, *His Defiance to Envy* in *Micro-Cynicon* (1599); John Weever in prefatory verses, *Epigrammes* (1599); Thomas Cutwode, a prose preface, *To the Conceited Poets of Our Age* in *Caltha Poetarum* (1599).[14]

Book 1, Satire IX: *An Obscene Poet*

> Envie ye Muses, at your thriving Mate,
> *Cupid* hath crowned a new *laureat*:
> I saw his *Statue* gayly tyr'd in greene,
> As if he had some second *Phoebus* beene.
> His *Statue* trim'd with the Venerean tree,
> And shrined faire within your Sanctuarie.
>
> (1-6)

Hall has overtly mentioned or covertly alluded to many authors by this point in the satires: Spenser, Sidney, Marlowe, Stanyhurst, the poets of the *Mirror for Magistrates*, sacred poets, sonneteers, the poets of Roman hexameters, legendary and romantic poets, and drunken poets. But he has not noted Shakespeare, whose two long poems, *Venus and Adonis* (1593) and *The Rape of Lucrece* (1594), were still popular.

Hall now deals with a poet whom critics have been unable to identify. It has been conjectured that he was some obscure scribbler of the day, but the poet is successful ("thriving") and Cupid has crowned him a "new laureat," a poet of acclaim. The Muses should feel envy at the superiority of the author. Hall sees fit to devote a whole satire to him.

When one thinks of a popular poet who was newly being acclaimed as Cupid's laureate, and who wrote so well that the Muses should envy him, Shakespeare has to be considered. The name was publicly unknown until 1593, when it first appeared in print on *Venus and Adonis*. That work was a bawdy, sophisticated and beautifully written poem about love that was avidly read by the public and the court, but was thought to be obscene by Loyal Puritans. It, along with *The Rape of Lucrece*, had been published in numerous editions.[15]

The poet's statue or likeness is gaily attired in green. As has often been noted, the French word for "green" is "vert" and is a homophone of "Ver," an alternate spelling of de Vere's name. The pronunciation of *vert/Ver/Vere* rhymes with "fair." "Green" had become a frequent covert indicator for de Vere in the literature of the 1590s. Thomas Nashe combined "Ver" and "green" in *Summer's Last Will and Testament*, first performed in 1592, but not published until 1600 (another noteworthy event, as all of Nashe's works had been banned by the Bishops). Ver, a character representing Spring, merrily enters the stage with a large number of singers and dancers dressed all in green moss. Rita Lamb, a Stratfordian, has identified Ver as de Vere.[16]

Hall, in his *Virgidemiarum*, says that it's as if the poet is a second Phoebus. De Vere had been compared to Phoebus Apollo by Gabriel Harvey in the widely known *Gratulationes Valdinenses* (1578). Apollo is named in the Latin motto on the title page of *Venus and Adonis*, from Ovid's *Amores*, Book I, Elegy 15. Marlowe translated it: "Let base-conceited wits admire vile things, /Fair Phoebus lead me to the Muses springs."[17]

"Trim'd with the Venerean tree" means adorned with myrtle, which was considered a wanton tree that grew on laurel stock. Erato was crowned with myrtle when erotic poetry was the subject. The word "Venerean," in Early Modern English, meant connected with or related to Venus. "Shrined faire within your Sanctuarie" employs a usage of the word "faire" that, when applied to literature, meant eloquent or polished. *Venus and Adonis* was an eloquent and polished poem. "Faire" is also suggestive of an allusion to Ver. In Old English, *F* in the initial position of a word was always pronounced as *V*.[18] The same pronunciation was sometimes found in the middle of a word, such as "behoofe" for "behoove." The carryover to Early Modern was common; for example, in the 1580 will of Agnes Arden, Mary Arden's stepmother, the body of the will contains a bequest to a Richard Petyvere, who becomes at the end of the will a witness, Richard Petifere.[19] In *King Lear*, Edgar says in IV.v, "without vurther 'casion...let poor volk pass... zo long as 'tis by a vortnight." Thus, "faire" could be synonymous with "Ver." The covert indicator "faire," added to Phoebus in the motto of *Venus and Adonis,* points to de Vere.

A definition of "Shrined" or "enshrined" was to conceal within a shrine. The Oxford English Dictionary gives an example of this usage from Spenser in *Hymne in Honour of Beautie,* (1596), "What booteth that celestiall ray, if it in darkness be enshrined ever?" In this sense, Hall suggests that de Vere is concealed in the Muses' sanctuary, a place of safety. He is a hidden poet. Spenser's line is evocative of de Vere's hiddenness as well, but it is a sidetrack that won't be followed.

Whiles th'itching vulgar tickled with the song,
Hanged on their unreadie poets tongue.
     (11-12)

The public was "tickled" with what he wrote and eagerly read everything. However, the "unreadie poet" didn't want to be recognized. He was not ready or was unavailable for use. It is again emphasized that de Vere was a hidden poet. The public was enthralled with *Venus and Adonis*.

But Arts of Whoring: stories of the Stewes,
Ye Muses, will ye beare and may refuse?
Nay, let the *Divell* and *Saint Valentine*
Be gossips to those ribald rimes of thine.
     (33-36)

The Muses are asked not to accept or condone overt, lewd, sexual poetry like *Venus and Adonis*. Then Hall makes reference to "the *Divell* and *Saint Valentine,*" two works by Thomas Nashe: *Pierce Penniless his Supplication to the Divell* (1592) and *The Choice of Valentines* (early 1590s).[20] *Pierce Penniless* was Nashe's most successful work, a satire in prose that addressed the wickedness and evil in the world. The title character has been identified as an allusion to both de Vere and to Nashe.[21] *The Choice of Valentines* was an extremely erotic poem, not printed until 1899, but widely circulated and known. A definition of "gossip" in Early Modern English was godparent. Hall is saying that Nashe's two works, not the Muses, should represent the obscene author's "ribald rimes."

Within the first six lines are three words with strong covert meanings that allude to de Vere: "greene," "Phoebus" and "faire." The poet is a challenge to the Muses, is thriving, is Cupid's new laureate, is entwined with an erotic Venus, is obscene and is hidden in the Muses' sanctuary. Cupid's new laureate is William Shakespeare, the author of *Venus and Adonis,* and he is Edward de Vere, a hidden poet. If this seems like a huge leap without enough evidence, coming satires will provide more clarity. Hall's elliptical writing makes it imperative to read to the end to fully understand preceding allusions.

This is the first satire that deals covertly with de Vere as Shakespeare.

Or beene the Manes *of that Cynick Spright,*
Cloth'd with some stubborn clay and led to light?
...That so with gall-weet words and speeches rude,
Controls the maners of the multitude.
Envie belike incites his pining heart,
And bids it sate it selfe with others smart.
...angrie Nemesis*...that scourge I beare,*
And wound and strike and pardon whom she list.
(Book 2, Prologue, 1-12)

Hall asks if Diogenes of Sinope, the Cynic who could mock Alexander the Great and the elite and get away with it,[22] has come back to life with his bawdy and biting work that is so popular with the public. The prologue and the following satire refer back to the immediately preceding satire, Book 1, Satire IX, *An Obscene Poet*. The laureate whom Cupid has newly crowned was extremely talented and, by implication, could mock Elizabeth and the mighty and get away with it. His lewd *Venus and Adonis* was so popular with the public that it influenced public behavior. Hall recognizes the "smart," the scathing wit, the biting humor of the author even as he scourges the content of his work.

At this point, Hall reveals himself in his guise as Nemesis. He feels entitled to go after anyone with his scourging or to pardon them. He has told us he will attack the proud, but he himself has assumed an arrogant, godlike persona.

For shame, write better, *Labeo,* or write none,
Or better write or *Labeo* write alone.

(Book 2, Satire I: *Immodest Poetry,* 1-2)

Labeo is told not to be lewd, but to "write cleanly," as the last couplet of this satire says, or not to write at all. He's also told to write by himself, "alone," under his own name (this translation will be seen as accurate when a later satire is introduced). Labeo is the author with whom Diogenes wants to sate his pining heart. Labeo is the author whom Hall compares to Diogenes.

The source of the name Labeo has two strong contenders, who, when added together, more fully reveal de Vere. Using a name associated with two plausible historical figures is a literary device that Hall used frequently. One candidate is Labeo Attius, a court poet of the emperor Nero, who became the eponym for a bad poet. Hall indicates that his Labeo is a bad poet, although "bad" is directed at content and not skill, and tells him to "write better." Hall says that, in large part, he writes his satires in the manner of Persius.[23] Persius derided Labeo Attius in his Satire I: "Do you, who are old enough to be wiser, put together such obscene and filthy stuff in order to be food for your libidinous hearers? I tell you plainly, and without disguise, that you are an old trifler, to pretend to wit or poetry."[24] The whole of Persius's Satire I concerns bad writing like Labeo's, who, near the end says, "Tell me the truth about myself," to which Persius replies, "You are just a fool, you old bald pate, ye blue-blooded patrician."[25]

A second candidate for Hall's Labeo is Quintus Fabius Labeo, from an old, distinguished family associated with Rome's beginnings.[26] He was a Praetor in 189 BCE and was later Second Consul of the Republic. He also wrote plays. The Roman biographer Santra (c. 44-39 BCE) surmised that Terence was more likely a front for this Labeo (or for Gaius Sulpicius Gallus or Marcus Popillius) as the author of the plays for which Terence was given credit, than for Laelius or Scipio, who were younger men.[27]

Both Labeos point covertly to de Vere. They are upper class, mature men, poets and playwrights. Labeo Attius is a fool, he is bald, he has written obscene and filthy works to feed lascivious readers. He asks for the truth about himself. Quintus Fabius Labeo's heritage is associated with the founding of Rome, as de Vere claimed his was, and it is suggested that someone else was given credit for this Labeo's work. A compelling and complicated picture of de Vere is seen in the two Labeos.

Hall detracts from de Vere's name both as an author and, as we shall see, as a person. John Marston, in *Reactio*, Satire IV of *The Metamorphosis of Pigmalion's Image & Certaine Satyres* (1598), which was a direct response to *Toothlesse Satyrs and Byting Satyres* before *Virgidemiarum* of 1599 was published, says: "What cold Saturnian/Can hold and hear such vile detraction?" He used a prefatory poem, "To Detraction," in *The Scourge of Villainie*. Marston saw Hall's work as detraction, he personified him as "Detraction," and he saw his work as vile. Marston also specifically identified Labeo as the author of *Venus and Adonis*.[28]

Another small hint to Labeo's identity may be the last two letters of the name—*eo*. Edward de Vere was variously known as Edward Oxenford or the Earl of Oxford and he used the initials *E.O.* on poems and song lyrics from his early years. Hall plays with the end of names in other satires, i.e., Cyned becomes Cynedo, Pontice becomes Pontian.

> Nay, call the *Cynick* but a wittie foole,
> Thence to abjure his handsome drinking bole:
> Because the thirstie swaine, with hollow hand,
> Convey'd the streame to weet his drie weasand.
>
> (Lines 3-6)

Hall is again comparing Labeo with Diogenes, who is called a witty fool, and we have seen Persius's use of a fool who pretends to wit. Hall is saying that Labeo has given up something of value to behave like a commoner. He is stooping from his high position. De Vere's association with the public theater would have been a disgrace within the social mores of the day. It would have been considered base or common or vile for a nobleman, especially one of highly esteemed lineage who was also Lord Great Chamberlain, to write for or act on the public stage, although it was acceptable to write or act for the entertainment of the court. Diogenes was singularly odd, to use a phrase applied to de Vere,[29] who was widely known for his wit and for being a fool.

A riddle

> *Write they that can, tho they that cannot doe:*
> *But who knowes that, but they that doe not know?*
>
> (Lines 3-6)

Those who are able to write (and publish), *do so, though those who aren't able to write* (because of their high position), *also do. But who knows that they write? Only those who have said that they do not know that they write* (who have sworn not to reveal the authors).

The riddle is an important part of Hall's message. It tells of concealed aristocratic writers. Labeo is one. The riddle says that those who know their identities keep that knowledge hidden. In Book 4, Satire IV, *Plus beau que fort*, a motto by Hall, he says, "Have I not vow'd for shunning such debate/ (Pardon ye satyres) to degenerate?"—the debate being about Shakespeare.

> So, lavish ope-tyde causeth fasting-lents,
> So extravagant spring causes the leanness of Lent.
>
> (3-6)

An archaic translation of "ope-tyde" is early spring. It was the time when flowers first started opening, or the time before Ash Wednesday. "Ver" means spring in Latin and we remember the character Ver, who represented Spring, in Nashe's play. In the context of the satire, Hall is saying that de Vere needs to stop writing so voluminously, which causes a shortage of paper and quills for lesser writers and makes them expensive. In his personal life de Vere was called lavish and spent money extravagantly.

And each man writes: *Ther's so much labour lost.*
That's good, that's great: Nay much is seldome well,
Of what is bad, a littl's a great deale.
Better is more: but best is nought at all.
Lesse is the next, and lesser criminall.
Little and good, is greatest good save one,
Then Labeo, or write better, or write none.

(3-6)

Italicized sentences always indicate that Hall is saying something important. Hall makes an allusion to Shakespeare's *Love's Labour's Lost*. He includes references to Shakespeare in parts of the satires that deal with de Vere, and links them repeatedly. The line also shows his disapproval of the writings of most authors. On a covert level, the use of "each man," meaning *every* man, is an allusion to de Vere, and Hall specifically decries his voluminous writing. "Every" alludes to E. Ver or Edward de Vere, who used "ever" in his own *Echo Verses*: *Sitting alone upon my thought in melancholy mood* and in *Ann Vavasour's Echo* (c. 1580) to refer to himself as E. Ver and as an anagram of Vere.

There are three colons in this section. "Labour lost" follows the first, an evident allusion to the title of the play. Following the second colon are "much" and "well," and following the third are "nought" and "all." They are simple words, but used together, and following the example of "labour lost," they evoke *Much Ado About Nothing* and *All's Well that Ends Well*.

Tush, in small paynes can be but little art,
Or lode full drie-fats fro the forren mart
With *Folio-volumes*, two to an Oxe-hide.

(27-29)

The lines are a specific allusion to Oxford/de Vere. The "Folio-volumes" alluded to are *Venus and Adonis* and *Lucrece*. The hide of *one* ox produced *two* folios. It isn't difficult to see the de Vere word *Oxe*. We now have "greene," "Phoebus," "faire," "Oxe," "lavish," and "ope-tyde/Spring."

"Drie-fats" were vats used to ship dry items. They were often lined with waste paper from printers to protect the items. Hall means the lines as an insult to *Venus and Adonis*, that it should be so used.

So may the Giant rome and write on high,
Be he a Dwarfe that writes not there as I.

(35-36)

Earlier critics with deep classical backgrounds have not been able to understand this couplet.[30] With our eyes on de Vere, the meaning appears. He was the premier earl, a giant, but he was rather short.[31] Hall refers to small stature numerous times in relation to de Vere. The giant, great, ancient Oxford writes for the court, the highest social level. It's all right with Hall that he writes there, but again the implication is that it isn't acceptable for him to write for the public. The word "high" is an indicator for de Vere. A quote from Sidney's *The Lady of May* (1598) uses similar language: "The highest note comes oft from basest mind, / As shallow brooks do yield the greatest sound…." It corresponds with Hall's frequent reference to de Vere as base, even though he is of highest station.

The use of "rome" is an obscure allusion to de Vere's claim to trace his ancestry to Aeneas, the legendary founder of Rome, and to Troy, as Aeneas was a Trojan hero. The lines immediately following this section refer to Troy. There are further allusions to Rome, Troy and Aeneas. We can add them as indicators that make us look for covert meanings that point to de Vere.

But well fare *Strabo*, which, as stories tell,
Contriv'd all *Troy* within one walnut shell.
His curious ghost now lately hither came,
Arriving neere the mouth of luckie Tame.
I saw a *Pismire* struglling with the lode,
Dragging all *Troy* home towards her abode.
(37-42)

Strabo is wished well. According to myth, Strabo made all of Troy in miniature; he essentially made the history of Troy in miniature. Someone like him, "new Straboe," as Hall will refer to him in line 52, has recently appeared near the mouth of the Thames (in London at the public theaters, or at Hampton Court at the royal theater), and is making the history of England in miniature, "new Straboes Troy" (on the stage). Even the least of those in London can take it into their lives. They can learn English history and understand it by watching a play. Hall approves of New Strabo/Labeo/de Vere/Shakespeare's heroic writings of kings and victories. He specifically says so in Book 6, Satire I, *Semel Insaniuimus*, "Tho Labeo reaches right (who can deny?)/ The true straynes of heroicke poesie." Having jumped ahead, we can see "true" as another word attached to Labeo that points to de Vere, as "vere" in Latin means "true."

Hall is referring to new Strabo's history plays, new Troy, and thinks well of them since everyone can identify with what it means to be English, a unifying theme for both Catholics and Protestants. "All Troy within one walnut shell" is an allusion to *Hamlet*, II.ii, "I could be bounded in a nutshell and count myself a king of infinite space…."

> Now dare we hither, if we durst appeare,
> The subtile *Stithy-man* that liv'd while eare;
> Such one was once, or once I was mistaught,
> A Smith at *Vulcans* owne forge up brought,
> Another Smith, brought-up at Vulcan's own forge,
> that made an iron-chariot so light,
> The coach-horse was a Flea in trappings dight
> The tame-lesse steed could well his wagon wield
> Through downes and dales of the uneven field.
> Strive they, laugh we....
>
> (43-51)

At this point, Hall wants us to have courage and to draw nearer to what he's really saying. It's a strong hint to a hidden meaning. The words "dare" and "durst" emphasize that he realizes the danger in writing of it.

The clever "Stithy-man," or Smith, Vulcan, is the learned and brilliant Sir Thomas Smith who had lived a little earlier ("while eare"). Smith died in 1577. The other Smith, "such one was once...a Smith," is de Vere, who was brought up at Thomas Smith's ("Vulcan's") own home ("owne forge"). De Vere spent a large part of his childhood in Thomas Smith's home.[32]

The other Smith/de Vere created a strong, but frothy, light, iron vehicle—a comedy—that was seen everywhere in public and was commanded or led by an untamed little steed all dressed up in trappings or in lavish clothing. The "chariot" is made of "iron," and the French word for iron is "fer," which, we have seen with the interchangeability of the letters *f* and *v*, can also refer to Ver. The untamed "Flea" is de Vere himself, referring to his rash behavior and his small stature. He was known as among the best for comedy of his day.[33]

They work hard to create. We laugh at their creations. What they create and we laugh at are the comedies. Hall approves of them because he laughs at them. His dual opinion of de Vere's writing is evident, as he recognizes his intelligence and ability in the history plays and the comedies, but scourges his misuse of it in *Venus and Adonis*.

> ...meane while the black storie
> Passes new *Strabo*, and new *Straboes Troy*.
> Little for great: and great for good: all one:
> For shame or better write or *Labeo* write none.
>
> (51-54)

Continuing with his satire, Hall comes back to Labeo after dealing with the history plays, "new *Straboes* Troy," and the comedies, "an iron-chariot so light," and approving them. He returns to shaming Labeo for writing so lewdly in *Venus and Adonis*. He says that writing of little worth is considered great because it's so popular with the public. If it's so popular, it must be good. It's all considered the same. "All one" may be an allusion to Southampton's motto, "One for All and All for One," and to him as the dedicatee of *Venus and Adonis*.

> But who conjur'd this bawdie *Poggies* ghost,
> From out the *stewes* of his lewde home-bred coast;
> Or wicked *Rablais* dronken revellings,
> To grace the mis-rule of our Tavernings?
> Or who put *Bayes* into blind *Cupids* fist
> That he should crowne what Laureats him list?
> (55-60)

The *Factiae* by Poggio was particularly obscene. Hall compares Poggio's writing to *Venus and Adonis*. He says that Labeo wrote it from his own experiences in brothels. Hall means real brothels, he brings them in often, and he may also mean the public theater, which was associated with brothels in people's minds. He says that the writer was a wicked, giant, drunken reveler. De Vere was accused by Arundel of being drunk in taverns[34] and he had a reputation for vile behavior early in his marriage to Anne Cecil, while he lived at Wivenhoe on the coast of Essex.[35]

    Cupid ignores lewd writing, a reference to Cupid's new laureate of Book 1, Satire IX, *An Obscene Poet*.

> Both good things ill, and ill things well; all one?
> For shame! write cleanly, *Labeo*, or write none.
> (63-64)

Labeo has turned evil into good and good into evil in *Venus and Adonis*. In Hall's Puritan opinion, he's a bad poet. Hall shames him with even more emphasis by using an exclamation point; it's the fourth time he's used the phrase and he opens and closes the satire with it. He again tells him to either write decently or to stop writing.

    "Labeo," the "curious ghost of Strabo" (new Strabo), and the "smith brought up at Vulcan's own forge" are all de Vere and respectively represent *Venus and Adonis*, the Shakespeare history plays (new Strabo's Troy) and the comedies. They are all Shakespeare, who is a new poet. He has been crowned Cupid's laureate. Hall is showing that he knows that de Vere is Shakespeare and he knows everything that he has written, but, as the riddle says, Hall won't say that he knows. It is his "gentle" way of identifying de Vere as Shakespeare and is the second satire in which he does so.

> To what end did our lavish auncestours
> Erect of old these stately piles of ours?
> For thred-bare clearks, and for the ragged Muse,
> ...Here may you, *Muses*, our deare *Soveraignes*,

Scorne each base *Lordling* ever you disdaines,
And everie peasant churle, whose smokie roofe
Denied harbour for your deare behoofe.

(Book 2, Satire II: *Neglect of Learning*, 1-14)

Why did our ancestors build stately buildings for universities? Was it merely for poor scholars whose poetry Hall considers rough and vulgar? He then invokes the Muses to scorn a base little Lord whose poetry they disdain. He is once more alluding to de Vere's small stature and is disdaining his *Venus and Adonis*. The phrase "each base *Lordling* ever" brings in the strong de Vere word "ever," and as noted, "each" means "every." The word "base" appears again to indicate that de Vere has stooped from his high position. This phrase is one of Hall's clearest allusions, with "Every," "base," "little Lord," and "E. Ver."

The beginning of the couplet—"And everie peasant churl"—is strange. What miserly peasant was asked, but refused to keep safe in his smoky rafters, works of the Muses for their own good? It seems like an allusion to William Shakspere and to his assuming the name of Shakespeare, but his refusal to harbor something for the Muses doesn't make sense with what we know, which is that William Shakspere of Stratford is credited with the works of William Shakespeare. The coupling of "everie" with "peasant churle" is a significant combining of de Vere and Shakspere.

I offer a speculation, based on my research on Book 4, Satire II, *Arcades Ambo*, which concerns a rustic becoming a gentleman: William Shakspere of Stratford might have refused to be an openly recognized allonym for William Shakespeare, the poet and playwright, while he, Shakspere, was alive, even though he may have plagiarized some sonnets for personal effect. His father, John, had been trying to become part of the gentry for a long time, which would have meant that William, as eldest son, would also be elevated. It was a continuing desire, a passion. John first applied for a coat of arms in 1569 when William was five, but it was not granted until 1596, some twenty-seven years later. Neither William nor his father would have wanted him to be identified as an actor for the public stage, as it was considered a common, base occupation which would have barred him from rising into the gentry. William could play the role of a gallant around London and be involved in somewhat nefarious activities, or even go into debt, but he could not openly act on the stage or write for it for pay, and be granted a coat of arms. The earlier allusion to "everie peasant churle" who "denied harbour" for the Muses benefit has some suggestion that Shakspere's position was to deny that he was the author Shakespeare.

Ye palish ghosts of *Athens*, when, at last,
Your patrimonie spent in witlesse wast,
Your friends all wearie, and your spirits spent,
Ye may your fortunes seeke: and be forwent
Of your kind cosins and your churlish sires,
Left there alone midst the fast-folding Briers.

Have not I lands of faire inheritance,
Deriv'd by right of long continuance
To first-borne males...?
(33-41)

The plural "ghosts" is used here. Hall uses the plural in other places to mask the singular, and he shifts into the singular in line 39. The allusion to Athens may be to Pallas Athena, the virgin patron of Athens, the goddess of the arts associated with the theater. A statue of Pallas Athena was said to have guaranteed the safety of Troy and was later taken to Rome by Aeneas to guarantee its safety as well.

Academics referred to Cambridge University as Athens. De Vere was associated with Queen's College in 1558 when Thomas Smith placed him there after Queen Elizabeth's ascension. He matriculated at St. John's College in 1559, but never graduated, having been taught by private tutors, as was the custom for noble scholars. He received an honorary Master of Arts degree from the University in 1564. William Cecil, his guardian and father-in-law, was a graduate of St. John's College and became Chancellor of the University.[36] De Vere's connection to Cambridge was strong, although he spent little actual time there.

By the 1590s the only route left for de Vere was to marry wealth ("your fortunes seeke"), since he wasn't getting the preferment he sought from Queen Elizabeth, his "kind cosin," and he had sold or pawned his properties to churlish usurers. If he married a fortune, he could forgo asking for financial help. He moved to Stoke Newington and later to Hackney, both at that time in the country ("midst the fast-folding Briers"), after marrying Elizabeth Trentham in late 1591, whose well-to-do family paid his debts over a period of time.[37] He was "left there alone," a rather bleak picture, evocative of *Timon of Athens* left alone in the country with no friends. De Vere was said to be friendless during the years of intrigue surrounding the succession to the crown.[38] He insists that he still has ancient Ver lands inherited by being the firstborn son of a long line.

"Churlish sire," which follows the earlier "peasant churle," is used again later to refer to a usurer. This is an example of Hall's elliptical writing, where a usage in one satire is brought up in a later one and refers to the same thing or person.

Or doth thy glorie stand in outward glee?
A lave-ear'd Asse with gold may trapped bee.
(63-64)

Here is another allusion to Shakespeare, to Bottom in *A Midsummer Night's Dream*. It's also an insult to de Vere, as he had long earlobes and he was entitled to use gold on his clothing as a member of the higher nobility. "Asse" is capitalized, indicating a person. Hall uses the allusion to drooping ears many times. If one looks at portraits of other men of the era, their earlobes are much shorter than de Vere's long lobe in the Welbeck Portrait, a copy of the original painted in Paris in 1575.[39]

Some say my Satyrs over-loosely flow,
Nor hide their gall inough from open show:
Not ridle-like obscuring their intent:
But packe-staffe plaine uttring what thing they ment.
(Book 3, Prologue, 1-4)

This is the first indication that someone has criticized Hall's content as being too plainly recognizable and not obscure enough. We shall see more of this.

The Conclusion:

Thus have I writ in smoother Cedar tree,
So gentle Satyrs, pend so easily.
Henceforth I write in crabbed oake-tree rinde,
Search they that meane the secret meaning finde.
Hold out ye guiltie, and ye galled hides,
And meete my far-fetch't stripes with waiting sides.
(*Tooth-lesse Satyrs*, 1-6)

As noted, Hall says that he will write with a rougher intent in *Byting Satyres* and specifically tells readers to search for his secret meaning. He warns the guilty, whom he has already scourged, to be ready for even more.

BYTING SATYRES: The last three Books (March 1598)

Hall supplies Italian, French, Latin and Greek mottos in *Byting Satyres*. They give a hint to his covert message. A few of them are nicknames for well known works, i.e., *Semel Insaniuimus* and *Arcades Ambo*. Hall also uses nicknames in the body of the satires, i.e., *Hos Ego* and *Arma Virum*. They will be discussed below.

Book 4, Satire I: *CHE BAIAR VUOL, BAI* ("Vile tho his principles, his conduct base [his heap'd treasure protects him from disgrace]"[40]). The motto is from Ariosto, Satire II (1518).

De Vere married Elizabeth Trentham in late 1591. Her wealthy family paid his huge debt over time, and invested his remaining assets.[41] Queen Elizabeth continued a grant to him of £1,000 per year.[42] He did possess "heap'd treasure," although he had lost most of his lands. The rough treatment that Hall has threatened begins immediately, with the use of vile principles and the emphasis on base conduct as a description of his character.

Who dares upbraid these open rimes of mine
…Which who reads thrise, and rubs his rugged brow,

And deepe intendeth every doubtfull row,
Scoring the margent with his blazing stars,
And hundreth crooked interlinears,
(Like to a merchants debt-role new defac't,
When some crack'd *Manour* crost his book at last).

(Lines 1-10)

Someone is upset about Hall's earlier satires, which originally circulated as pamphlets, and has criticized them. He has put angry stars and notes in the margins of his copies. "Blazing stars" is an allusion to the de Vere family badge of a star that was prominent on the coat of arms, was carried into battle on a flag, and was inscribed in buildings with a de Vere connection.[43] There is much marginalia, something that is also seen in de Vere's personal copy of the Geneva Bible at the Folger Shakespeare Library in Washington, DC.[44]

The parenthetical remark about a merchant finally being paid from the sale of a decrepit manor is an allusion to de Vere's loss of lands and patrimony. "Merchant" has a double meaning of a buyer and seller of commodities, but, more strongly in Hall's satires, of a usurer.[45] We have previously seen references to a churl in the sense of a usurer. They are all related to the merchant who is introduced here and usury is the important link. We will see this merchant again.

De Vere had recognized himself in Book 2, Satire I, *Immodest Poetry*, as Labeo/Shakespeare and was angry.

Stamping like *Bucephall*, whose slackned raines
And bloody fet-lockes fry with seven mens braines.

(Lines 13-14)

Bucephalus, Alexander the Great's horse, had a star on his forehead and the shape of an ox head on his flank, both allusions to de Vere. The name in Greek translates to Ox Head.[46] "Fry with seven mens braines" is an allusion to *Henry VI, Part I*, I.iv, "Your hearts I'll stamp out with my horse's heels / and make a quagmire of mingled brains."

The word "fry" has various senses to do with undergoing fire or intense heat by fire. Buchephalus's reins were slackened. He was given his head, or license to do as he chose, to satirically go after, or fry, a number of men; "seven" is used here to suggest an indeterminate number. Since Hall alludes to de Vere as Alexander's horse, it was Alexander who slackened the reins, an allusion to Queen Elizabeth. She gave de Vere license to write what he did. She knew what he was doing.

Yet wel bethought…reads a new;
The best lies low, and loathes the shallow view,
Quoth old *Eudemon*, when his gout-swolne fist
Gropes for his double ducates in his chist;
Then buckle close his carelesse lyds once more,

To pose the pore-blinde snake of *Epidaore*.

After more thought, de Vere decided it was best not to say anything. He felt he could control the situation using his wealth. He was well aware that Hall was referring to him as Labeo and as Shakespeare, but decided not to say anything because he saw that the reference was deeply hidden.

Hall is suggesting that de Vere had gout, a possible reason for the unwell body and lame hand that are mentioned in his later letters.[47] It is in addition to his lameness from a wound. Gout comes and goes; a person can function well at times, but be painfully laid up at others. It mainly affects the big toe, but can disable other joints including heels, knees, wrists, and fingers. This allusion is also suggestive of William Cecil, who had great wealth and was well known to have gout, showing that Cecil knew de Vere was Shakespeare and that he used his wealth to keep it hidden.

"Double ducates" in his chest refers to *The Merchant of Venice*. In my research, all of the Early Modern search results for "double ducates" were to *The Merchant of Venice*, II.viii, "A sealed bag, two sealed bags of ducats/ Of double ducats, stolen from me by my daughter!"

Lines 37-44:
Labeo is whip't, and laughes mee in the face;
Why? for I smite and hide the galled place.
Gird but the *Cynicks* helmet on his head,
…Long as the craftie *Cuttle* lieth sure
In the blacke *Cloude* of his thicke vomiture;
…Who list complaine of wronged faith or fame,
When hee may shift it to anothers name?

Hall now identifies his character as Labeo, whom he has already scourged, but Labeo laughs in his face because he recognizes that Hall has hidden his meaning so well that no one can see it. When Labeo is put into Diogenes's place of mocking the mighty in the guise of a witty fool, no one can complain of libel or betrayal of secrets, because he has shifted his writing to someone else by using their name. A helmet signifies hiddenness and it is related to the name William.[48] Hall is referring to Labeo as a hidden witty fool, a writer named William. Labeo feels safe in his voluminous writing and no one can complain about what he writes. He feels safe to "fry" many men. Hall again intimates that de Vere wrote voluminously, yet we have only small amounts that have come through the ages, unless, as openly stated, he wrote using other men's names.

Lines 66-75:

Now see I fire-flakes sparkle from his eyes,
Like a *Comet's* tayle in th' angry skies;
His pouting cheeks puffe up above his brow,
Like a swolne Toad touch't with the Spider's blow;

> His mouth shrinks sideward like a scornfull *Playse*,
> To take his tired Eares ingratefull place;
> His Eares hang laving like a new-lug'd swine,
> To take some counsell of his grieved eyne.
> Now laugh I loud and breake my splene to see
> This pleasing pastime of my poesie.
>
> (19-24)

A wonderful picture of an angry de Vere is presented, where fire shoots from his eyes, reminiscent of Harvey's *Gratulationes Valdinenses*. The allusion to a comet is astronomical, as opposed to astrological. De Vere was well versed in astronomy, as was Shakespeare.[49] His cheeks are puffed out, his brow is furrowed, his mouth is pulled so far sideways in a wry expression that it almost meets his dangling ear, and his eyes are unhappy at what he's reading. Hall loves his own verse and delights to see the effect it has had. Was this merely the unheeding work of a brash, arrogant, young Puritan, academic or did he feel safe because he knew that he had powerful Puritan supporters?[50]

There is reference to dangling ears again, like a male swine, a boar, with a lug or ring in its ear, an allusion to the de Vere heraldic crest of the blue boar.

> Shall then that foule infamous *Cyneds* hide
> Laugh at the purple wales of others side?
> Not, if hee were as neere, as by report,
> The stewes had wont to be to the Tenis-court;
> Hee that while thousands envie at his bed,
> Neighs after Bridals and fresh mayden-heade;
> While slavish *Juno* dares not looke awry,
> To frowne at such imperious rivalrye,
> Not tho shee sees her wedding jewels drest,
> To make new Bracelets for a strumpets wrest;
> Or like some strange disguised *Messaline*,
> Hires a nights lodging of his concubine....
>
> (92-103)

Hall becomes specific, though he uses Latin names and a different one for Labeo. He again accuses de Vere of going to brothels and brings in the tennis court in reference to his infamous argument with Sidney. De Vere shouldn't laugh at others, or mock them on the stage, when he has so many faults himself. Hall has shifted the name to Cyned; it is still Labeo he writes about. Cyned comes from the Latin *cinaedus* which translates as "adulterer," "effeminate man," or "homosexual." Hall probably means all three, although most of his allusions are to brothels and prostitutes (presumably female prostitutes), except for one mention of an "obsequious page" later in this satire as a possible object of Cyned's "dog days rage," or sexual desire of an older man.

Hall refers to de Vere's marriage to Ann Cecil and to the fact that other men wanted to marry her, i.e., Sidney and Rutland, but then he "neighs after" or sexually desires "bridals," a wedding, with "fresh mayden-heade," a virgin Queen Elizabeth who is the "imperious," royal rival. The faithful wife had to look away and not frown at their dalliance. The bed-trick is alluded to, as Ann had to disguise herself as a wanton woman ("Messaline") and bribe his mistress to let her sleep with her own husband.

Most of this was common gossip about de Vere and is found in contemporary accounts. "As by report" shows that Hall heard of it from others. The bed-trick, the tennis court, plus his flirtation with Queen Elizabeth particularly evoke de Vere. No one else fits the whole of this commentary. It clearly, although covertly, identifies him as Cyned and starts Hall's personal attacks on him.

O *Lucine*! barren *Caia* hath an heire
After her husband's dozen yeares despaire.
And now the bribed Mid-wife sweares apace,
The bastard babe doth beare his fathers face;
But hath not Lelia past hir virgine yeares?
For modest shame (God wot) or penall feares.
He tels a Merchant tidings of a prise,
That tells *Cynedo* of such novelties;
Worth little lesse than landing of a whale,
Or *Gades* spoyles, or a churles funerale:
Go bid the baines and point the bridall day,
His broking Baud hath got a noble prey.
A vacant tenement, an honest dowre
Can fit his pander for her paramoure,
That he base wretch, may clog his wit-old head
And give him hansell of his Hymen-bed.
(114-129)

De Vere's marriage to Elizabeth Trentham is now scourged. The model, new wife, who had never had a child, has now delivered an heir after her husband had despaired of one for a dozen years. There was a span of about twelve years after de Vere reunited with Ann Cecil in late 1581 to resume his marriage and try to produce a male heir, until Henry de Vere was born in February 1593 to the new wife, Elizabeth Trentham. Finally, an heir for the venerable de Vere line, one of the most respected and ancient in Europe. The new wife was past her virgin years. Elizabeth Trentham was thirty-one when she married de Vere, and she didn't have to worry about being thrown into prison, like Ann Vavasor, because the queen approved this marriage.

Cynedo tells his merchant-usurer that he's had a huge prize, and can now pay his debts. Hall adds a final *o* to Cyned's name, another hint that he is Oxford. So go ahead with the wedding. The bawd, Elizabeth Trentham, has made a business deal and her prize is a noble title. She is depicted as a predatory "broking Baud," a deal-making prostitute who has captured her "noble prey." Hall intimates that her child, Henry, "the bastard babe," wasn't de Vere's, but was instead her lover's son. He also intimates that de Vere gave her lover "hansell of his Hymen-bed," or first use of his marriage bed, which prevented him from being a cuckold. One again wonders how did Hall dare write such things and where did he get the information?

The satire continues with debauchery in brothels by a man similar to Cynedo, with a hint that he had syphilis and was treated for it by a barber. It also deals with prostitution by a woman similar to his bawd-wife that would evoke a "For Shame!" from Hall had it been Labeo writing. It is this portion that would have drawn the attention of the bishops for lasciviousness. The following satire drew attention for coming too close to exposing a highly placed person.

Book 4, Satire II: *ARCADES AMBO* ("A Pair of Rascals"). From Virgil, Eclogue VII (c. 39 BCE). In Virgil's eclogue, one poet dominates in skill over another. The winning poet sings that the myrtle is dearest to lovely Venus and the laurel is dearest to Phoebus. Hall is hinting to the educated in his audience, who would know this eclogue, to remember similar allusions in Book 1, Satire IX, *The Obscene Poet,* which identify de Vere as the author of *Venus and Adonis* and as a laureate. In this satire, someone is merely a plagiarist of the poetry of another, who is Caesar's laureate. They are both rascals.

Arcades Ambo is, in my opinion, the key satire in *Virgidemiarum*. The ensuing satire—Book 4, Satire IV, *Plus beau que fort*—refers back to it and suggests the trouble Hall incurred because of it. Ben Jonson's *Every Man Out of His Humor* (1599) significantly parallels it.[51] Other authors allude to it: John Marston in *The Scourge of Villainie,* Satire III (1599); Gervais Markham and Lewis Machin in *The Dumbe Knight: A Historical Comedy* (c. 1601); the anonymous, academic play *The Comedy of Timon* (c. 1602); Thomas Dekker collaborating with Thomas Middleton in *The Honest Whore, Part I* (1604); Ben Jonson in *The Devil Is an Ass* (1616); Thomas Middleton with William Rowley in *The Changeling* (1622); Thomas Middlelton with William Rowlely in *The Spanish Gipsy* (1623).[52] The Induction to *The Taming of the Shrew* has parallels to *Arcades Ambo.*[53] The bishops put *Virgidemiarum* at the top of their list and it was, I think, *Arcades Ambo* that was the main reason for its proscription.

I see one other allusion, which, if accurate, is compelling. In *Measure for Measure,* V.i, Lucio says about Duke Vincentio who is in disguise as a friar, "Here comes the Rascal I spoke of," then, "This is the Rascal; this is he I spoke of," and finally, "Come Sir, come Sir; Why you bald-pated Rascal, you must be hooded must you?" I see Lucio in part as Hall, while others have identified Duke Vincentio as a de Vere character.[54] Lucio berates Duke Vincentio when he is in disguise as a friar, while Hall berates de Vere in his disguise of Shakespeare, which is what made him a rascal. Other parallels in *Measure for Measure* will be discussed in connection with a later satire.

Arcades Ambo garnered attention even a few decades after it was written, not coincidentally, in 1616 when William Shakspere of Stratford died, and again at the time of the printing and publication of the First Folio in 1622-23. What was it that was so strongly intriguing?

Old driveling *Lolio* drudges all he can,
To make his eldest sonne a Gentleman;
Who can despaire that sees another thrive,
By lone of twelve-pence to an Oyster-wive,
When a craz'd scaffold, and a rotten stage,
Was all rich *Naevius* his heritage.
(1-6)

The theme of the satire is introduced in the first three couplets. Old foolish Lolio, a rustic, petty usurer, is trying to rise into the gentry and make his eldest son a gentleman, while rich Naevius has nothing left of his inheritance except the morally corrupt public theater, which implies that he has spent his heritage on the stage. There is an immediate linking and contrasting of Lolio and his son with Naevius, who, I propose, are John and William Shakspere, here linked to and contrasted with Edward de Vere.

There are at least two possible sources for the name Lolio. One is Marcus Lollius, known as Maximus,[55] a Roman politician who was a "homo novus" or new man, someone about whose ancestors nothing is known. He was the first of his family to serve in the Senate and rose to prominence under Caesar Augustus, but later had a fall. He was described as a hypocrite who was only interested in amassing wealth.[56] He had a son, also named Marcus Lollius, who was often confused with his father. These brief characteristics resemble John and William Shakspere.

In a different vein, Horace wrote an ode to this Lollius in 13 BCE. He prefaces it: "To Lollio that his Writings shall never perish: Vertue without the help of Verses is buried in Oblivion. That he will sing Lollio's praises, whose vertues he now also celebrates."[57] In the poem Horace sounds slightly defensive in praising his "potent friend" Lollio, whose reputation is now very bad, and it seems that he is attempting to rehabilitate him.[58] This aspect of Lollio resembles de Vere.

The second source for the name Lolio is Chaucer's Lollius,[59] from *Troilus and Crysede* (c. 1381-86), a tale taken from Boccaccio's *Il Filostrato* (c. 1336), which was itself based on *Le Roman De Troie* (c. 1155-60) by Benoit de Sainte-Maure. Chaucer implies that he is merely translating *Il Filostrato*, but he never mentions Boccaccio and wrongly attributes it to a Lollius, who is unknown as an author. The controversy over Chaucer's Lollius continues to this day.[60]

Putting these two Lollios together, as is Hall's wont, we find a combined picture of John Shakspere and his son William. At the same time we see a slight image of de Vere. No trace can be found of John's ancestors beyond his father Richard, who was a tenant farmer, a husbandman. John was the first in his family to rise to serve as mayor and chief alderman, which gave him the right to apply to be a gentleman. He was known to have dealt in large, usurious loans and to have amassed wealth.[61] William of Stratford is unknown as an author in his own name, as no literary trail can be found for him in contemporary records.[62] There are literary records that relate to the name Shakespeare, but that is what is being questioned. Who is he? Was the name only a front? To this we add the Lollius with a greatly fallen reputation, whose "Vertue" will fall into oblivion without verses, and whose writing, it is wished, shall never perish. This is de Vere. All very complicated, but typical of satirical writing of the Elizabethan era, and not beyond the ability of the brilliant, young Hall.

Next we have Naevius, a Roman poet and playwright. He was noted to have originated Roman history plays and to have parodied the life of the elite.[63] He is cited by Francis Meres in *Palladis Tamia* (1598) as among the best of the Latin writers of comedy and his name appears in the same sentence as de Vere, who (as Oxford) is cited as among the best of the English writers of comedy.

Naevius, in Hall's satire, has lost his heritage; all he has left is the stage and the cheering crowds who applaud his work. In him, we see de Vere associated with the public theater, where he presented history plays, comedies and tragedies, and in which he parodied members of court. He is identified as a poet and a playwright. He has lost his lands and patrimony because of the stage.

The intertwining of John Shakspere and his eldest son William with Edward de Vere was hinted at earlier in Book 2, Satire II, *Neglect of Learning*, in the "each base *Lordling* ever" and "everie peasant churle" who wouldn't give harbor to the Muses.

Himselfe goes patched like some bare *Cottyer*
...Let giddie *Cosmius* change his choyce aray,
Like as the *Turke* his tents thrise in a day.
...Bearing his pawne-layd lands upon his backe,
...Who cannot shine in tissues and pure gold,
That hath his lands and patrimonie sold?
(9-16)

Lolio, who is actually thriving as noted earlier in line 3, dresses in old, patched clothing and scrimps on everything to get ahead and to make his son a gentleman. By further contrast, "giddie Cosmius" (meaning worldly or cosmopolitan) wears expensive clothing and changes it three times a day, and like a Turk moves his tents three times a day. He has pawned and sold his lands and his patrimony to afford such luxury.

When we know that Queen Elizabeth nicknamed de Vere her "Turk" (or "torc," which means boar in Gaelic and is pronounced as "turk"),[64] we see the covert connection between Cosmius and Turk. "Giddie" is the adjective for Cosmius, a synonym of fickle, a word which was used to describe de Vere in a letter from Gilbert Talbot to his father, the Earl of Shrewsbury ("If it were not for his fickle head, he would pass any of them shortly"[65]). De Vere was known for changeable and strange behavior.

It is implied that Cosmius wears luxurious fabrics and has pure gold on his clothing. Only royalty or the higher nobility could wear pure gold on their clothing according to sumptuary laws,[66] and we have yet another reference to someone who has sold not only his lands but also his patrimony. De Vere had lost Castle Hedingham, his patrimony, to William Burghley and had incurred so much debt that he had no more lands to sell to pay for it.

Else is he stall-fed on the workey day
With browne-bread crusts softened in sodden whey,
Or water-grewell, or…paups of meale……
Let sweet-mouthed *Mercia* bid what crowns she please
For halfe-red cherries or greene garden pease,
Or the first Artichoks of all the yeare,
To make so lavish cost for little cheare.
                    (31-50)

More contrast, this time between Lolio and a woman named Mercia, who pays much for the first items of spring, but receives little in return. Lolio, as usual, is miserly; he's still saving and amassing wealth. "Sweet-mouthed" has the sense of ironic sweet-talking or flattery. "Halfe-red cherries" are Royal Ann cherries, the first to appear in the spring. Green garden peas are an early spring vegetable, as are the first artichokes.

I see Mercia as Elizabeth Trentham, since the ancient kingdom of Mercia was centered on the river Trent;[67] furthermore, we have just read a satire that has her paying large amounts of money to buy a noble title, but one that has lost its lands and patrimony. Some have seen Queen Elizabeth as Mercia who bid many crowns, 1000 per year, for "green" or "spring" (i.e., referring to de Vere's thousand-pound annuity). In either case, it is de Vere being bid for.

For else how should his sonne maintained bee,
At Inns of Court or of the Chancery,
There to learne law, and courtly carriage,
To make amendes for his meane parentage,
While he unknowne and ruffling as he can,
Goes currant ech-where for a Gentleman.
While yet he rousteth at some uncouth signe,
Nor never red his tenures second line.
What brokers' lousy wardrop cannot reach,
With tissued paines to pranck ech peasants breech?
                    (53-62)

We finally meet our Lolio's son, William Shakspere, and learn something about his "lost years." He is striding around London as a young, foppish gallant, learning how to be a gentleman at his father's behest and with miserly financial support, so the family can finally gain a coat of arms and rise into the gentry. This is the simplest and most reasonable explanation for what William did during those years,[68] and Hall provides evidence for it. The foppish, rustic character Ruffio/Shak-forke, mentioned earlier, prefigures Lolio's son. The only character with such a large role in a satire without a name of his own is Lolio's son, but we can speculate that his name is Ruffio. His father has sent him to London to mingle with gentlemen at the Inns of Court or the Chancery and to learn some law. He's unknown there, but struts around in the latest fashion as if he's already part of the gentry. He doesn't live at the Inns or Chancery, but at rough taverns, doesn't stay long at any one place and leaves without paying the bill. He wears a broker's old wardrobe, tailored to look like the latest fashionable gentlemen's clothing.

All of the foregoing fits William Shakspere. His having no name of his own is significant if he was being confused with the famous and talented William Shakespeare, author of *Venus and Adonis*. Hall hints in the motto, *A Pair of Rascals*, that this is the case.

A subsequent section of the satire describes Lolio's son as staying in his room most of the time because he's afraid of being caught by a debt collector. He only goes out at night when it's dimly lit and he can't easily be recognized. Then he runs into a rustic countryman from home who eagerly calls out to him in his father's name and crosses the street to shake his hand.

Could never man worke thee a worser shame,
Than once to minge thy fathers odious name,
Whose mention were alike to thee as leefe
As a Catch-pols fist unto a Bankrupts sleeve;
Or an *Hos ego* from old *Petrarch's* spright,
Unto a Plagiarie sonnet-wright.
                    (79-84)

Lolio's son is ashamed of his father's name. A scholar at Oxford in 1487, Hugh Shakspere changed his name to Hugh Sawnders because Shakspere was considered too base and common, "vile reputatum est."[69] "Minge" meant to mingle or to mix. Perhaps Shakspere used or mingled Arden, his mother's family name, which was more respectable. (A search for a William Arden in London in the late 1500s might produce some interesting information.)

Hall suggests that Lolio's son was afraid of being caught by a debt collector and he adds, as an equally bad thing, of being accused of plagiarizing sonnets. Was Lolio's son pretending to be the author of sonnets? We have the earlier comment that the "peasant churle" would not give harbor to the Muses. There is an important connection between Shakspere and Shakespeare in this part of the satire and it shows that Shakspere is a plagiarist, not the author. It is evident that the name William Shakespeare, as author of the courtly, elegant poems *Venus and Adonis* and

The Rape of Lucrece, and their association with the Earl of Southampton, would have conferred new status on the similar name, William Shakspere, and would have helped in the quest to gain a coat of arms.

A long section of the satire deals with Lolio's son returning home and impressing the rustic neighbors with his gentlemanly behavior and dress. They ask for his advice on mundane matters of law, like a goose getting into a neighbor's pasture. His father has finally acquired a coat of arms, which makes Lolio's eldest son a gentleman as well.

So new falne lands have made him in request,
That now he lookes as lofty as the best.
                    (115-116)

Lolio's son purchases new property, New Place, which makes him landed gentry, more acceptable than being a mere gentleman, and makes him "as lofty as the best." He is now "in request." It has been asked why William purchased property in Stratford in 1597, when he was supposedly in the midst of his work in London as the playwright William Shakespeare, and how could he afford it. The hidden account that Hall tells helps us to understand. John Shakspere had been reaccumulating wealth, both as a usurer and as a landlord-farmer, and he scrimped on everything. He sent William to London to learn the behavior of a gentleman. John was granted a coat of arms in October 1596, which made William, as eldest son, a gentleman as well. William purchased New Place in 1597 (impliedly with John's help) to enhance his status and become landed gentry.[70] It all fits with John and William's desires to be recognized as gentlemen of the better sort. His father had finally fulfilled his dream.

His father dead, tush, no, it was not hee,
He findes recordes of his great pedigree,
And tels how first his famous Ancestor
Did come in long since with the conquerour.
Nor hath some bribed Herald first assign'd
His quartered Armes and crest of gentle kinde.
The Scottish Barnacle (if I might choose)
That of a worme doth waxe a winged goose.
                    (133-140)

The description of how Lolio became a gentleman is a common one, but it specifically fits John Shakspere's route to gentlehood. He lied about who his ancestor was and claimed to be descended from someone who had served Henry VII. He claimed that his or Mary Arden's ancestor came in with William the Conqueror.[71] Lolio said that he hadn't bribed the herald to get his coat of arms, but John Shakspere's name was later on a list of those who shouldn't have been given a coat because they were of base birth,[72] which implies that he did bribe the herald.

Hall makes fun of the coat of arms by alluding to the "Scottish Barnacle" that, in myth, grew on a tree, fell into water below, became a worm and eventually became a goose. This is another complex combining of de Vere and Shakspere, as the word "ver" means worm in French. The barnacle was in a high position in a tree, but fell (became base by associating with the public theater). The worm then evolved into a goose. Hall's choice of the Scottish barnacle is a clever, scathing allusion to Edward de Vere as Shakespeare and to William Shakspere as somehow being a front for him.

Who were borne at two pide painted postes
And had some traunting Chapman to his syre.
(144-145)

Painted posts were placed outside the mayor's or other local magistrates' homes; public documents were posted on them. John Shakspere had been mayor of Stratford. In Lolio's case, the posts were pied or multicolored. The word "pied" was used to refer to the coat of a fool, one that was of many colors.[73] Hall is reinforcing the earlier foolishness of "driveling" and of a worm becoming a goose.

A "traunting Chapman" was a peddler, someone who moved around and sold goods. Peddlers were among the most base of people and would not have been considered worthy to become gentlemen. To a twenty-first century mind, all of this carries a connotation of snobbishness, but it simply reflected the social customs of the time. Snobbishness has nothing to do with the identification of Edward de Vere as Shakespeare. Only the analysis of Hall's words and the search to find his hidden meaning are relevant.

O times! Since ever *Rome* did kings create,
Brasse Gentlemen and *Cesar* Laureates.
(147-148)

The final line recognizes the pair of rascals of the Latin motto, John and William Shakspere (gentlemen who are created by bribery), and William Shakespeare/Edward de Vere (laureate poets who are chosen by Caesar/Queen Elizabeth).

"Ever *Rome*" refers to de Vere, making it clear that he has been chosen by Elizabeth to be crowned a laureate. *Julius Caesar* played on the stage to great public recognition, its first known presentation in 1599, but this indicates an earlier date of 1597-98 (or its circulation in manuscript). "*Cesar* Laureates" refers to the play, another Shakespeare allusion.

To recap this important satire: Lolio and his son depict John and William Shakspere as a foolish, rustic, landlord-farmer and petty usurer who scrimps to send his eldest son to London to learn how to be a gentleman and lift the family into the gentry; the son struts around the Inns in the latest fashions, moves from place to place, goes into debt, plagiarizes sonnets, returns home and buys new property; Lolio has gained a coat of arms but he has lied about his ancestry and bribed the herald; neither he nor his son are worthy to be gentlemen as they are baseborn.

In Naevius/Cosmius/Mercia/Cesar Laureates, and even in the name Lolio, we have Edward de Vere who is Shakespeare. He is a rich man of bad reputation, who has lost his heritage and has nothing left but the stage; he is good at history, comedy and at mocking the elite; he is a fickle man who dresses extravagantly but has lost his lands and patrimony; he is of the higher nobility and is entitled to wear pure gold on his clothing; he is compared to a Turk; he is associated with a woman who has spent lavishly on Spring, but who gets little in return; he is a poet laureate and Caesar's laureate. This representation of de Vere as Shakespeare is very clear if one looks past the abstraction of several characters combined into one.

Arcades Ambo intertwines William Shakspere and Edward de Vere/Shakespeare, a pair of rascals, two distinct people. William Shakspere of Stratford is not the poet and playwright William Shakespeare, but is a plagiarist of sonnets. John Shakspere plays a prominent role in this satire as he does in allusions made by Marston, Jonson, Markham, Middleton and others. It is interesting to look more fully into his role. A coming satire presents some controversial ideas.

This is the third satire in which Hall identifies de Vere as Shakespeare and this one differentiates him from William Shakspere of Stratford. This satire caused trouble for Hall.

Book 4, Satire III: *FUIMUS TROES. VEL VIX EA NOSTRA* ("We once were Trojans. Truly, these things are barely ours, or we are only stewards"). *Fuimus Troes* is from Virgil, *The Aeneid,* Book II. *Vel vix ea nostra* is from Ovid, *The Metamorphosis*, Book XIII (c. 8). The motto is another reference to descendants of Troy and to Oxford's pride about his lineage. The *Aeneid* has direct relevance to de Vere as a descendant of Aeneas, and *The Metamorphosis* has direct relevance to Shakespeare, as it is recognized to be his most quoted source. Hall doesn't miss a chance to draw them together.

What boots it *Pontice*, tho thou couldn'st discourse
Of a long golden line of Ancestors
...painted faces...ever since before the last conquest
...bead roles...since *Deucalions* flood
...church-windowes to record
The age of thy fayre Armes;
...Crosse-leg'd Toombe...*Buckle* that did tie
The Garter of...greatest Grand-sires knee,
...reliques...silver spurs, or spils of broken speares;
...cyte olde *Oclands* verse...
Of the wars in Terouane and Tournai?
(1-17)

The opening couplet is an almost direct quote from Juvenal's Satire VIII. Pontice boasted of his antiquity and great deeds of the past but was without virtue himself. Hall goes on to list things that his Pontice/de Vere brags about, all of which are part of de Vere's background. "Spils of broken speares" refers to Shakespeare. The allusion to descent from before the Conqueror is another parallel to Shakspere of Stratford and to his ancestral claim.

Or hide what ever treasures he thee got
…in desperate lot,
…Or if (O shame!) in hired Harlots bed
Thy wealthie heyre-dome thou have buried;
…little boots thee to discourse
Of a long golden line of Ancestors.
Of a long line of noble ancestors.
(20-27)

More chastisement from Hall, including returning to the "O shame!" he used on Labeo, saying that if Pontice has lost his fortune in desperate gambles, and if he's lost his ability to have an heir because he's been with prostitutes (by implication, having contracted syphilis), he shouldn't brag about a long genealogical line that will be ending. Hall has already intimated that Henry de Vere was not his child and thus not his true heir.

Ventrous *Fortunio* his farme hath sold,
And gads *to Guiane* land to fish for gold,
Meeting, perhaps, *if Orenoque* denye,
Some stragling pinnace of *Polonian Rie*.
(20-27)

The allusion is to Raleigh, who went to South America to search for gold but failed to find it. He returned to England in 1595 from his first voyage to Guiana. Intercepting Polish ships by the English was also a topic of the time. Hall is using Raleigh as an example of a highly placed person who has done rash, but better, things than de Vere.

Wiser *Raymundus* in his closet pent,
Laughs at such danger and adventurement;
When half his lands are spent in golden smoke
And now his second hopefull glasse is broke.
But yet, if haply his third fornace hold,
Devoteth all his pots and pans to gold.
(34-39)

Baconians were correct when they saw Bacon's family motto in the "*mediocria firma*" allusion in Marston's *Reactio* of *Certaine Satyres;* they were incorrect to find that he was Labeo. Bacon is Raymundus, who spent much time experimenting in turning other metals into gold. He is called the father of modern science because of his careful experimentation. Hall gives a satirical example of his methods. Raymundus was a searcher for the Philosopher's Stone and he was wiser. Bacon wrote learned papers on alchemy and was also a philosopher. Hall is citing Bacon as another example for de Vere to follow.

So spend thou, *Pontice*, if thou canst not spare,
Like some stout sea-man or *Philosopher*.
(40-41)

By implication, Hall is telling de Vere not to spend his money on the public theater. It's better to speculate on seeking gold or on trying to create it through alchemy. Did de Vere make money/gold from the theater? Hall seems to be hinting that he did. His brief allusions to Raleigh and Bacon and his comments about them as a seaman and a philosopher, with no hidden allusions to Shakespeare's works, makes it clear that he sees neither of them as the poet/playwright.

And were thy fathers gentle? that's their praise,
No thanke to thee by whom their name decays;
...Right so their titles beene, nor can be thine
Whose ill deserts might blanke their golden line.
(42- 49)

Your ancestors were noble and deserved their titles, but your bad behavior has brought shame on your family name; having gone to brothels and slept with prostitutes, you might not have a true heir because you have syphilis. Hall is again hinting that Henry de Vere was not Oxford's son.

Tell me, thou gentle *Trojan*, dost thou prise
Thy brute beasts worth by their dams qualities?
Say'st thou this *Colt* shall proove a swift-pac'd steed,
Onely because a *Jennet* did him breed?
Or say'st thou this same Horse shall win the prize,
Because his dame was swiftest *Trunchefice*,
Or *Runcevall* his Syre, himself a *Gallaway?*
Whiles like a tireling Jade he lags half-way;
Or whiles thou seest some of thy *Stallion-race*,
Their eyes boar'd out, masking the Millers-maze,
...Or dragging froathy barrels at his tayle.
(50- 61)

The question is asked of de Vere whether an animal is judged by the mother's qualities. In the Elizabethan era, a father was thought to be the dominant factor in a son's genetic inheritance. His qualities would dominate and the son would be like him. A picture is painted of a horse that comes from a great line of thoroughbred dams and of Runcevall, the sire, who is of a great line, but he (Pontice) is only a "Gallaway," a small, common horse. The horse is like a tired nag who falters halfway through the race. De Vere started with great promise but quickly lost it by his bad behavior. The horse of the great line might be seen set to common chores well beneath his station, such as walking in circles to grind wheat or pulling a wagon loaded with beer (or writing plays or acting).

"Eyes boar'd out" points to de Vere and the family symbol of the blue boar.

Ah, me! how seldom see we sonnes succeed
Their Fathers praise in prowesse and great dead?
Yet certes if the Syre be ill inclin'd,
His faults befal his sonnes by course of kind.

(84- 87)

An ill inclined father has an ill inclined son. Critics of the early 1800s say this entire satire is an imitation of Juvenal's Satire VIII on Family Madness and Pride of Descent. Hall is insinuating that de Vere was unstable or mad and that he inherited it from his father, John, the 16th Earl of Oxford. His pride in his ancient Vere heritage is emphasized again here.

Book 4, Satire IV: *PLUS BEAU QUE FORT* ("More Handsome than Strong"). From *D'un Lieu de Plaisance* (From a Place of Pleasure, 1532) by Clemont Marot, a renaissance poet of the French court.

An important digression:

Can I not touch some upstart...
Of *Lolio's* sonne...
Or taxe wild *Pontice* for his *Luxuries,*
But straight they tell me of *Tiresias* eyes?
...*Collingborns* feeding of the crowes,
...hundreth *Scalps* which *Thames* still underflowes,
But straight *Sigalion* nods and knits his browes,
And winkes and waftes his warning hand for feare,
And lisps some silent letters in my ear.
...Have I not vow'd for shunning such debate
(Pardon ye satyres) to degenerate?
...Let *Labeo*, or who else list for mee,
Go loose his eares and fall to *Alchymie.*

(1-15)

The beginning of this satire is important to understanding what has become Hall's primary covert message, that Edward de Vere is the poet and playwright William Shakespeare. A large portion of *Byting Satyres* deals with the topic and with other de Vere scandals. We now have an abrupt, angry interpolation. Hall is self-righteously indignant. He resentfully asks why he is not permitted to deal with the boastful, new gentleman, Lolio's son/Shakspere, or take wild Pontice/de Vere to account for his lascivious ways. He's been summoned by someone in power who demands that he stop writing about them and threatens him with awful consequences if he doesn't. Hall is being disingenuous in shifting the warning to be about Pontice and his lasciviousness. That isn't the biggest problem.

Why would anyone care what Hall wrote about Lolio's son, an "upstart" (which means someone who was promoted to gentlehood by dishonest means[74]), a rustic of relative unimportance, one who should be safe from Envy or from the lightning strikes of the gods because he is so lowly? Pontice/Labeo, on the other hand, is one of Ida's pines who needs to fear Envy as he is highly placed and comes from a long, illustrious line of ancestors. What was it that Hall wrote about them that made Sigalion, the Egyptian god of silence (possibly a Bishop or even Burghley, because of the wink and lisp[75]), nod, knit his brows, wink, and wave his hands in fear to silence Hall? And what "debate" had Hall vowed to shun writing about?

When one follows the single, covert thread in Hall's satires—from the Obscene Poet, to Labeo, to New Strabo, to the Smith brought up at Vulcan's forge, to Eudemon, to Cyned, to Naevius/Cosmius/Mercia/Caesar's Laureate, to Pontice—it becomes clear that Hall has vowed not to write, at least not openly, about de Vere as Shakespeare. Specifically, he has vowed not to write about de Vere's relation to Lolio's son and to the debate about them, which is about Shakespeare and Shakspere. Hall knew the story, but couldn't tell it openly or completely.

He ends his indignant rant by telling Labeo to stop reading his satires, free his ears (another reference to lugged, droopy ears) and go do alchemy instead. We see again that Labeo has complained about Hall. We've already seen Labeo's anger, and then his ultimate laughter and acceptance that he remains safely hidden, but now he's angry about the satire that concerns Lolio's son. In *Arcades Ambo* Hall too clearly identified de Vere as Shakespeare and exposed the misdirection to William of Stratford. Hall is being warned not to write about William Shakspere and Edward de Vere. It is such a serious warning that he is threatened with a possible cruel and disgraceful death if he doesn't stop.

The authorship of Shakespeare's works is the dire problem, and somehow William Shakspere of Stratford is involved. We don't see all of the connection, although we do see that he is not the famous poet and playwright. Hall accuses him of plagiarizing sonnets, but he also says that he refused to harbor works for the Muses' benefit.

We can now understand why other contemporary authors found Lolio and his son so fascinating. We can also understand why allusions to Lolio, or to controversial topics in *Arcades Ambo,* reappeared in works in 1616, 1622 and 1623. The literary grapevine was at work and those who knew the story were again dealing covertly with the true identity of Shakespeare.

Onely, let *Gallio* give me leave a while
To schoole him once, or ere I change my style.
Martius...in Buffes be drest...iron plates upon his brest,
...from the *Belgian garrisons*;
What shall thou need to envie ought at that,
...thou smellest like a *Civet cat*;
...thine oyled locks smooth platted fall,
...a plum'd Fanne may shade thy chalked face,
...lawny strips thy naked bosome grace.
(16-17, 41-50)

Hall now returns to the flow of his satires as if nothing has happened. He writes of Gallio, a much pampered young man who resembles Southampton with his long, smooth locks and white face. The name Gallio is similar to Gullio of the *Parnassus Plays* (c. 1599-1602), and the characters are similar. Some see a close connection between Hall and the Cambridge plays, and even feel that he wrote them, but the writing style is quite different.

The rest of the satire gives the description of the same vain young man. Hall shows Gallio examples of the bravery of many other young men, but Gallio is as soft as the most delicate things.

Now, *Gallio*, gins thy youthly heat to raigne
In every vigorous limme, and swelling vaine;
Time bids thee raise..headstrong thought on hy
To valour and...chivalry
Gallio may pull me roses ere they fall,
...net...Tennis-ball...tend...Spar-hawke
...yelping Begles...halter Finches
...list...in courting...lovely dame,
Hange on... lips...melt in...eyes
Dance...joy in her jollity;
...Hy wanton *Gallio*, and wed betime,
...Seest thou the rose-leaves fall ungathered?
Then hye thee wanton *Gallio* to wed;
Hy thee and give the world...one dwarfe more,
Such as it got when thou thy selfe wast bore
...Can never happiness to soone begin.
(76-101)

Hall urges Gallio to valor and chivalry, but Gallio is only interested in entertaining himself. Hall then says that Gallio should marry quickly and not let his "rose-leaves" fall, but should give the world a child just like himself. Roses and rose-leaves are allusions to the name Wriothesley, which was pronounced variously as "Rosely" or "Risely." Encouraging him to marry young and produce an offspring like himself is an echo of Shakespeare's first seventeen sonnets.

Book 4, Satire V: *STUPET ALBIUS AERE* (Albius is mad for brass or he is money-crazy). From Horace's *Sermones*, Book I, Satire IV. It immediately follows a section about Latin writers and it invokes one of them to write better or not to write at all, which, as we have seen, is a request Hall addresses to Labeo. Albius Tibullus was a Roman knight and poet who had inherited a large estate, but most of it was confiscated by Octavian and Marc Anthony. His death was commemorated by Ovid in *Amores*, Book 3, Elegy 9 (c. 16).[76] The elegy mentions Venus's boy, Aeneas's funeral, the wild boar that gashed Adonis's thigh, and Troy, all of which evoke de Vere and *Venus and Adonis*.

I hesitate to include this satire because it is so controversial in what it is saying. It carries forward the character of the prior rustic, churlish usurer, the merchant usurer and the petty usurer Lolio, forming an ellipse with Tocullio of this satire. I discuss it because I think Hall shows that de Vere (as Cyned) is involved in taking out a loan, and John Shakspere's role in it.

Tocullio was a wealthie usurer,
Such store of Incomes had he every yeare,
By Bushels was he wont to meet his coyne
As did the olde wife of *Trimalcion*.
                    (39-42)

The name Tocullio means petty usurer.[77] We see that the rustic usurer is now wealthy. The "olde wife of Trimalcion" is Fortunata, the wife of Trimalchio, from a tale in the *Satyricon* by Gaius Petronius. Fortunata "measures her money by the peck."[78] Referring to bushels to store Tocullio's money is an allusion to grain hoarding, another source of his wealth.

Hall returns to the churlish, rustic, petty usurer and grain hoarder, Tocullio/Lolio/John Shakspere. The names are different but the essence is the same. By referring to the old wife Fortunata, Hall insinuates that Mary Arden was the brains behind John Shakspere. The story in the *Satyricon* describes a strong woman who is in charge of things while the husband, Trimalchio, an upstart, is wealthy, vulgar, foolish, but personable. Mary's father, Robert Arden, had appreciated her abilities. He designated her one of the executors of his will even though she was the youngest of his eight children. He also left her a sixty-acre farm, Asbies, which was his most valuable possession. It was located in Wilmcote, a parish three miles from Stratford.[79] Interestingly, it was the neighboring parish to Billesley.

Could he doe more....
Of his old pillage, and damn'd surplusage?
                (43-44)

These lines point more specifically to usury and grain hoarding. Tocullio is a pillaging small usurer and damned grain hoarder, as is Lolio. They both have the desire to advance socially and are amassing wealth. They are the same person. They are John Shakspere, who didn't do many good deeds with his wealth.

Shouldst thou him credit that nould credit thee?
Yes, and maiest sweare he swore the verity;
The ding-thrift heire, his shift-got summe mispent,
Comes drouping like a pennylesse penitent,
And beats his faint fist on *Tocullios* doore,
It lost the last, and now must call for more.
                (55-60)

Should Tocullio give a loan to someone who would not give him "credit," meaning to acknowledge him as a gentleman? Yes, and you can swear that he swore the truth. We add another word in "verity" as a reference to de Vere. "True" and "truth" were widely recognized as relating to the name de Vere or to his motto, *Vero nihil verius*, "Nothing truer than truth." The spendthrift, penniless heir has spent his unearned inheritance and needs a loan. He's dejected and knocks faintly on the door. In Book 2, Satire II, *Neglect of Learning*, Hall said, "Thy spirits spent," meaning being depressed. It is the same character here. "Verity," "pennylesse," and "ding-thrift" are strong indicators for de Vere.

Soone is his arrand red in his pale face,
Which beares dumbe *Characters* of every case;
So *Cyneds* dusky cheeke and fiery eye,
And hayre-les brow tels where he last did lye;
So *Matho* doth bewray his guilty thought,
While his pale face doth say his cause is nought.
                (65-70)

These lines show that Cyned/Labeo is the dejected, penniless, beater on the door. Tocullio can see by Cyned's pale face that he needs a loan. Cyned's face betrays his character "of *every* case" with its reddish-brown cheek, bloodshot eye and loss of hair, which are all signs of syphilis,[80] as Hall intimates, the result of sleeping with prostitutes in brothels, his reiterated theme. In his description of de Vere's countenance, Hall seems to be saying that he is bald ("hayre-les brow"). Persius in Satire I referred to Labeo as "bald-pated." Could de Vere have been bald in his later years?

Matho is involved as an agent ("his cause") and has a guilty conscience. He is mentioned earlier in the satire as a lawyer who has taken a bribe to be quiet about a "brawl at any bar" and to "kiss the book to be a perjurer." This is a reference to Christopher Marlowe's death. Ingram Frizer (pronounced "freezer") was a lawyer and was Thomas Walsingham's business agent. He was the man who killed Marlowe.[81] In a later satire, Matho is described as "freezing Mathoe." I think that Matho is, partially, Ingram Frizer. Matho figures strongly in Cyned's debts, along with John Shakspere. Together, they are the merchant usurer and the rustic petty usurer.

Lines 71-73:

Seest thou the wary Angler trayle along
His feeble line, soone as the Pike too strong
Hath swallowed the bayte that scornes the shore,

Tocullio isn't used to giving such a big loan to such a big person. Once the big fish Cyned has swallowed the bait, Tocullio carefully trails him along and reels him in.

Write, seale, deliver, take, go, spend and speede,
And yet full heardly could his present need
Part with such summe; for but as yester-late
Did *Furnus* offer pen-worths at easie rate,
For small disbursement; He the banke hath broke,
And needs mote now some further playne orelook.
                    (80-85)

Cyned has such onerous debts that the large loan he's just taken barely covers his present need. De Vere had gotten so deeply into debt that he was constantly in need of more money. Furnus had given him small loans at a low rate of interest, but Cyned has asked for so much that he can't give him any more ("he the banke hath broke"). "Furnus" may be an allusion to Thomas Walsingham, who gave loans to fellow courtiers and heirs. He had been thrown into jail for debt before he gained his inheritance and he helped others to keep them from a similar situation.[82] He is a tie to Ingram Frizer.

Ah foole! for sooner shalt thou sell the rest,
Then stake ought for thy former Interest;
When it shall grind thy grating gall for shame,
To see the lands that bear thy Grandsires name
Become a dunghill peasants sommer-hall,
Or lonely *Hermits* cage inhospitall.
                    (93-98)

Hall again calls de Vere a fool. It would be better if he sold all his land than go further into debt simply to pay the interest on loans he already owes. De Vere is going to be deeply ashamed at the loss of all his lands, especially if one of the properties becomes the summer home of some peasant who had a dunghill at his door. A document from 1552 shows that John Shakspere was fined for having a dunghill outside his home.[83] If de Vere couldn't repay his debt, John Shakspere would own one or more of his lands.

The combination of Tocullio/Matho is the same merchant/usurer as in Book 4, Satire I, *Che Baiar Vuol, Bai*, who finally gets a ruined manor in payment and it is the same merchant/usurer whom Cynedo tells of a prize so big that he can now pay his debt.

As noted, I think that Hall tells of de Vere obtaining a big loan from John Shakspere. Accompanied by Matho, a shady merchant, Cyned approached Tocullio for the loan. There is no record that shows such a transaction, but it would have been off the books if it was an illegal, usurious loan, with the deal to be revealed only in default or at death, when repayment would be demanded, at a "churls funerale."

In *The Honest Whore, Part One* (1604) by Thomas Dekker in collaboration with Thomas Middleton, mention is made of Sir Oliver Lollio, which is an allusion to Oliver ("green" and "ver")/de Vere and to Lollio/John Shakspere. In a scene set in a brothel (II.i) it is said, "What an ass is that lord to borrow money of a citizen." To which it is replied, "Nay, God's pity, what an ass is that citizen to lend money to a lord." Hall referred to de Vere as an "Asse." That is, in my opinion, another covert allusion to de Vere taking a loan from John Shakspere, who is also an ass, and it refers back to Hall's *Virgidemiarum*.

Jonson's *The Devil Is an Ass* (1616, the year of William of Stratford's death) also contains the story of a loan from a citizen, Guilt-head, to a courtier, Everill ("Ever-ill"), an allusion to a dissolute de Vere. Guilt-head wants to make his eldest son, Plutarchus, a gentleman. These are strong echoes of Hall's *Arcades Ambo* and *Stupete Albius Aere*.

With Hall's account of the loan in *Virgidemiarum* and the allusions to it in *The Honest Whore, Part One*, and *The Devil Is an Ass*, we have three legs to the stool. It can now stand upright and be considered a legitimate thesis to be examined further.

It does seem implausible that de Vere obtained a loan from John Shakspere and that he did so before the name "Shakespeare" appeared on *Venus and Adonis* and before he married Elizabeth Trentham in late 1591 and her family paid his debts. But let us recall Book 4, Satire I, *Che Baiar Vuol, Bai*, and the merchant-usurer who is told of a prize that's huge, so "Go bid the baines and point the bridall day." The inference is that Cyned is going to marry a wealthy wife and now can finally repay the loan he got from his merchant-usurer John Shakspere (and somehow Matho/Frizer is involved). Further, as a possible incentive connected to the loan, did de Vere have anything to do with helping to make John Shakspere a gentleman? Could the name Shakespeare, with all of its ironical allusions in other ways, have also been part of a deal to give the base name Shakspere greater acceptance?

There are a few ties between de Vere and John Shakspere. One is by the proximity of Mary Arden's property, Asbies in Wilmcote Parish, to de Vere's grandmother Elizabeth Trussell's property, Billesley Manor, in the adjoining Billesley Parish, an easy walk.[84] (The Induction to *The Taming of the Shrew* concerns a rustic, Christopher Sly, son of Old Sly. He is passed out drunk at Wilmcote. A lord who has a manor in the area finds him, takes him home and satirically makes him into a gentleman. They then sit down together and watch a play by Shakespeare.)

A second possible tie was found by Charlotte Stopes, a Stratfordian, who suggested a connection of Mary Arden to a branch of the Trussell family, which would make her a distant cousin of de Vere.[85] If Mary Arden was claiming to be descended from the ancient family of Ardens, they did come in with the William the Conqueror. A number of allusions to William Shakspere make this claim, so de Vere could have felt a distant kinship with him through Mary. However, nothing has been found to show Mary's connection to this distinguished branch of the Ardens.[86]

A third tie with Billesley, but not to Shakspere, is that local legend has it that *As You Like It* was written at Billesley Hall, a legend still proudly referred to today.[87]

Book 6, Satire I: *SEMEL INSANIUIMUS* (Omnes) ("We have all been mad at some time"). This is a well-known phrase from the *Eclogues* of Baptista Mantuanus (1498). Thomas Nashe uses it in *Have With You to Saffron-Walden* (1596). He translates it, "Once in our dayes, there is none of us but have plaid the ideots." He calls it, "that wether-beaten peice of a verse out of the Grammar."[88] Hall is indicating that he has been slightly mad, an idiot, for writing *Virgidemiarum*.

Book 6 is one long, sarcastic satire, which says that all of Hall's scourging was a mistake. The time is truly a golden age and it was wrong for him to scourge anyone. Hall begins and ends with Labeo, indicating how important he has been throughout the satires, particularly in Book 2, Book 4, and now in Book 6.

Labeo reserves a long nayle for the nonce
To wound my Margent through ten leaves at once,
Much worse than *Aristarchus* his black Pile
That pierc'd olde *Homer's* side;
....Whiles he his frightfull Beetle elevates,
His angry eyne looke all so glaring bright,
Like th' hunted Badger in a moonelesse night;
...Now red, now pale, and swolne above the eyes,
...But when he doth of my recanting heare,
Away ye angrie fires and frostes of feare,
Give place unto his hopefull tempered thought,
That yeelds to peace, ere ever peace be sought.
(1-20)

Hall begins by saying that Labeo keeps a long fingernail on his satires to "wound" or edit them. By referring to Aristarchus, who heavily edited Homer's *Iliad* and *Odyssey*, and to Aristarchus's marginal symbol of a dagger,[89] which signified that a line was to be deleted, Hall is intimating that de Vere edited some of his satires "ten leaves at once." He uses the word "Pile" or *pilum* for the dagger, which also translates as "spear."[90] "Pile" is capitalized, signifying a name, another subtle allusion to Labeo as Shakespeare. "Long nayle" may also allude to de Vere's habit of drawing manicules with long fingernails in the margins of books he owned, as evidenced in his copy of the Geneva Bible and the Psalms. Hall shows fascinating personal glimpses of de Vere, who we know worked with many authors. This shows direct reference to Labeo's editing, but it appears that Hall did not welcome it. If de Vere did edit Hall's work, some rather damning things were left in, showing an honesty about himself.

It is clear that Labeo has caused Hall to be chastised, has demanded recantation, but then has granted forgiveness. Labeo's anger is reprised ("red…angrie fires") as is his fear of exposure ("pale…frostes of fear"). However, when Labeo hears of Hall's recanting, he becomes reasonable and hopeful and forgives Hall before ("ere ever") he even asked for it. *Ever* again. A new picture of de Vere is shown, as one who has "hopefull tempered thought" and who "yeelds to peace, ere ever peace be sought." He is not vile, as Hall has previously depicted him, but he shows a noble side. Hall has been repeating all the scandal and rumors that were in literary, court and Puritan circles, whether they were true or not. His satires do show the scandalous stories that were rife about de Vere, many of which were accurate.

A long retraction of Hall's criticism of the age and its vices intervenes. It is instead truly a golden age and no one should see any evil. Then we meet a new, but familiar, character.

But why doth *Balbus* his dead-doing quill
Parch in his rustie scabbard all the while,
His golden Fleece ore-growne with moldy hore,
As tho he had his witty workes forswore?
Belike of late now *Balbus* hath no need,
Nor now belike his shrinking shoulders dread
The Catch-poles fist; the Presse may still remaine,
And breath, till *Balbus* be in debt againe.
(163-170)

Lucius Balbus, the younger, built a theater in Rome, dedicated in 13 BCE, which is always described as magnificent. He also wrote plays.[91] Hall's Balbus has let his quill dry out in a rusty, unused scabbard, with the allusion to the quill as a sword or spear. "Golden Fleece" is a reference to a noble hide or parchment. Mold has grown on the fleece. It's as if Balbus has abandoned his "witty workes." A noble playwright and theater-builder has stopped writing. He has sheathed his quill. Using Balbus as a name suggests that de Vere was responsible for building a theater or theaters in London. There are no records to show his involvement.

Hall's supposition is that Balbus doesn't have financial need at the moment and doesn't fear the debt collector. There is again an implication that de Vere was involved with the theater because he was in need and that he profited from production of his plays, all he had left of his heritage. Hall cynically assumes that he will be in debt again soon.

By the two crownes of *Pernasse* ever-greene,
And by the cloven head of *Hippocrene,*
As I true Poet am, I here avow,
(So solemnly kist he his Laurell bow,)
If that bold *Satyre* unrevenged be,
For this so saucy and foule injurie;
So *Labeo* weens it my eternall shame,
To prove I never earned a Poets name.
                    (179-186)

Back to Labeo, who swears by the two "ever-greene" hills of Parnassus and by the fountain of Hippocrene that as a "true poet" (and he solemnly kissed his "laurel bow" as laureate), Hall's bold satires will be avenged for such a saucy and foul injury, and Hall will "never" be recognized as a worthy poet, to his eternal shame. To seek honor for a wrong was an act required of nobility. "Ever-green," "true poet," "laureate," "never," "eternal." Hall doesn't need to throw in any more clues. Solemnly kissing the laurel crown alludes to Queen Elizabeth having granted it to him. Labeo was one of her chosen laureates.

A thought concerning de Vere's vengeance for Hall's detraction from his name: as noted, it concerns Lucio in *Measure for Measure,* who is a "fantastick," someone who makes things up, an allusion, I think, to Hall. The title of the play connotes revenge; a measure is being meted for a measure that has been done. There are more important characters than Lucio, but he is one of the story lines, and, as usual in a satirical characterization, he is not a simple, single depiction. When we first see him, he is accused by a gentleman of making up diseases in him when he is in fact healthy. "Thou art always figuring diseases in me but thou art full of error; I am sound."

Throughout the satires, Hall intimates that de Vere has gone to brothels where he contracted syphilis, and, as a result, he can no longer produce an heir, which would end the illustrious, ancient de Vere line. He hints that Henry is not de Vere's son, but a bastard. Hall lists the symptoms of a reddish rash, red eyes and loss of hair. He also mentions gout in a different satire. In *Measure for Measure*, III.i, Duke Vincentio, who is in disguise as a friar and who is seen as de Vere in disguise, is speaking to Claudio about death and life. He says about himself, "For thine own bowels which do call thee Sire,/ ...Do curse the *Gout, Serpigo* and *Rheume.*" Gout is self-explanatory and Vincentio/de Vere seems to be confirming that he has it. Serpigo is a type of reddish rash. Rheum is a watery secretion from the eyes, accompanied with redness as in a cold. In V.i, we recall that Lucio says about the Duke who is still in disguise, "Here comes the Rascal I spoke of…. This is the Rascal; this is he I spoke of…Come Sir, come Sir; Why you bald-pated Rascal, you must be hooded must you?"

All of the diseases, or symptoms of them, that Hall has accused de Vere of having, are dealt with in *Measure for Measure* as ailments of everyday life, not as indications of syphilis. Lucio refers to the Duke as "bald-pated," another hint that de Vere may have been bald later in life. The allusions to the Duke as a "Rascal" are evocative of the satire *Arcades Ambo*, A Pair of Rascals. Lucio refers to the Friar/Duke as being hooded, as being in shadow or in disguise; Hall writes of Shakespeare/de Vere, his disguise for his writing for the public theater. They were both called rascals.

A final striking similarity between Lucio and Hall is that the Duke forgives Lucio at the end of the play, but makes him marry the prostitute he has forsaken, which is the revenge—the measure that is extracted. In *Virgidemiarum*, Labeo forgives Hall, but Hall is now identified by name in the Bishops' Ban and his initials are on *Virgidemiarum* as the author. No more anonymity. He has to live with his lascivious and scandalous writing.

Measure for Measure was not published until the First Folio in 1623, but its first known staging was in 1604,[92] a time frame within which it could be reasonably understood as a response to Hall's satires.

The first lines of *Virgidemiarum* demand that the proud bow their heads willingly in repentance, but now it is Hall who must bow his head, even though he does so with sarcasm.

O age well thriven and well fortunate,
When ech man hath a Muse appropriate,
And she like to some servile eare-boar'd slave,
Must play and sing when, and what he would have.
Would that were all! Small fault in number lies,
Were not the feare from whence it should arise.
(233-238)

At this point, Hall seems to be throwing in random pieces he has written. Maybe he thought they were too good to leave out. He has made his point clearly, but covertly, that de Vere is the topic of many of his satires, but he continues. He makes another reference to powerful, highly placed people who write plays and songs, and to de Vere, who caused Hall to be chastised. "Eare-boar'd" parallels "eye boar'd out" and "newly lugged boar" from earlier satires also suggests drooping ears. We see "ech man" again, signifying *every* man.

Sith *Pontian* left his barren wife at home,
And spent two yeares at *Venice* and at *Rome*;
Returned, heares his blessing askt of three;
Cries out, O *Julian* law, Adulterie!
(241-244)

Pontian Greeks inhabited the area around Troy. The name is similar to Pontice, whom we saw as de Vere. The addition of "an" to the name could be an allusion to Ann Cecil. The story in the two couplets parallels de Vere going to Italy for about two years. When he returned, his wife had a child whom he disowned as his, intimating an adulterous affair.

Tho *Labeo* reaches right (who can deny?)
The true straynes of *Heroicke* Poesie;
For he can tell how fury reft his sense,
And *Phoebus* fild him with intelligence;
He can implore the heathen Deities
To guide his bold and busie enterprise;
Or filch whole Pages at a clap, for need,
From honest *Petrarch*, clad in English weed;
While bigge *But Ohs* ech stanzae can begin,
Whose trunk and tayle sluttish and hartless bin.
He knows the grace of that new elegance
…In epithets to joyne two wordes in one

Forsooth, for Adjectives cannot stand alone;
…Lastly, he names the spirit of *Astrophel*,
Now, hath not *Labeo* done wondrous well?
(245-264)

For the last time, Hall returns to Labeo and describes his writing, which he now praises. Labeo writes heroic poetry in "true" strains. His stories of kings and battles and heroes are well done. No one can deny that they're good. He can write of great emotion almost leading to madness, which understanding came from "Phoebus" (*Lear, Hamlet, Timon*). He can implore heathen gods to help him write (*A Midsummer Night's Dream*). He can steal whole themes from Petrarch and put them into English (*Romeo and Juliet, Troilus and Cressida, Sonnets*). Big "But Ohs" start *ever*lasting stanzas. "Ech" is an Old English word meaning "everlasting" and an Early Modern word meaning "every." Since the word "stanzae" is plural, "every" doesn't make sense here, but "everlasting" does, though both words follow the pattern of allusions to de Vere. The middle and end of stanzas are full of lewdness and heartlessness (*Venus and Adonis*). He uses hyphenated words as adjectives because two words are better than one (*Venus and Adonis, Lucrece*). And finally, he invokes the spirits of Sidney and Spenser (*Venus and Adonis, Lucrece*). The parallels to Shakespeare and to de Vere are evident.

But ere his Muse her weapon learns to weild,
Or dance a sober *Pirrhicke* in the field,
Or marching wade in blood up to the knees,
Her *Arma Virum* goes by two degrees.
The sheep-cote first hath been her nursery,
Where she hath worne her ydle infancy,
...Or else hath beene in *Venus* chamber train'd;
To play with *Cupid,* till shee had attain'd
To comment well upon a beauteous face,
Then was she fit for an Heroicke place.
(265-280)

Before Labeo began writing heroic works about knights in armor and battles, his first words (*Arma Virum*: the familiar first words and the nickname of the *Aeneid*) were of two types, pastorals and love poems; the love poems culminated in *Venus and Adonis,* which lifted Venus to a heroic level. Hall has been forced to be positive about *Venus and Adonis* after all his chastising.

 He refers to the first words of the *Aeneid*, the epic poem by Virgil that details the life of Aeneas, to again allude to Labeo as de Vere. He says that Labeo's Muse tells the story of Aeneas/de Vere. His life is in his works. Even the word *Virum* evokes Ver. The Latin genitive suffix *um* means "of something," of the word it is attached to, in this case, of Vir/Ver. Consider the opening lines of the *Aeneid*: *Arma virumque cano, Troiae qui primus ab oris Italiam fato profugus Laviniaque venit litora* (I sing of arms and of a man who first, exiled by fate, came from the shores of Troy to Italy [Rome] and to the Lavinian shores [Lavinia was Aeneas' last wife]).[93] Aeneas, Troy, Rome. Exiled by fate. Edward de Vere.

 Hall abruptly ends his satires after a further twenty-line derogatory description of an aging, wrinkled mistress, heavily made up with Venetian chalk, with bad teeth, but whom all the poets praise. It fits a picture of Queen Elizabeth at age sixty-five. What a rash, young, Puritan poet!

 Joseph Hall probably wrote his satires between late 1595 and early 1598, when he became a fellow of Emmanuel College, the dominant stronghold of Puritanism in Cambridge, where he had spent seven years as a brilliant undergraduate. During the course of analyzing the satires, several questions arose in my mind. Was he writing at the behest of someone else, one or more of the powerful Puritans who supported him? Did they encourage him to write to denounce what they saw as evils and dissolution in Elizabethan life? Did they want to counter the strong influence that Edward de Vere, writing as Shakespeare, had on the lives of the public? Or did the naively arrogant Hall, who believed that God directed every step of his life, do it on his own?

 Hall's was only one voice telling the story. During the same time, many other authors wrote satires, epigrams, pamphlets and satirical plays of an extremely personal nature, with Edward de Vere as a major hidden target of friendly and antagonistic works.[94] These works were, in a sense, the social media of the day. The writers wrote about, and to, each other. Some of them also wrote in a covert manner that Edward de Vere was Shakespeare.

It is understandable that he became such a topic of discussion and of satire. The name William Shakespeare first appeared in print in 1593 on the celebrated but infamous *Venus and Adonis,* and was quickly followed by the celebrated, but less notorious, *The Rape of Lucrece* in 1594. Shakespeare's plays were appearing on the London stage to great applause during the rest of the 1590s, anonymously at first, then with attribution starting in 1598. The name William Shakespeare acquired a kind of celebrity status. Anything by him, even with only his initials, was eagerly seen or read by the public and, as Hall writes, "controls the manners of the multitude." De Vere's status as the premier earl of England, of an ancient, esteemed line, his scandalous life, his involvement as a patron of writers and the public stage, and, as Hall suggests in the character Balbus, a builder of theaters—all of this would only heighten the interest within the literary community. He was a larger than life figure, himself a celebrity, though of greatly fallen repute. His identity as Shakespeare was carefully effaced, as attested in his own Sonnet 72:

> My name be buried where my body is,
> And live no more to shame nor me nor you.
> For I am shamed by that which I bring forth,
> And so should you, to love things nothing worth.

The place to find his story is in hidden allusions in his own works and in the works of those contemporary writers who kept it alive.

The cumulative evidence that Hall is writing in a covert manner about Edward de Vere as Shakespeare in *Virgidemiarum* is powerful. Many allusions are remarkably specific to de Vere. The satires of Book 1, Satire IX, *An Obscene Poet,* of Book 2, Satire I, *Immodest Poetry,* and of Book 4, Satire II, *Arcades Ambo,* A Pair of Rascals, specifically tell that de Vere is Shakespeare.

Joseph Hall's arrogance caused him trouble. He was not proud of *Virgidemiarum,* he never claimed it in lists of his own works, but he savored the effect it had on people he attacked. It had an effect on de Vere. It may have helped force him into retirement from London and the stage around 1598.

As a nobleman, it was incumbent on de Vere to answer Hall's detraction, but he did so in a manner that was, in *Virgidemiarum's* own words, "hopefull and tempered." His troubled life and his anger are vividly portrayed, but so is his reasonable, forgiving nature and his brilliance as the author Shakespeare.

A suitable coda to *Virgidemiarum:*

SONNET 112

> Your love and pity doth the impression fill
> Which vulgar scandal stamp'd upon my brow;

For what care I who calls me well or ill,
So you o'ergreen my bad, my good allow?
You are my all the world, and I must strive
To know my shames and praises from your tongue;
None else to me, nor I to none alive,
That my steel'd sense or changes, right or wrong.
In so profound abysm I throw all care
Of other's voices, that my adder's sense
To critic and to flatterer stopped are.
Mark how with my neglect I do dispense:
You are so strongly in my purpose bred,
That all the world besides methinks are dead.

Endnotes

[1] Joseph Hall, *Virgidemiarum, Sixe Bookes. First three Bookes, Of Tooth-lesse Satyrs. 1. Poeticall. 2. Academicall. 3. Morall.*, London, Printed by Thomas Creed for Robert Dexter, 1597. *Virgidemiarum, The three last Bookes Of Byting Satyres*. Imprinted at London by Richard Bradocke for Robert Dexter at the signe-of the Brasen Serpent in Pauls Church yarde, 1598. *Virgidemiarum* is the title of the two books put together into the 1599 edition. *Virgidemiarum* is also part of the title of the last three books of *Byting Satyres*, published in 1598.

[2] Richard A. Cabe, "Elizabethan Satire and the Bishops' Ban of 1599," *The Yearbook of English Studies*, Vol. 11, *Literature and Its Audience*, 11 Special Number (1981), 188-193.

[3] Peter Hall, *The Works of Joseph Hall: Miscellaneous*. Oxford: Talboys (1839), 143-144.

[4] Arnold Davenport, *The Poems of Joseph Hall*. Liverpool University Press (1969), 294.

[5] Hall, Book 3, *The Conclusion of All*.

[6] Hall, Book 3, Satire V.

[7] Hall, Book 3, Satire VII.

[8] Hall, Book 4, Satire VII.

[9] Alexander Waugh, "From the Pulpit—A Few Home Truths," *Brief Chronicles* VI (2015), 2-3. This has already proven to be true. Waugh deals with Great Osmond, from Hall's Book 3, Satire II, where he shows a clear allusion to de Vere that I had failed to see.

[10] William Pickering, *Virgidemiarum: SATIRES, by Joseph Hall, Bishop of Exeter and of Norwich. In Six Books*. London: Chancery Lane (1825).

[11] Oliver Lawson Dick, *Aubrey's Brief Lives*. University of Michigan Press (1957), 505.

[12] De Vere Society, *De Vere Lineage*, http://herebedragons.weebly.com/de-vere-lineage.html.

[13] Alan H. Nelson, *Monstrous Adversary: The Life of Edward de Vere, 17th Earl of Oxford*. Liverpool University Press (2003), 34.

[14] Davenport, 160. I have added Thomas Cutwode as another example.

[15] Daniel Henry Lambert, *Cartae Shakespeareanae: Shakespeare Documents; A Chrono-*

logical Catalogue of Extant Evidence Relating to the Life and Works of William Shakespeare. George Bell (1904), 10, 11, 12, 13, 22, 31, 38, 45.

[16] Rita Lamb, http://sicttasd.tripod.com/ttheory.html. At the outset of her essay, Lamb issues a stern warning to Stratfordians not to read further because it identifies certain satirical characters with known Elizabethans, including de Vere as Ver or Spring. Donna Murphy, *The Mysterious Connection Between Thomas Nashe, Thomas Dekker and TM: An English Renaissance Deception?* Cambridge Scholars Publishing (2014), 5.

[17] Patrick Cheney, *Shakespeare, National Poet-Playwright,* Cambridge University Press (2004), 86.

[18] E-Intro to Old English – 2. Pronunciation, http://mich.edu/medieval/resources/IOE/pronunciation.html; Also in an email message from Leeds University, Department of English, in reply to *Ask a Linguist,* online.

[19] James Orchard Halliwell-Phillipps, *Life of Shakespeare.* London: John Russell Smith (1848), 12.

[20] Davenport, xliv.

[21] Mark Anderson, *Shakespeare by Another Name.* Gotham Books (2005), 272.

[22] *Diogenes the Cynic* http://penelope.uchicago.edu/~grout/encyclopaedia_romana/greece/hetairai/diogenes.html.

[23] Hall, Book 1, Satire I, "*Trumpets, and reed, and socks and buskins fine/ I them bequeath...*" is an imitation of the *Prologue* to Persius's Satires; Book 4, Satire I, suggests Persius's Satire I; Book 5, Satire I, "And to thy hand yeeld up the *Ivye* mace/ From crabbed *Persius* and more smooth *Horace*...."

[24] Rev. M. Madan, *A New and Literal Translation of Juvenal and Persius.* Oxford (1807), 253 n.22.

[25] G.G. Ramsey, *Juvenal and Persius.* William Heinemann (1928), 323.

[26] Alexander Waugh, *The Spectator,* Neue Shake-speare Gesellschaft, 8 November 2013. www.shakespeare-today.de/front_content.php?idart=733. Kurt Kreiler, *Anonymous Shake-Speare,* 3.5.1. Hall, *Virgidemiarum,* n.1. http://www.anonymous-shakespeare.com/cms/index.255.0.1.html.

[27] Antony Augostakis and Ariana Traill, *A Companion to Terence.* John Wiley and Sons (2013), 4.

[28] Anderson, 308: "Labeo, Marston notes, once wrote that 'his love was stone: Obdurate, flinty, so relentless none.' This is a quote from line 199 of *Venus and Adonis.* ('Art thou obdurate, flinty, hard as steel?') 'Labeo' is Shake-speare."

[29] Gabriel Harvey, *Speculum Tuscanismi* (1580), line 15, "In Courtly guiles a passing singular odd man."

[30] Davenport, 175.

[31] Thomas Nashe, *Strange News* (1592), "He is a little man, but hath one of the best

wits in England." Shakespeare Oxford Fellowship, *The Many Nicknames of the Earl of Oxford*. www.shakekspeareoxfordfellowship.org/?s=many+nicknames+of+earl+oxford.

[32] Stephanie Hopkins Hughes, "'Shakespeare's' Tutor: Sir Thomas Smith (1513-1577)," *The Oxfordian* vol. 3 (2000), 19-44.

[33] Francis Meres, *Palladis Tamia* (1598).

[34] Nelson, 201-202.

[35] Anderson, 59-61.

[36] Anderson, 9, 29.

[37] Jeremy Crick, "Elizabeth and Ffrancis Trentham of Rocester Abbey," *De Vere Society Newsletter* (February 2007), 1-12

[38] Nelson, 415.

[39] N.P.G., "Edward de Vere, 17th Earl of Oxford (1550-1604), Courtier Images of Edward de Vere." Npg.org. Web. Accessed 12/16.

[40] Temple Henry Croker, *The Satires of Ludovico Ariosto*. A. Millar (1759), 50.

[41] Crick, 1-12.

[42] B.M. Ward, *The Seventeenth Earl of Oxford*. J. Murray (1928), 355.

[43] The House of Vere: References, http://www.bibliotecapleyades.net/dragons/esp_sociopol_dragoncourt02_13.htm; Wikipedia, *St. Peter and St. Paul's Church, Lavenham*, https://en.wikipedia.org/wiki/St_Peter_and_St_Paul%27s_Church,_Lavenham.

[44] Roger A. Stritmatter, *The Marginalia of Edward de Vere's Geneva Bible*. University of Massachusetts (2001).

[45] J. Aubrey Rees, *The Grocery Trade, Its History and Romance*, Duckworth & Co. (1910), vol. I, 101-114. "In fact, he was as much a professional money-lender as a grocer (merchant)...." I am grateful to Julie Sandys Bianchi for discovering this reference.

[46] Basil Tozer, *The Horse in History*. Methuen (1908), 54. Wikipedia, *Bucephalus*, http://en.wikipedia.org/wiki/Bucephalus.

[47] William Plumer Fowler, *Shakespeare Revealed in Oxford's Letters*. Peter E. Randall (1986), 524 ("I have not an able body"); 593 ("If my health had been to my mind"); 607 ("by reason of my sickness, I have been unable to write"); 653 ("with a lame hand to write"); 739 ("by reason of mine infirmity, I cannot come among you").

[48] Wikipedia, *William (Given Name)*, https://en.wikipedia.org/wiki/William_given_name.

[49] Hank Whittemore, *No. 84 of 100 Reasons why the Earl of Oxford was "Shakespeare": He was Involved in the Revolutionary Expanding Universe of Astronomy*. Feb. 7,

50 George Lewis, *A life of Joseph Hall, D.D., Bishop of Exeter and Norwich, Part 4*. Hodder and Stoughton (1886), 38-43. Among the Puritans: Henry Hastings, 3rd Earl of Huntingdon; Henry Mildmay, Chancellor of the Exchequer and founder of Emmanuel; Laurence Chaderton, Master of Emmanuel; Sir John Popham, Chief Justice.

51 Carolyn Morris, "Did Joseph Hall and Ben Jonson Identify Oxford as Shakespeare?" *The Oxfordian* vol. 15 (2013), 3-26.

52 These allusions call for an essay of their own and are too extensive to go into here. The main links are to characters named Lollio or to situations that strongly parallel the content of *Arcades Ambo*, which deals with a rustic squire who wants his eldest son to be a gentleman and who claims to have come to England with the conqueror.

53 The Induction to *The Taming of the Shrew* deals with a rustic who is satirically made into a gentleman; a farmer's eldest son claims his ancestor came in with the conqueror.

54 Michael Delahoyde, *Measure For Measure*, http://public.wsu.edu/~delahoyd/shakespeare/measure5.html.

55 Livius.org, *Marcus Lollius*, http://www.livius.org/person/lollius/; Encyclopaedia Britannica, *Lollius, Marcus*, http://en.wikisource.org/wiki/1911_Encyclop%C3%A6dia_Britannica/Lollius,_Marcus; Wikipedia, *Marcus Lollius*, http://en.wikipedia.org/wiki/Marcus_Lollius.

56 Peter Bayle, *The Dictionary Historical and Critical of Mr. Peter Bayle*, vol. 3, 859-860. He was "a man in everything more fond of money than behaving well, and, under the highest appearances of virtue, the most vitious of men."

57 William Dolle and Alexander Brome, *Poems of Horace, Consisting of the Odes, Satyrs, and Epistles. Rendered in English and Paraphrased by Several Persons*, Book 4, Ode 9. London (1680).

58 Richard F. Thomas, *Horace: Odes IV and Carmen Saeculare*. Cambridge University Press (2011), 198-199: "What Horace writes, grand and dignified though the sentiments are, sounds like an attempt at rehabilitation and is a little on the defensive—an awkward situation for the poet."

59 Chaucer, *Troilus and Criseyde*, http://hompi.sogang.ac.kr/anthony/chaucer/troilus.htm; Malissa Kent, "The Many Faces of Lollius: A Study of Chaucer's Auctour in Troillus and Criseyde," unpublished MSS.

60 Jacqueline de Weever, *Chaucer Name Dictionary: A Guide to Astrological, Biblical, Historical, Literary and Mythological Names in the Works of Geoffrey Chaucer*. Routledge (2014), 218.

61 Park Honan, *Shakespeare: A Life*. Oxford University Press (1998), 36-38.

62 Diana Price, *Shakespeare's Unorthodox Biography, New Evidence of an Authorship*

[63] *Problem.* Greenwood Press (2001).

[63] Encyclopedia Britannica, http://www.britannica.com/EBchecked/topic/401487/Gnaeus-Naevius.

[64] Paul Hemenway Altrocchi, *Malice Aforethought: The Killing of a Unique Genius.* Xlibris Corporation (2010), 163-164. Paul Altrocchi and Hank Whittemore, *My Name be Buried: A Coerced Pen Name Forces the Real Shakespeare into Anonymity* (2009), 106.

[65] Anderson, 66-67.

[66] *Who Wears What*, http://elizabethan.org/sumptuary/who-wears-what.html, 2-25-2012.

[67] Barbara Yorke, *Kings and Kingdoms of Early Anglo-Saxon England.* Routledge (2002), 102.

[68] Davenport, 238: "It grew more and more customary for the sons of the better class yeoman to try their fortunes in London."

[69] John S. Hales, *The Name Shakspeare.* The Athenaeum (1903), 230-233.

[70] Karl Elze, *William Shakespeare: A Literary Biography.* G. Bell and Sons (1888), 482-488.

[71] Samuel A. Tannenbaum, *Shakesper's Coat of Arms* (1908).

[72] Ralph Brooke and John Leland, *A discoverie of certaine errours published in print in the much commended Britannia, 1594, very prejudicial to the discentes and succession of the aunciente nobilitie of the realme. By Yorke Herault.* John Windet (1599).

[73] Oxford English Dictionary: A quotation from *Brieff discours of the troubles begonne at Franckford Germany* A.D. 1554 by W. Whittingham: To weare the pied coat of a foole.

[74] Oxford English Dictionary: Upstart 1555 H. Braham, *Inst. Gentleman* sig. Ciiij, These gentlemen are now called vpstartes, a term lately invented by such as pondered not ye groundes of honest meanes of rising or commyng to promocion.

[75] Charlton Ogburn, Jr., *The Mysterious William Shakespeare.* Dodd, Mead & Co. (1984), 511: "At all these love matters my Lord Treasurer winketh and will not meddle in any way." Paul Hemenway Altrocchi, "A Portrait Analysis of William Cecil," *Shakespeare Matters*, vol. 1, no. 1 (Fall 2001), 8. Altrocchi shows that Cecil had a cleft palate which would have produced a slightly lising speech.

[76] Encycopedia Britannica, *Albius Tibulllus*, c. 55-19 BCE. http://www.britannica.com/EBchecked/topic/595039/Albius-Tibullus.

[77] Joseph Esmond Riddle, *A Complete English-Latin Dictionary.* Longmans, Orne, Brown, Green & Longmans (1838), 288.

[78] W.C. Firebaugh, *The Satyricon of Petroniuis Arbiter*, vol. 1. Boni & Liveright (1922), 80-82.

[79] C.C. Stopes, *Shakespeare's Family, Being a Record of the Ancestors and Descendants of William Shakespeare with some Account of the Ardens.* Elliot Stock (1901).

[80] Patient Trusted Medical Information and Advice, http://www.patient.co.uk/health/syphilis-leaflet.

[81] Charles Nicholl, *The Reckoning: The Murder of Christopher Marlowe.* University of Chicago Press (1992), 83-88.

[82] Constance Brown Kuriyama, *Christopher Marlowe: A Renaissance Life.* Cornell University Press (2010), 99; En.wikipedia.org/wiki/Thomas_Walsingham_(literary_patron).

[83] Elze, 8.

[84] *Walk in the footsteps of Shakespeare*—a guided trail around Wilmcote, Billesley and Aston Cantlow. http://www.visitchurches.org.uk/Assets/BillesleyShakespeareprojectassets/WalkingintheFootstepsofShakespeareTrail.pdf?1331133288.

[85] Stopes; William Farina, *De Vere as Shakespeare.* McFarland (2005), 66.

[86] N.W. Alcock and Robert Bearman, "Discovering Mary Arden's House: Property and Society in Wilmcote, Warwickshire," *The Shakespeare Quarterly* vol. 53, no. 1 (Spring 2002), 70 (see also p. 70 n.61: Only half a century after Robert's [Arden] death did John Shakespeare rewrite history by identifying him as a gentleman. Robert himself never aspired to being more than a husbandman, although he could surely have described himself as a yeoman).

[87] Warwickshire.livingmag.co.uk/Billesley-manor.

[88] A.H. Bullen, *The works of Thomas Nashe: Have with you to Saffron-Walden. Nashe's Lenten stuffe. Summer's last will and testament. Shorter pieces. Doubtful Works* (1905), 79.

[89] Mental-floss, *5 Characters from the Margins of Ancient texts*, http://mentalfloss.com/article/52758/5-characters-margins-ancient-texts.

[90] Davenport, 250 n.3.

[91] "Balbus," *Encyclopaedia Britannica,* 1911, vol. 3, online edition modified 19 July 2014.

[92] J.W. Lever, ed., *Measure for Measure*. London: Methuen (1965), xxi-xxv.

[93] R. Allen Smith, *Virgil.* John Wiley & Sons (2010), 105.

[94] Quakespeare Shorterly, http://lookingforshakespeare.blogspot.com/2015/08/a-sin-oth-state.html; The Festival Robe, http://www.thefestivalrobe.com/ These are two sites that show covert allusions to de Vere in the works of other authors of the era.

Teaching the Sonnets and de Vere's Biography at School – Opportunities and Risks

Elke Brackmann and Robert Detobel

Teachers are facing a new situation for which they are not really prepared. Being forced by the media (e.g., Roland Emmerich's 2011 film, *Anonymous*) to take a stance on the authorship question, they are at a loss. Up to now the authorship issue has been considered a topic dealt with at university level, but the universities in Germany prefer not to respond. Although doubters of all kind belong to academia the universities refuse to develop an appropriate interest in the issue. Brunel University in London (thanks to Prof. William Leahy) seems to be an exception.

True, a huge amount of work pressure, not to speak of endless correction tasks, has increased at public schools and made it more difficult for teachers to do some extra research on Shakespeare. There exist, in addition, some mental barricades, which make the issue even appear annoying. The feeling of safety that the Stratfordian version offers is too tempting to be abandoned, especially when one has no idea about the questions connected with it.

The question remains: "What am I to tell my students?" Not knowing what to do, teachers have clung to two seemingly convincing means of escape:

1: No biography is needed to understand the works of the Bard. A convincing argument, no doubt, because it has led to great results and not detracted from the depth, topicality and grandeur of Shakespeare's works. But the argument is also misleading, as it brutally undermines new and better ways of understanding. In addition, people are often inconsistent, e.g., the staunch Stratfordian Harold Bloom, who puts forward the thesis that both Hamlet and Falstaff are Shakespeare's most biographical characters.[1] Or Helen Vendler, the outstanding commentator on the sonnets, who claims the speaker of the sonnets feels as a social outcast (Sonnet 71) without putting it in a special social context.[2] Whenever possible, commentators refer to biographical experiences, constantly violating the conviction that the works speak for themselves.

2: The Elizabethan worldview as a substitute for the missing biographical facts. Generations of students have been made familiar with the idea of the chain of being as essential for the Elizabethans. Needless to say this is correct, but it does not really help to explain any drama, with the exception of *Macbeth*, and ignores historical reality to an unbearable extent. What kind of complex police state existed when Elizabeth I was in power, how unsafe the throne was, how her position was continually under attack, how aristocracy defined itself —all these essential aspects are left out.

The educational publishers hesitate to respond accordingly. *Green Line Oberstufe*[3] does write about different candidates; but the authors do not realize that the Stratford biography is totally inconsistent with what they wrote beforehand about the Bard's comprehensive knowledge of languages.

Relating Edward de Vere's biography to his works does involve chances and risks, which we would like to discuss openly. W. H. Auden's saying that Shakespeare's sonnets are "naked autobiographical confessions" is well known, just like Browning's counterargument that the sonnets are nothing but "literary exercises." For us, personally, it is incomprehensible that the depth, the suffering and sincerity that pervade the sonnets should have no relation to the author's own experiences. The question arises whether we know of any other poet who voiced his own weaknesses and shortcomings with such honesty —to admit all that in front of yourself, so to speak, makes Shakespeare a citizen of the 21st century and goes far beyond viewing the sonnets as stylistic exercises.

With the example of Sonnet 29 we would like to show practicable and one-sided or simply wrong ways of approaching this poem.

The schoolbook *Shakespearean Sonnets and Elizabethan Poetry*[4] shows consistency in dealing with the sonnets. There is not even a hint to whoever wrote them in this book, nor is the Earl of Southampton is mentioned as the addressee, although a great number of orthodox scholars agree on it. The author, Elena Gross, offers useful worksheets on the Elizabethan worldview mentioned above, even though they do not play a decisive role in interpreting the sonnets. As an introduction to Sonnet 29, she offers a list of quotations on "envy" to prepare the students for the key topic, according to her view. In doing so, she builds a bridge for the students and helps them to train their competence in questions dealing with the beautiful language of the poem. Thus, she leads them to a better understanding of the topic "envy."

In contrast, Helen Vendler[5] evokes the two levels of reality, the hierarchy of the social world and the hierarchically structured world of nature—it is exactly in this place the so-called Elizabethan worldview could come in, but Gross does not mention it here. Vendler, as usual, makes the text speak. As she does not need to help students, she can neglect any didactical reduction and, as a consequence, comes to a more comprehensive interpretation. Indeed, she is sure that biography plays a part when she says: "The self-pity of the opening is based on genuine misfortune, if the domestic fiction of the poem is to be believed; we do not doubt that the speaker is *"outcast"* (emphasis added). The fact that we have no information as to why the speaker feels outcast is painful unless one has been conditioned into thinking that biographical parallels do not matter anyway.

Many books dealing with the Elizabethan Age have not helped to solve this puzzle. Can the authorship issue come to more plausible conclusions? Yes, it can: In his book *Will, Wunsch und Wirklichkeit*, Robert Detobel writes:

> If we see the Sonnet as a poem written by an immensely gifted courtier, who, out of aesthetic delight, has violated a certain code of behavior and, as a consequence, was excluded from court life, at least temporarily, we not only approach the drama of the poem, but also the drama of the poet. Assuming that Edward de Vere was the author this interpretation makes sense.[6]

It has to be clear about what we can achieve with a biography and what we cannot. Hans Albert Koch, in his review of a biography of the brothers Grimm, defined biography as follows:

> One of the oddest things in modern literary studies is that the biographical approach is looked at with scorn – at a time when the literary genre "biography" is very successful. What is being withheld is the fact that an author's biography does *not* offer a *sufficient* but a definitely *necessary condition* for the understanding of his work.[7] (Emphasis added)

What we are trying to do is to work according to objective criteria, to structure the tasks in a way useful for students and to present material that appeals to them both emotionally and intellectually. But before dealing with such a task, the risks must not be denied. To deal with it in a freewheeling manner would have disastrous consequences. When James Shapiro associates the opening lines of Sonnet 27 ("Weary with toil, I haste me to my bed/The dear repose for limbs with travel tired") with Shakespeare's concern about the bad state of the highway between London and Stratford, for the repair of which he supported a petition in 1611, the term "freewheeling" is rather an understatement.[8] Of course, Oxfordians and other Non-Stratfordians as well are not necessarily immune to this type of hazardous allusion spotting, fossilizing each metaphor into the concreteness of a street name in the index of a city map or, vice versa, diluting a particular phrase to the windy metaphorical meaning that fits one's own strained interpretation. Such approaches not only overstretch the idea of biographical factors, they also destroy all feelings for a poem as a piece of art and ignore the value of the phonetic level.

In an attempt to use the chance of the release of Emmerich's *Anonymous*, Sony Pictures promulgated a study guide for students. It subscribes to a crude way of dealing with an author's biography, and does not really challenge the student's critical thinking with tasks like "Use the information on this sheet to research the theory that William Shakespeare of Stratford-upon-Avon was not the author of the plays."[9] Such tasks are simply not interesting and, sorry to say so, sheer manipulation. We can imagine that brilliant students see through it and feel repulsed. We should not repeat the mistakes the orthodox theory continually makes. In this case we definitely side with Shapiro, when he makes fun of such a didactic concept and labels teachers who are willing to take part in it "tired and unimaginative."[10]

In an attempt to make the *Sonnets* speak and to connect them to de Vere's authorship, we tried to approach the following three sonnets in a way that we hope meets academic standards. We follow that with an approach to three more sonnets.

Activities

Try to approach this topic by starting from personal experiences and observations:

1. You have come to realize that your peer group has treated you like an outsider for days. What strategies can your group employ to make you feel this way? Write them down:

    -
    -

2. Think of <u>different</u> ways of reacting that YOU may show:

    -
    -

    Before concentrating on the sonnets, find out what Elizabethan aristocracy expected of peers and how outsiders were treated, then compare them to your findings: Are there any similarities and differences?

Nobility: Not Just a Matter of Title

Characteristics I - spending

Being a nobleman or an aristocrat not only denoted you were a person of high social rank, but it also implied a certain attitude towards life.

In order to be a real aristocrat you were expected to spend or waste money to a great extent. Sir Thomas Smith, an Elizabethan scholar, wrote: "in England no man is created baron, except he may spend of yearly revenue thousand pounds or one thousand marks. Viscounts, earls, marquesses and dukes more according to the proportion of the degree and honour."[11]

When in June 1586 the Earl of Oxford was granted by the Queen a pension of 1,000 pounds a year to prop up his ruined estate, it was in all likelihood to allow him to spend according to his rank.

Characteristics II - Learning

Just as it is difficult for us to understand that social prestige in the 16th and 17th centuries was based on spending, it is equally difficult to realize that at the beginning of the 16th century the aristocracy was, by and large, hostile to learning. A nobleman was supposed to be good at blowing the horn, skilled in hunting or training a hawk—this was enough to be properly educated.[12] The ability to write was regarded as sufficient for the son of a nobleman. Due to the change in the social landscape, however, the aristocracy could no longer afford to cultivate a negative view on learning, for in the long run they would have lost their influence and power. So, they were forced to educate themselves and their children and keep playing an important part in the affairs of the state.

Characteristics III - Honesty

To be a nobleman meant to conform to a certain mode of behavior, which was not written down, but built on the common sense of people reputed to be "honest." The term covers a wide field of meanings such as:

Appropriate social behavior (comparable to today's idea of "political correctness");

Sincere; Noble; Of good reputation: It depends on how one is esteemed by others, seen "through men's eyes," thus good reputation may conflict with self-esteem;

Civil: civil manners paved the way to a civilized society governed by law instead of violence.

Both honest manners and learning, in other words, came to be seen as requirements for participating in the government as a political leader. The crux of the matter, however, is: Who actually decides who really is honest or dishonest, when there is no written law to judge by?

Inward and outward honesty

When honesty refers to certain rules of outward behavior, people may follow them for the sake of success only; they completely forget the other meaning of honesty, namely being sincere and being true to one's values. In Elizabethan aristocratic society honesty was essential. No matter how corrupt you were inwardly, as long as you played your social role correctly, nobody seemed to mind. In other words, the ethics of the court were ethics of behavior, not ethics of inner conviction or mentality. Moreover, this society was characterized by fierce rivalry and competition for favor. Small wonder people were tempted to discredit others by exposing their behavior as dishonest, even if this was not the case. One is painfully reminded of the present day, where competition may lead to uncontrollable bullying as well. Yet there is an essential difference. Nowadays you may live and communicate with people from different classes whereas in Elizabethan times a member of the upper class was irrevocably bound to this class. It was practically impossible for him to live outside it; to become an outcast, as a consequence, meant to be socially dead.

The Earl of Oxford was honest and hated all empty ceremonies. That is why he sums up his state of mind in Sonnet 121 by saying, *"I am that I am."*

An unwritten code of behavior is as powerful as a written one, because an informal group of people decides who should be condemned morally. This strategy of ostracizing a person makes him defenseless, even if he is innocent, even if he is honest or has broken a rule that is worth breaking. It is enough to be punished with a contemptuous look by others. This penalty is worse than imprisonment because it meant isolation and loneliness; being outcast is a prison-like experience indeed. Isolation was the high price Shakespeare had to pay for real honesty.

Sonnet 29

When in disgrace with Fortune and men's eyes,
I all alone beweep my outcast state,
And trouble deaf heaven with my bootless cries,
And look upon myself and curse my fate,   4
Wishing me like to one more rich in hope,
Featured like him, like him with friends possessed,
Desiring this man's art, and that man's scope,
With what I most enjoy contented least;
Yet in these thoughts myself almost despising,   8
Haply I think on thee, and then my state
(Like to the lark at break of day arising
From sullen earth) sings hymns at heaven's gate;   12
For thy sweet love rememb'red such wealth brings
  That then I scorn to change my state with kings.

1 in disgrace out of favor

1 Fortune fortune was the goddess of luck, either good or bad, in Roman religion. She was represented turning a wheel the direction of which she could at any time change, so symbolizing the mutability of luck

2 state social status

3 bootless hopeless, useless

6 featured with features like his, beautiful

7 art skill of any kind

7 scope: area of activity, sphere of influence

10 state state of mind, feeling

14 state social status

Activities

1. What exactly is meant with the first line?
2. Lines 2 to 9 describe the speaker's reaction after realizing he is an outcast; explain them in your own words.
3. Work out what helps him to regain a balanced mental state.
4. Sonnet 29 obviously covers a wide range of feelings and thoughts, which are given emphasis by the use of various stylistic elements. Match the elements that are given in alphabetical order (some are used more than once) to the correct lines or phrases and discuss their effect in this particular context:

anaphora, antithesis, chiasmus, enjambment, ennumeration, personification, simile

The thought of his beloved leads the speaker out of his depression. Is this a satisfactory solution for you? Why? Why not?

Language awareness

This poem deals with a variety of positive and negative feelings. Try to formulate them and visualize them in this "thermometer," finding at least two expressions for one line (one example is given):

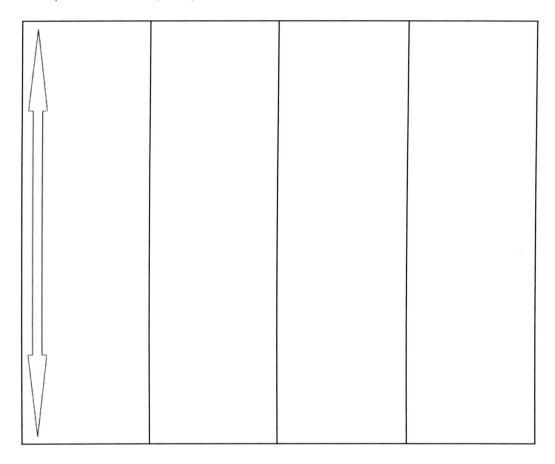

Sonnet 121

To prepare: One person must volunteer to be an outcast.
Everyone then writes down on a slip of paper a statement that is intended to damage this person's reputation. Next form a passage through which the outcast has to pass. In turn, each person hurls his or her accusation, then gives the outcast the slip of paper. In the end the outcast talks about his experiences and tries to formulate an appropriate verbal response. While he or she is thinking, the others also write down what they expect him or her to say.

Or

"The others say...the others say...the others say...." Discuss the importance of the others' judgment of you. Should we be immune towards it or take it seriously?

> 'Tis better to be vile than vile esteemed,
> When not to be receives reproach of being,

And the just pleasure lost, which is so deemed
Not by our feeling but by others' seeing. 4
For why should others' false adulterate eyes
Give salutation to my sportive blood?
Or on my frailties why are frailer spies,
Which in their wills count bad what I think good?
No, I am that I am, and they that level 8
At my abuses reckon up their own;
I may be straight though they themselves be bevel;
By their rank thoughts my deeds must not be 12
shown
Unless this general evil they maintain:
All men are bad and in their badness reign.

2 receives reproach of being if one is not so and is nevertheless reproached to be so

3 so deemed regarded as immoral

5 adulterate the Latin "adulter" means both "adultery " and "false." "False adulterate" would be "false false"

6 give salutation pronounce their blessing

6 sportive playful

8 which who

8 wills wishes, desires

9/10 level at to aim at, to shoot at

11 bevel not straight, not upright

12 rank foul, rancid, smelling bad

Activities

1. Below are paraphrases of two lines in a jumbled order. Match the paraphrases to the two appropriate lines in the sonnet:

- Even true joy is lost if it is only considered true joy in the others' view and not because I feel the joy.

- My personal integrity cannot be attacked by anybody; indeed, I think the

- others do not realize that they merely fight their own devils when judging me.

- I'd rather be immoral than seem immoral as the others' judgment does not differentiate anyway.

- Why should the others who are even more wicked than I am watch me and criticize deeds that I consider good?

- The others who are even more false than I—why should they be the ones to bless my playful deeds?

- Perhaps it is I who is honest and direct and it is they who are dishonest and have no right to judge my deeds.

- What counts is that they are convinced in general that all men are bad and corrupt by nature.

2. The speaker meditates upon the difference between *being* and *seeming*. Why was it difficult in Shakespeare's days to be authentic? Why is it even difficult nowadays?

3. Do you agree with the first line or do you see it as an overreaction of a vulnerable person? Discuss.

4. In his letter to Lord Burghley from 30 October 1584 Oxford furiously included the sentence "I am that I am." Briefly explain the circumstances leading to this statement, which is also part of this sonnet.

5. In groups prepare a shared reading of the sonnet, trying to agree on the poem's tone and mood: Melancholic? Aggressive? Defiant? Lighthearted? Ironic? Does the mood change or remain the same throughout the sonnet?

Language Awareness

There are many ways of cementing your command of English vocabulary. The golden rule to follow is always "Use them or lose them." This sonnet is full of verbs dealing with judgment:

1 esteem

2 reproach
3 deem
7 spy (also: "to spy")
8 count (bad)
10 reckon

First find synonyms for the given words. Then (as homework or pair work or group work), invent a gap text for your neighbor in which the above mentioned words and/or their synonyms are used. Make a little story out of the sentences with the missing words, then it is more interesting! There should be eight gaps.

Or

Fill in the right words, using the words underlined above and their synonyms:
All her life she ___ it clever not to marry one of her suitors; among them were highly ___ kings and adventurers. No doubt, some people ___ this one of her great virtues. Moreover, her secret service depended on a network of ___. As an unmarried woman on the throne she was in constant danger and rebellions were common. She ___ Sir Walter Raleigh among her closest friends, but in the end he suffered her bitter ___, ended up in the Tower and was eventually beheaded. It would be interesting to find out what would have happened to England if her sister Mary Tudor had outlived her—would England still be ___ for Shakespeare? After all it was her interest in the theater that made her ___ it worth supporting.

"I Am That I Am"—Oxford's Letters to Burghley Between 1575 and 1584 and Shakespeare's Sonnet 121

In January 1575 Oxford leaves England for Italy. In March he is in Paris and receives a letter from Lord Burghley that his wife is with child. Oxford is satisfied for two reasons. The first reason he gives relates to his travels, only the second to a possible successor. "For now it hath pleased god to give me a son of mine own (as I hope it is), methinks I have the better occasion to travel, since whatsoever becomes of me, I leave behind me one to supply my duty and service either to my prince or else my country." Knowing that he possibly will have a son to continue the ancestral line, he can more lightheartedly proceed with his travels.

From a letter of 24 September 1575 one could conclude he is less concerned about his health than about the restrictions his weakness will impose on the time available for traveling. "Yet with the help of god now I have recovered the same and am past the danger thereof though brought very weak thereby, and hindered from a great deal of travel. Which grieves me most, fearing my time not sufficient for my desire."

On 27 November 1575: "And as concerning my own matters, I shall desire your Lordship to make no stay of the sales of my land, but that all things according to my determination before I came away." In Oxford's letter of 3 January 1576 emerges the fundamental and irreconcilable opposition between Oxford's and Burghley's worldviews. Oxford wants to go on with the sale of his land so that he may continue his travels; Burghley advises him otherwise. "In doing these things your lordship shall greatly pleasure me. In not doing them you shall as much hinder me.... Mine is made to serve me and my self, not mine."[13] In Italy Oxford was looking to satisfy his thirst for learning and art. The phrase expresses that aesthetic self-realization was his supreme aim, to which anything else was subordinated.

A very important letter in connection with Shakespeare's Sonnet 121—its importance seems to have passed unnoticed thus far—is that of 10 July 1576. Oxford writes to Burghley: "Now if your Lordship shall do so, then you shall take more in hand than I have, or can promise, for always I have and I will still prefer mine own content before others." B.M. Ward and Conyers Read have transcribed it this way.[14] It is more appropriately written with genitive apostrophe: "for always I have and I will still prefer mine own content before others.'" That is, "I'll do what contents me and not what contents others," or "If what seems good to me but what others look askance at and think bad, I'll nevertheless do what in my view is right."

In lines 3 and 4 of Sonnet 121 Shakespeare expresses the same determination: "Others' seeing" are the "men's eyes" of the opening line of Sonnet 29.

Then, in the letter of 30 October 1584: "My lord, this other day your man[15] Stainner told me that you sent for Amis my man, and if he were absent that Lyly should come unto you. I sent Amis for he was in the way. And I think very strange that your Lordship should enter into that course towards me, whereby I must learn that I knew not before, both of your opinion and good will towards me. But I pray, my Lord, leave that course, for I mean not to be your ward nor your child, I serve Her Majesty, and I am that I am, and by alliance near to your lordship, but free, and scorn to be offered that injury, to think I am so weak of government as to be ruled by servants, or not able to govern myself."

Oxford was then financially engaged in the theater. He had leased the Blackfriars theater in 1583 and subleased it to John Lyly. "Sportive blood" in line 6 of the sonnet may refer to that. Probably it was for this reason Burghley had sent for Lyly. If not a perfect one, the correspondence between Oxford and Burghley between 1575 and 1584 offers a close match with Shakespeare's Sonnet 121 and provides an excellent background for it. An autobiographical background!

Sonnet 111

> O for my sake do you with Fortune chide,
> The guilty goddess of my harmful deeds,
> That did not better for my life provide
> Than public means which public manners breeds   4
> Thence comes it that my name receives a brand,
> And almost thence my nature is subdued
> To that it works in, like the dyer's hand.
> Pity me then, and wish I were renewed,   8
> Whilst like a willing patient I will drink
> Potions of eisel 'gainst my strong infection;

No bitterness that I will bitter think,
No double penance to correct correction. 12
Pity me then, dear friend, and I assure ye
Even that your pity is enough to cure me.

1 Fortune The Roman goddess presiding over good and bad luck. The young man reproves her for the sake of the poet
1 chide rebuke, scold
2 guilty goddess It is the goddess who is made responsible for some things the poet has done and which have caused him troubles.
4 public means It may mean "governmental means"; it may also mean "income from the public," for instance, the public stage. It may mean both.
4 public manners in this case it rather means "vulgar," causing inappropriate behavior
5 brand stigma, in Elizabethan times the hand or face of a criminal was branded with a hot iron
6 is subdued cannot escape; is subject to
10 Potions of eisel medicine mixed with vinegar, often used against the plague and other infections
12 double penance I will not be against suffering twice the punishment

Activities

1. Modern publications often stress the fact that actors in Elizabethan times had a very low status, but this is only a half-truth when we look at the biography of the sonnet-writer. Sum up what deeply troubled Shakespeare when writing this sonnet with the unforgettable line, "Thence comes it that my name receives a brand."

2. This is a prose version of sonnet 111. It contains four mistakes. Find them and correct them:

On my behalf, my friend, you scold the goddess Fortune whose changeability influenced my doings that proved so hurtful and left no other means of living to me than those created by the public stage where I learned to behave properly in public.

It is this connection with the public stage that has brought me into disrepute and has impregnated my habits no more than the dye impregnates the hand of the dyer, whose hand takes on the color of the material he is working with.

Then lament me and wish that I may renew myself, and I, against my will, shall be a patient pleased to obey; I shall swallow any bitter medicine in any quantity to cure my illness and not refuse to be punished over and over again to correct myself steadily.

Have compassion for me, but I cannot certify that your compassion will be sufficient to put me back on the right path.

3. Analyze the meaning and function of the powerful imagery used in lines 5, 6-7 and 9-10.

The Narrative Underlying Sonnet 111

Together with Sonnet 110, Sonnet 111 tells us a story about the author's life. Again, together with some sociohistorical information and a particular piece of documentary evidence, the story, insofar as we can reasonably expect to uncover it, points to author other than William Shakespeare to whom authorship is generally attributed. Why?

A Motley to the View

Sonnet 110 opens: Alas, 'tis true, I have gone here and there

And made myself a motley to the view.

A "motley" is the multi-colored dress of the court jester. The word can be understood literally or metaphorically. But "view" here means "exposure to the public," such as a professional actor was regularly exposing and had to expose himself to. For an aristocrat, this was a serious breach of the behavioral code of his class and almost equivalent with committing "social suicide." Hence, the rueful reflection in the third line of sonnet 110.

In 1531 Sir Thomas Elyot published his *Book named the Governor*, a sort of manual for the re-education of the old feudal aristocracy to the new court aristocracy. "Governor" here means "political leader." According to Elyot the new aristocrat, the "governor" or political leader, ought to possess two things: learning (the majority of the old feudal aristocracy had considered learning as effeminate and only proper for a clerk, not for a knight) and refined or "honest" manners. Training in different arts such as poetry, music and painting was also part of this re-education. However, the aristocrat should reserve such artistic performances to his leisure time and privacy, and should never expose himself to the public view performing music, painting, etc. The Roman emperor Nero is held up as the negative example, because he used to sit in the theater where the people of Rome could watch him. Elyot reveals that he is aware of the danger that the loss of respect caused by the behavior of even one individual aristocrat might rebound on the whole ruling elite. The pressure of the aristocracy, as an entire class, on each member to conform to the aristocratic behavioral code, which was a basic element of their legitimating ideology, was enormous. Elyot's assessment of Nero in 1531 does not differ in essence from that of the Roman historian Tacitus. Tacitus's unconditional damnation of Nero's behavior is not rooted in the emperor's predilection for poetry, playing and singing as such, but rather in his not restricting it to the private sphere.

Harmful Deeds

If Shakespeare was really an aristocrat who had acted on the public stage, the poet's complaint that "thence comes it that my name receives a brand" becomes perfectly understandable in the light of the values of a courtly aristocratic society. The poet speaks of his "harmful deeds," not of his harmful "profession."

In 1572 Parliament enacted an "Act for the punishment of vagabonds for relief of the poor & impotent." Paragraph 5 stipulated that rogues and vagabonds included "all Fencers, Bearwards, Common Players in Interludes & Minstrels, not belonging to any Baron of this Realme or towards any other honorable personage of greater degree."[16]

On 10 May 1574 the Privy Council issued a patent to Leicester's Men, a company of players in the service of Robert Dudley, Earl of Leicester, the queen's favorite, giving them "authority to perform music, and plays seen and allowed by the Master of the Revels [revels or festivities were an important part of court life; they were supervised by the master of the Revels, himself a subordinate of the Lord chamberlain of the Queen's Household], both in London and elsewhere, except during the time of common prayer, or of plague to London."[17] The 1572 act against rogues and vagabonds did not apply to this company. About 1579 several other companies of players existed in the service of a peer or a knight. The 1572 act did not apply to those players because they officially belonged to the household of a lord.

The statement that players were of base status needs qualification. In no way can it be evidenced by reference to the 1572 act. Officially, those players were servants of some lord, not itinerant players. In 1583 a new company was set up with the best players from other companies, including as the Earl of Leicester's Men and the Earl of Oxford's Men: it was known as the Queen's Men. They were sworn in by Sir Francis Walsingham, secretary of state, as "grooms of the Queen's chamber," hardly a low social status.

At the same time that the Court and the Privy Council promoted and protected the playing companies the authorities of the City of London were not so well disposed towards the theater. That is why nearly all of the theaters were situated in so-called "liberties," precincts over which the city of London had no legal jurisdiction. This aversion was primarily directed at the theater as a place where all sorts of people congregated: whores and panderers, thieves and other lewd people; besides, it was also seen as a focus of epidemics, mainly the plague. Without doubt, something of this deprecatory view of the theater did rub off on the players themselves. Puritans were principled enemies of any form of theater, which in 1642 led to the closing of all the theaters. Andrew Gurr calls it the "prime paradox" of the history of the theater "that the survival and the growing prosperity of such companies, the King's Men above all, was due almost entirely to the support and consistent protection given them by the highest authority in the land" (*The Shakespearian Playing Companies* [Oxford, 1996], 9).

Sonnet 111 remotely indicates that the poet had performed on the public stage. However, from another source we can safely conclude that he did, and that this was the cause of his disgrace. In a courtly society, "disgrace" or "loss of favor" nearly always meant "banishment from Court," the center of power.

Sometime before 1611 John Davies of Hereford, an epigrammatist and literary insider, wrote an epigram "To our English Terence, Mr. Will Shake-speare" [modernized spelling and punctuation]:

> Some say, good *Will*, whom I in sport do sing,
> Had'st thou not played some kingly parts in sport,
> Thou hadst been a companion for a *King*.

"A companion for a king" in an absolute monarchy was one who regularly attended the monarch, i.e., a courtier. Shakespeare was banished from Court for having acted on the stage. Davies of Hereford indicates a reason, most likely THE reason why Shakespeare's name received a brand.

Finally, at the end of sonnet 110, lines 10 and 11, and, more overtly, in lines 9-12 of sonnet 111, the poet promises correction to the friend. That implies that the young aristocrat, too, had uttered his disapproval of the poet's "harmful deeds," while it is nearly impossible to imagine that a professional actor's name would receive a "brand" from what is, in another sense, his very brand, namely his profession.

Language Awareness I

The goddess "Fortuna" or "Fortune" has become part of our everyday language as well. Work with the *OED* to locate and find:

Compounds with "fortune"	Idioms with "fortune"	Adjectives derived from "fortune"	Prefix un + "fortune"

Language Awareness II

Rephrase the given sentences with the words at the beginning without changing their meaning:

a. Although I will try out all sorts of medicine, your pity will have a healing effect on me as well.

   Despite ___.

b. You cannot possibly remain the same person if you work with common players every day.

It is impossible ___.

c. You accused me of my harmful deeds, but I think you should blame Fortune for them.

You'd rather not ___.

d. My situation is in a way hopeless, but I promise to take measures against it.

In spite of ___.

e. My name has received a brand because of my involvement in the common theater.

My status should have prevented me ___.

f. Being disgraced by your peers is worse than being in prison.

Being in prison is not ___.

g. The brand in the face of a criminal prevented him from being taken seriously by others.

Because ___.

Sonnets 71, 72 and 81: Self-doubts, suffering, oblivion and – ever-living poetry

Sonnet 71

No longer mourn for me when I am dead
Than you shall hear the surly sullen bell
Give warning to the world that I am fled
From this vile world with vildest worms to dwell;   4
Nay, if you read this line, remember not
The hand that writ it, for I love you so
That I in your sweet thoughts would be forgot,
If thinking on me then should make you woe.   8
O if (I say) you look upon this verse,
When I (perhaps) compounded am with clay,
Do not so much as my poor name rehearse,
But let your love even with my life decay   12
Lest the wise world should look into your moan,
And mock you with me after I am gone.

2 surly bad-tempered and rude
2 sullen bad-tempered and dull
2 bell funeral bell
4 vile disgusting, terrible, extremely bad, wicked
8 make you woe make you suffer deeply
10 compounded mixed, combined
11 rehearse repeat, utter
12 Lest for fear that

Sonnet 71-Activities

1. **No longer mourn for me when I am dead**: Take this first line of a famous sonnet as an opening statement in a letter you want to write to a close friend. Think of what such a line might imply (e.g., illness, old age, threat of suicide or even longing for death).

2. Make a list of what the speaker requests the addressee not to do.

3. Explain the lines which show that the speaker's relationship to the world is despondent.

4. Analyze the stylistic means that underline the speaker's feelings and say why they are so effective.

5. Do you think it is a sign of true love to intend to spare one's lover any feelings of mourning?

6. Write the addressee's possible answer **or**

    Imagine the two people meet and have a detailed conversation about this important topic. Write down this conversation.

7. You are asked to recite this poem for a radio program. Apart from your voice or voices, some background music will be used along with it. What kind of music or musical instruments do you think might be appropriate?

Language awareness

In this sonnet there are many words from two-word fields. Fill in these tables:

Transience of human life

Nouns	Verbs	Adjectives
mourning	mourn	mournful
		dead
	decay	
	remember	
	forgot	

Feeling of being rejected by the world:

Nouns	Verbs	Adjectives
warning	fled (flee)	sullen
moan	mock	vile
		poor
		wise

Sonnet 72

This sonnet resumes topics from Sonnet 71, doubting the speaker's merits and his works.

1. Put the jumbled lines in the right order, then compare your solution with other pairs and talk together about your choice.

> That you for love speak well of me untrue,
> O lest the world should task you to recite
> Unless you would devise some virtuous lie
> What merit lived in me that you should love,   4
> For I am shamed by that which I bring forth,
> Than niggard truth would willingly impart:
> For you in me can nothing worthy prove,
> To do more for me than mine own desert,   8
> After my death (dear love) forget me quite;

> And so should you, to love things nothing worth.
> And hang more praise upon deceased I
> O lest your true love may seem false in this,   12
> My name be buried where my body is,
> And live no more to shame nor me nor you:

2 lest for fear that
6 niggard mean, miserly
7 prove find, show
8 desert deserving
11 hang more praise In those days it was common practice to hang epitaphs on the hearse or funeral monument
12 in this In this respect

2. Write the main messages the speaker tries to convey in your own words and in the form of imperatives (8-12 messages might be possible).
3. Work with a partner. Which three lines or expressions do you consider most essential?   Why? Compare your findings with the results of other pairs.
4. One student wrote about this sonnet:

> Stating clearly that neither he as a human being nor his works have any value whatsoever seems absurd to me. For me it simply does not make sense that the speaker's personality seen through the eye of his beloved should lead to his suffering. If Shakespeare was the author, I am really at a loss when it comes to interpreting this sonnet.

In the light of what you know about Oxford's biography, formulate an answer that may satisfy the student.

Language awareness

Use the OED and explore the word family of the key words of this sonnet. You may devise word trees or any other form that helps you to remember these expressions:
merit
worthy/worth
desert (deserve)
true
shame
lie

Sonnet 81

Or I shall live your epitaph to make,
Or you survive when I in earth am rotten,
From hence your memory death cannot take,
Although in me each part will be forgotten.   4
Your name from hence immortal life shall have,
Though I (once gone) to all the world must die;
The earth can yield me but a common grave,
When you intombed in men's eyes shall lie: 8
Your monument shall be my gentle verse,
Which eyes not yet created shall o'er-read,
And tongues to be your being shall rehearse,
When all the breathers of this world are dead   12
You still shall live (such virtue hath my pen)
Where breath most breathes, even in the mouths of men.

1 Or…Or Whether…or
3 hence these sonnets
4 in me in my case
8 intombed remembered in an exquisite tomb
9 gentle here: gentlemanly, i.e., noble, lovely
11 tongues to be people not yet born, future generations
11 rehearse utter
12 breathers of this world all the people alive in those days

Activities

1. True or false? Correct the following statements concerning the content of the sonnet if necessary:

    a. The speaker imagines two future scenarios, that either he or his beloved will outlive the other.

    b. The speaker is convinced that both he and his beloved will cease to live on in the memory of others.

    c. Posterity will definitely continue talking about the speaker.

d. The beloved will always be remembered because of the sonnets written for him.

e. The grave the speaker expects to be laid in is not one that fits a poet of such quality.

f. The splendid tomb the beloved will be given is the reason that the speaker will never be forgotten.

g. The speaker has already provided a different monument for his beloved, which will be read and appreciated by generations to come.

h. Future generations will not enjoy repeating the name of the beloved.

i. Due to the powerful words the beloved person formulates he will be immortal.

2. Explain the different fates the two people will face in case the speaker dies first:

Speaker's fate	Fate of the beloved
❖	❖
❖	❖
❖	❖

Even though not explicitly said, Sonnet 81 is a love poem—this is hidden in its form: The American scholar Helen Vendler pointed out that the structure of the lines suggests that the two people "embrace" each other. Lines 1 and 4 "embrace" the beloved, lines 5 and 8 "embrace" the speaker. From line 9 on they share a common destiny, being mentioned together.

To make this visible and audible, prepare a shared reading of the sonnet. Pay special attention to the use of personal pronouns, **or**

If you prefer painting or drawing, try to make the connection of the two visible in a picture or any other form of visualization.

3. Explain why, under the orthodox view that Shakespeare of Stratford wrote the sonnets, the assertions in line 4 and in line 13 (brackets) are contradictory and not understandable. Then explain why they make sense in the context of the historical background offered by the scholar Robert Detobel below.

Language awareness

This sonnet covers a number of expressions referring to the sense of sight: l. 8 "men's eyes," l. 10 "eyes not yet created," l. 10 "shall o'er read," l. 1 "epitaph."

Find seven useful or idiomatic expressions dealing with the word "eye" and with the word "sight" in the *OED* and be prepared to explain them in the next lesson.

Looking back on Sonnets 71, 72 and 81, which are the key points that should be kept in mind? Write them down on a poster.

What were the most striking insights for you? Why?

All of Shakespeare's sonnets are sprinkled with unforgettable phrases. Choose at least two you are likely to remember and explain why.

Sonnets 71, 72, and 81

A term existed in the Middle Ages for how the poet urges the young man to behave after his death in Sonnet 71 and its continuation in Sonnet 72. It is *damnatio memoriae*, "damnation of memory." In ancient Rome the same phenomenon was called *abolitio nominis*, abolishment or eradication of the name. The worst curse one Jew can pronounce on another is "may his name and memory be obliterated." "Damnation of memory" was applied to persons who had committed particularly horrible crimes such as high treason or who through their behaviour were thought to have drawn scandal on their community. One act that could entail damnation of memory was suicide. Damnation of memory, though no longer explicitly so called, continues into our own time. The most famous case is probably that of the English rock singer and songwriter Gary Glitter, whose name was removed from the Wall of Fame of the Cavern Club in Liverpool (commemorating among others the Beatles and the Rolling Stones) after he was convicted of child pornography charges.

The essential difference is of course that in our case the poet proclaims damnation of memory on himself. Obviously, the speaker's disgust with the world is real, existential, hence biographical. To illustrate the poet's self-indictment one could chose two sentences from the Book of Job and replace the second person plural in the first one and the third person singular in the second one by the first person. "My memory may be compared unto ashes, and my body to a body of clay" (Job 13,12). And: "My remembrance shall perish from the earth, and I shall have no name in the street" (18,17). Or else Revelation 3, 1-2: " I know thy works, for thou hast a name that thou livest, but thou art dead... for I have not found thy works perfect before God."

Indeed, sonnet 72 concludes:

> For I am shamed by that which I bring forth,
> And so should you, to love things nothing worth.

From the distance of several centuries, the poet's pejorative view of himself and his works—which are now honoured, admired, and even idolized as works of literary genius—is an astounding, if not bewildering, confession. It is the more so if we do not overlook the active verb "to flee" in lines 3 and 4 of Sonnet 71. "When I am fled from this vile world," the poet writes. He does not write "When I'll be gone from this vile world," or "When I shall have departed this vile world," or "passed away from this vile world." "To flee" from a world of which he has grown weary indicates a deliberate, premeditated action. It means "to commit suicide."

In Sonnet 81 this negative picture is not only bewildering but also bewilderingly paradoxical.

If the poet survives the youth, he will write his epitaph. An epitaph generally consists of a few verses inscribed on a grave or tomb. It is important to stress the fact that such an epitaph would be written on a one-time occasion, namely the youth's death, from which one is inclined to infer that at the moment of writing these lines the poet is envisaging the youth's death as an imminent real possibility.

The sonnets are not that epitaph. The sonnets will be the friend's everlasting monument, outliving the memory of "tyrants," as is stated elsewhere (see Sonnet 107). The poet's pen immortalizing a beloved lady, an admired hero or some other honoured person was a favourite topic of Renaissance lyric poetry. The primal simile expressing the idea of the poet as the essential agency of eternity was the story about Alexander the Great weeping at the tomb of the Greek mythological hero Achilles for lacking a poet like Homer to sing his feats. In the minds of Renaissance poets, Achilles rather participated in Homer's fame than vice versa. Homer's fame, of course, was not blotted out from men's memory. Nor do we find such a statement on obliteration, a curse on their own work and name in the sonnets of Shakespeare's contemporaries Edmund Spenser, Samuel Daniel, Michael Drayton, etc., who all are making similar promises of eternity. Yet Shakespeare is fully aware of the supreme excellence and everlasting value of his poetry. It is the "virtue of his pen" from which the eternal memory of the youth will spring. In spite of this, he seems to be sure that nobody will remember him, or, put differently, that his authorship will not be connected with his *own name*.

How can this dilemma be satisfactorily solved? Some scholars have tried to explain that these lines could be interpreted ironically, though, in our view, not in a way that can said to be satisfactory. They leave us in the lurch as to why or how Shakespeare might have come to think so gloomily about the fate of his own name, contrary, it must be stressed, to that of any other contemporary poet. And what made him think about the death of the much younger friend, who under normal circumstances would have a longer life expectancy than the poet himself?

Hamlet might answer: "Yea, there's the rub." The circumstances under which Sonnet 81 was written might not have been "normal." The youth's life might have been threatened, because of a dangerous illness or from some other cause. That assumed, the opening line of the sonnet would be all but trivial; it would suddenly take on a piercing dramatic quality which, however, would evaporate if we are set to squeeze out of the sonnets any biographical content.

The case for Henry Wriothesley, third Earl of Southampton, as the young man addressed in the sonnets can now be considered firmly established. We know of one point in time in his life (and also within the generally accepted period of composition of the sonnets) when he was in great danger and/or about to die. This was in February 1601, when he was sentenced to death for high treason. It is also useful in this context to recall that the use of the word "epitaph" is suggestive of death in a foreseeable future, whereas the "monument" of the sonnets is to last forever. Shortly after Shakespeare had dedicated *Venus and Adonis* (1593) and *The Rape of Lucrece* (1594) to him, possibly in between, Southampton had moved away from the poet into the orbit of Robert Devereux, 2nd Earl of Essex, born in 1565, eight years before Southampton. Essex was a prominent military commander, though rather more dashing than effective. He had been a favorite of Queen Elizabeth, but since 1596 (if not earlier) his fortunes were declining and reached rock bottom by the end of the century after his disastrous military campaign in Ireland. Southampton had participated in the military expedition to the Azores (1597) and in Ireland (1599), both under the command of Essex. In brusque contempt of the queen's orders, the disappointed Essex had returned to England. As a consequence of his disobedience, a lucrative monopoly (the duties on imported wine) was not renewed in 1600, which deprived him of his major source of income. Not willing to reflect on his own mistakes and inadequacies, Essex made Sir Robert Cecil responsible for his loss of the queen's favor. By 1600 Cecil, Secretary of State, had succeeded his father, Lord Burghley, as the queen's most influential minister. Essex sought to gain control of the levers of power by disempowering Cecil. The episode is known as the Essex Rebellion, in the planning and execution of which Southampton was deeply involved.

The attempted coup started in the morning of Sunday, 8 February 1601. At the end of the same day the rebellion was quelled. On 17 February Essex and Southampton were indicted of high treason. The trial was held on 19 February. Essex and Southampton were both convicted and condemned to death. Essex was beheaded on 25 February. Southampton's penalty was commuted into lifelong imprisonment. The exact date of the commutation is not known, but it must have occurred before the end of March.

Sonnet 81 could have been written between February and March when Southampton's life was in the balance. It could also have been written later in the year, during the first six months or so of Southampton's imprisonment in the Tower, when Southampton was reported to have been very sick.

If Shakespeare of Stratford wrote Sonnet 81 between February and March or in September 1601, the poet's statement that "each part of me will be forgotten" is incomprehensible. For soon after the publication of *The Rape of Lucrece* in 1594 the name of the author acquired great notoriety. In 1598 Richard Barnfield, himself a poet, hailed him:

> And *Shakepeare* thou, whose hony-flowing Vaine,
> (Pleasing the World) thy Praises doth obtaine.

> Whose *Venus*, and whose *Lucrece* (sweete, and chaste)
> Thy name in fames immortall Booke have plac't.

And wished him along with Edmund Spenser, Samuel Daniel and Michael Drayton, to

> Live ever you, at least in Fame live ever;
>   Well may the body dye, but Fame dies never.

Allusions by contemporaries do exist from which could be gleaned that the name Shakespeare was indeed a pseudonym. But they are couched in the dark oblique language of the time, although the messages are not lost beyond recovery.

One hint, however, is not that oblique. In 1596 Thomas Nashe (1567-1600/1), the foremost satirist of the last decade of the sixteenth century, pays tribute to a famous poet and patron in his pamphlet *Have With You to Saffron-Walden*. Nashe is thought to have been well acquainted with the author William Shakespeare. Yet Nashe never mentions the name Shakespeare. Had Nashe meant William Shakespeare of Stratford, there would have been no reason not to name him: the name was known, by then even famous, it stood beneath the dedications to Southampton of *Venus and Adonis* and *The Rape of Lucrece*. Nashe's eulogy is directed at an unnamed author, and implies that this author is not writing under his own name: He wishes that this author acquire no other fame than that merited by his pen, precisely the fame Shakespeare states in the sonnets will be lost to him, devoured by oblivion.

In his pamphlet Nashe reproaches his literary foe, the rhetorician Gabriel Harvey, of having assumed, during a visit of the queen to the then Secretary of State Sir Thomas Smith in Audley End in 1578, the role of preceptor of two persons in his book *Gratulationes Valdinensis* ("Congratulations from Walden"; Saffron-Walden was Harvey's birth town). The book consists of four volumes with a total of six speeches Harvey had planned to deliver. Volume I contains the speech to the queen, volume II to the Earl of Leicester, volume III to Lord Burghley, and volume IV to the Earl of Oxford, Sir Christopher Hatton and Sir Philip Sidney. Nashe writes that Harvey had taken "the wall[18] of Sir *Philip Sidney* and another honourable Knight (his companion) about Court attending; to whom I wish no better fortune than the forelocks of Fortune he had held in his youth, & no higher fame than he hath purchased himself by his pen; being the first (in our language) I have encountered, that repurified Poetry from Art's pedantism, & that instructed it to speak courtly. Our Patron, our *Phoebus*, our first *Orpheus* or quintessence of invention he is...."

The person meant is a courtier, still alive, who in his youth had been fortunate, i.e., had enjoyed the queen's favor but had later lost it. The statement could apply to Edward de Vere, 17th Earl of Oxford. In fact, only Oxford can be meant. He is unequivocally identified by the process of logical elimination. Of the six persons addressed by Harvey, three were dead by 1596: Sir Philip Sidney (1586), the Earl of Leicester (1588) and Sir Christopher Hatton (1591). The queen herself and Lord

Burghley were alive, but they could neither be addressed as Sir Philip Sidney's "knight companion" nor as poet, let alone as the foremost poet, the Phoebus (Apollo) and Orpheus of the age. The statement implies that Nashe feared Oxford would not earn the fame merited by his writings (his pen). Nashe's fear concords with Shakespeare's complaints about the obliteration of his name.

Endnotes

[1] Harold Bloom, *Shakespeare. The Invention of the Human* (New York, 1988), 403.

[2] Helen Vendler, *The Art of Shakespeare's Sonnets* (Harvard University Press, 1999),. 328.

[3] Green Line Oberstufe, published by Stephanie Ashford et al (Ernst Klett Verlag, 2009), 174-189.

[4] Elena Gross, *Shakespearean Sonnets and Elizabethan Poetry* (Ernst Klett Verlag, 2011).

[5] Vendler, 161.

[6] Robert Detobel, *Will, Wunsch und Wirklichkeit* (Verlag Uwe Laugwitz, 2010), 84 .

[7] Hans-Albert Koch, *Frankfurter Allgemeine Zeitung*, 10 March 2010.

[8] Detobel, 149-150.

[9] www.ymiteacher.com/pdf/AnonymousCollege.pdf

[10] *Shakespeare Beyond Doubt*, ed. by Paul Edmondson and Stanley Wells (Cambridge University Press, 2013), 236-237.

[11] Sir Thomas Smith, *de Republica Anglorum*, ch. 17. 1 mark = 2/3 pound, 1000 marks = 666.66 pounds.

[12] J.H. Hexter, "The Education of the Aristocracy the Renaissance," in *The Journal of Modern History* Vol. XXII (March 1950), 2.

[13] *Mine*: Material possessions

[14] B.M. Ward, *The Seventeenth Earl of Oxford 1550-1604* (London: John Murray, 1928), 126; Conyers Read, *Lord Burghley and Queen Elizabeth*, Vol. II (New York: Alfred A. Knopf, 1960), 137. Alan Nelson so renders it on his website; it is not mentioned in his biography of Oxford, *Monstrous Adversary*.

[15] My man= my servant

[16] Edmund K. Chambers, *The Elizabethan Stage*, 1923, Vol. IV, 270.

[17] Chambers, 272.

[18] To take the wall: see *Romeo and Juliet*, I.i.10-11. "I will take the wall of any man or maid of Montague's." To take the wall of somebody is to take the best and surest side of the path and thereby to show one's superiority to that person.

Oxford and *The Arte of English Poesie*

Richard Malim

In my book *The Earl of Oxford and the Making of "Shakespeare": The Literary Life of Edward de Vere in Context* (McFarland 2011), I suggested that Puttenham's *The Arte of English Poesie* (1589, hereinafter *Arte*[1]) could be an important piece of evidence in the process of establishing the actual date of many of Shakespeare's plays or early versions of them, because of its numerous references to already existing works, including those plays. At the time of writing I was able to use W.L. Rushton's little book,[2] but I did not have access to Whigham and Rebhorn's more recent critical edition, which has rendered previous studies of *Arte* obsolete. This paper owes a great deal to both works, but of course both are locked into the "orthodox" ideas of dating and attribution of the plays, and so I am trying to unlock that erroneous connection.

There is some doubt as to the authorship of *Arte*; I follow Whigham and Rebhorn and do not consider the validity of the claim of George Puttenham as author.[3] The date of publication is vital. The title page tells us that it was printed by Richard Field in 1589, and no one has ever suggested that that date is wrong or that Field ever misdated the title pages of the works he printed.[4]

Nearly as unimportant is the career and character of George Puttenham. He was the worst type of well-born courtly chancer, one who makes the rest of the Elizabethan courtiers look like nineteenth century gentlemen. He made life hell for a number of women who crossed his path and his general attitude towards them can be evidenced from *Arte*. To what extent was a Puttenham a scholar? Why did he venture upon his great work? The answer clearly was, to assist in his campaign to re-establish himself in the good books of the Queen. In *Arte* he flatters her grossly, quoting some eleven times from his earlier work *Partheniades* (Serenade to the Virgin Queen, c. 1579), a collection of seventeen poems which had failed (even if it had ever reached her) to sway her. In *Arte* he also sought to impress her as a polymath with the sweep of his scholarship. He spent time at Christ's College Cambridge and the Inns of

Court. It is not necessarily a mark against him that he is not recorded as being given a degree, as this was quite common. He would have attained a good standard in both Latin and perhaps Greek. There must, however, be a substantial question mark over the scholarship and originality in *Arte*. He did own at one time some one hundred books, likely to include a number of works on grammar and poetical collections; from these (or from those to which he had access) he quotes with accuracy. His knowledge of Greek seems to be quite limited, as he uses Latin translations for Theocritus, Aristotle and Plato: as a typical show-off he sets out the first line of the *Iliad* (Book 3, Chapter 24) and occasionally scatters the odd Greek word to maintain what may well be an illusion. Puttenham owned a number of books of French and Italian literature and shows his familiarity with those genres.

If this view seems harsh, we ought next to look at those Latin sources. Of the 121 "tropes" and "figures" identified by Puttenham, 115 come unacknowledged from *Epitome Troporum ac Schematicum* (1540) by Johannes Susenbrotus (1485-1543), a German Grammarian, and the remaining six from two other works. Puttenham attempts to disguise his total indebtedness to these writers for their classifications, but Whigham and Rebhorn effectively destroy any claim to scholarly originality.[5] Well educated classicists like the Queen and Oxford would readily have seen through that disguise, even though Puttenham suggests alternative English names for some of the tropes and figures. Puttenham's originality lies in mixing the grammatical critique with a dissertation on contemporary good behavior, illustrated by a swath of stories from the court about current and past rulers and those who served them, the latter mostly taken from Erasmus.[6]

In Chapter 31 of Book 1 *The Arte* reviews English poetry to date, beginning with Chaucer, Gower, Lydgate, Langland, Hardyng "the chronicler," and, coming into the current century, Skelton, Wyatt and Surrey. For Wyatt (eight quotations and three possible adaptations), Surrey (nine), "anonymous" (eight quotations and adaptations), and Vaux (adaptation), Puttenham is clearly using *Tottel's Miscellany* (1567 and later editions). *The Arte* claims authorship for the Vaux and one of the anonymous adaptations. Then he comes up to date with the famous quotation beloved of all Oxfordians:

> And in her Majesty's time that is now there is sprung up another crew of courtly makers, noblemen and gentlemen of her Majesty's own servants, who have written excellently well, as it would appear if their doings could be found out and made public with the rest. Of which number is first that noble gentleman Edward Earl of Oxford, Thomas Lord of Buckhurst when he was young, Henry Lord Paget, Sir Philip Sidney, Sir Walter Ralegh, Master Edward Dyer, Master Fulke Greville, Gascoigne, Breton, Turberville, and a great many other learned gentlemen, whose names I do not omit for envy [dislike], but to avoid tediousness, and who have deserved no little commendation.
>
> (1.31)

The same chapter commends the poetry, "eclogue and pastoral poetry [of] Sir Philip Sidney and master Chaloner and that other gentleman who wrote the late *Shepheardes Calender*.....Phaer and Golding for a learned and well-corrected verse, especially in translation.... But last in recital but first in degree is the Queen...." However, the author has clearly heard or seen Sonnet XIV of Sidney's *Certain Sonnets* in manuscript: from it he misremembers the line "For true it is, that they fear many whom many fear" as "Fear many must he needs, whom many fear" (319).

Puttenham quotes from Oxford, "a most noble and learned gentleman ... for his excellence and wit [intelligence, wisdom, cleverness]," twelve lines from "When wert thou born, Desire?" (3.19). For the others Puttenham quotes Sidney, Ralegh, and Dyer three times each, Gascoigne five times,[7] Turberville nine times, and the Queen three times. Ten further anonymous quotations and references come from *Tottel's Miscellany*. From the list at 1.31 above he omits Sir Arthur Gorges, but quotes him once.

All these are from the "crew of courtly makers," and Puttenham would most likely want us to add his name to this list. In addition to the eleven citations from *Partheniades*, there are four scraps from works which have not otherwise survived and at least twenty-three others from unknown and untitled works; Whigham and Rebhorn maintain that many of the latter were "surely composed expressly as examples for the *Arte*" (16).

Before we turn to dramatic poetry, there is one further example, not by a courtly gentleman, which is castigated by Puttenham as *Soriasmus* or Mingle-Mangle,

> as when we make our speech or writings of sundry languages, using some Italian word, or French, or Spanish, or Dutch, or Scottish, not for the nonce [particular purpose] or for any purpose (which were in part excusable) but ignorantly and affectedly. As one that said, using the French word *roy* to make rhyme with another verse, thus:
>
> O mighty Lord of Love, dame Venus' only joy.
> Whose princely power exceeds each other heavenly roy.
>
> (Turberville: "The Lover to Cupid for Mercie," *Epitaphs and Epigrams* [1567] 45r-v: 1-4)
>
> The verse is good, but the term peevishly [foolishly] affected. Another of reasonable quality in translation, finding certain of the hymns of Pindar and Anacreon's odes and other lyrics among the Greeks well translated by Ronsard the French poet and applied in the honour of a great Prince [Henry II] in France, comes our minion and translates the same out of French into English, and applieth them to the honour of a great nobleman in England (wherein I commend his reverent mind and duty).
>
> (3.22)

The "minion" is John Soothern, believed to be a Frenchman, a follower of Lord Oxford and a sometime spy for Oxford at the French Court, whose English might not have satisfied Puttenham's high standards. In 1584 Soothern published his long poem *Pandora*. Ode I is the dedicatory ode to Oxford, and in my book I quoted a long extract. Puttenham writes: "our said maker not being ashamed to use these French words—freddon, egar, superbous, filanding, celeste, calabrois, thebanois, and a number of others." "Celeste" does not appear in Ode I but the others do, and Puttenham misses out some fairly obvious such as "brute (bruit)," "digne" and "louanges." The suspicion arises that Puttenham was relying on his memory and did not have the work at hand, though he quotes two couplets and a further single line with accuracy save that Soothern's word "fredone" appears as the more anglicized (and less effective from the point of view of Puttenham's argument) "freddon."

We may now consider dramatic poetry. The first point is that writing for the stage was considered beyond the social pale for any aristocrat; no names of dramatists are included as authors of any of the excerpts or references employed by Puttenham. For Latin he introduces his own free translations. Thus he purloins without acknowledgement the *Medea* of the pioneer Latin dramatist Ennius and puts the Nurse's opening speech in the mouth of Medea herself:

"Woe worth the mountain that the mast bare
Which was the first causer of all my care." 3.17.

This displays a faint recollection of the speech, which is accurately translated:

"Would that the firwood timbers had not fallen to earth hewn by axes in a Pelian grove [on mount Pelion]; and that thereupon no prelude had been made to begin the ship.... For thus never would my misled mistress Medea sick at heart, smitten by savage love, have set foot outside her home."[8]

In the same way he treats Gager's Latin *Dido* (1583):

"Hie thee, and by the wild waves and wind
Seek Italy and realms for thee to reign
If piteous gods have power amidst the main
On ragged rocks thy penance thou may find."

(3.20)

Puttenham is clearly writing from memory, as the accurate translation[9] reads: "Go follow the winds, seek you kingdom by crossing the waves, the ocean to the land promised to you by the fates. If prayers and entreaties have any power, I am confident you will pay the penalty for this outrage, grounded on shoals and reefs, or bobbing your head among your smashed hulls crying for me...." The first couplet is reasonably accurate but the second is sketchy indeed.[10]

The only exceptions to Puttenham's rule of not mentioning current dramatists come at the end of Book I: "Of the later sort [of poets] I think thus: that for tragedy, the Lord Buckhurst and Master Edward [sic, he means George] Ferrers for such doings as I have seen of theirs do deserve the highest price. The Earl of Oxford and Master Edwards of her Majesty's Chapel for comedy and interlude...."

He then goes back to discussing poets.

The only dramatist *qua* dramatist from whom he quotes by name is himself. These quotations are the only bits from the plays which survive and a cynic might think that the plays did not otherwise exist: from *Ginecocratia* a comedy, four lines; from *Lusty London* an "Interlude," two quotations of four lines each; and from *The Wooer*, also an "Interlude," two quotations, one of two lines and one of four lines. Apart from *Partheniades,* there are perhaps a dozen more quotations and references from other works all otherwise totally lost. In addition, to illustrate his tropes and figures, he includes snippets of self-identifying poetry and from some others he omits any self-identifying label. These passages are left anonymous, but the way they are used may well lead us suspect that they could be Puttenham's self-produced examples.

The most important point is that all these references are from works that existed in 1589: Puttenham, I maintain, is the taker, not the exemplar. In order to keep the show on the road, as my correspondence with Professor Wiggins (above) demonstrates, "orthodoxy" is forced to demonstrate that none of the other references below is from an existing work: the Shakespearean ones must all have been taken (by Shakespeare) from *Arte*. Such is the volume of these references that orthodoxy requires us to imagine the opposite of that piece of Saintsbury's wisdom epitomized by this quotation:

> When a man writes...a good piece of prose [let alone dramatic verse], he does not say to himself, 'Now I shall throw in some hyperbaton; now we shall exhibit a little anadiplosis; this is the occasion, surely for a passage of zeugma. He writes as the spirit moves him and the way of art leads.

This vital point entirely escaped W.L. Rushton in 1909: the value of his book is that he does pick, first in a few pieces of poetry and then in a quantity of Puttenham's critical apparatus, references to Shakespeare's plays. There are no absolutely accurate renditions—indeed, with none of the plays in print, it would be surprising if there were: Puttenham presumably relies on his memory. The following plays are those commonly referred to, and after each I have put in a putative Oxfordian date[11] and the number of references: *Love's Labour's Lost* (1581, twenty-nine references), *Hamlet* (1586, twenty-eight), *Henry V* (1584, fifteen), *Richard III* (1582, fourteen), *Richard II* (1582, thirteen), *The Two Gentlemen of Verona* (1577, eleven) and *Troilus and Cressida* (1584, ten). There are no references to *Titus*

Andronicus, Pericles or *The Two Noble Kinsmen* (perhaps because Rushton did not accept them as by Shakespeare), or to *King Lear*. For several plays only one reference is cited, and few of them are at all impressive: *All's Well That Ends Well* (1581, but possibly never actually performed contemporaneously because of the too obvious connection with Oxford's own marital problems), *1 Henry VI* (1586, perhaps not accepted by Rushton), *Henry VIII* (perhaps also not accepted by Rushton and probably written too late, i.e., after 1589), *Measure for Measure, The Merry Wives of Windsor* and *The Tempest* (all written too late).[12] That leaves the remainder of the canon with between two and eight references each.

These are vital pieces of evidence for the actual date of the writing of early version(s) of the plays mentioned. Some modern critics advance the problems of "intertextuality": in short, the determination of who borrowed from whom, e.g., was it "Shakspeare" who borrowed from Nashe, or Nashe who borrowed from "Shakespeare," or both possibilities? In the case of Puttenham this "intertextuality" does not apply: Puttenham unlike the vast majority of contemporary authors is not writing a composition or a history, he is writing a compendium, a digest of grammatical usages which he claims to have identified from literature in English, all of which must be in existence by 1589 for him to extract the material for the examples of his "figures." I repeat that, for poetry as contrasted with dramatic verse, Puttenham seems happy to identify his source: it is only when he comes to dramatic verse and to "Shakespeare" that he becomes silent as to his sources: perhaps it was beneath his dignity to identify these sources when the 'low' class art of drama was concerned. The dry cataloguing of *Arte* has nothing by way of quotation or inspiration to offer the artist/writer, be he/she poet, dramatist, historian or even critic, when material full of life and vigour can be borrowed or stolen from contemporaries of genius. Puttenham is not writing for the applause of contemporary writers: he is writing to boost his standing among the Elizabethan cultural upper class. In his Conclusion he claims to "write to the pleasure of a Lady and a most gracious Queen, and neither to priests nor to prophets or philosophers," let alone to poets, dramatists, historians or critics, save to instruct them, as in the terms of the quotation in n.3 below.

The contrary (or 'intertextuality') idea that "Shakespeare" and his fellows had *Arte* on their desks as they wrote, ready to consult whenever they wished to throw in a piece of hyperbaton, exhibit some anadiplosis or zeugma in their compositions, as Saintsbury put it, flies in the face of common sense. Indeed "Shakespeare" seems implicitly to rule this out with his well-known anathematising of small beer and grammar rules, to the extent in (no doubt) one of the post-1589 rewrites of *Love's Labours Lost* (IV.i.60-92) in Armado's love-letter to the simple peasant-girl Jaquenetta he incudes Puttenham's 'figures' of Asyndeton, Synarithismus, Anthypopora, Emphasis, Parenthesis and Periergia (and no doubt others if one had the energy and ingenuity to track them down). *Arte* is unlikely to have been available to any, say, of the University wits, and perhaps would only swim into the ken of a writer in the position of Oxford.

Two words of caution must be here introduced. First, some of Rushton's more than 250 references are pretty slight; if I were writing his book I might not have included many of them. Individually few of them prove anything, but the sheer volume of them shows that Puttenham's mind was susceptible to the small amount of English literature available: he may not have had printed volumes to hand (there were none of Shakespeare in 1589, as far as we know) but he did have access from time to time to the court and to the great houses where the plays were performed. This puts him among a very small band of writers able to take in these quotations which he could have read in manuscript or heard read or declaimed aloud. Second, I have not identified any references from plays which are juvenilia and were clearly written before 1589 (except one rather feeble one which occurs in both *Arden of Feversham* and *Thomas of Woodstock*), although I have tried but failed to find cross-references to *The Famous Victories of Henry V*, *The Troublesome Reign of King John* and *The True Tragedy of Richard III*. That is most likely the fault of my defective literary self-education and may yet afford a qualified student a richer source for investigation; or it may be that the more sophisticated later versions had made their appearance at court by 1589, replacing the first efforts in Puttenham's memory, and possibly making his version difficult to link and identify.

There are in Rushton's book some twenty pieces of Puttenham's poetry, which are unrelated (with possible exceptions to his own dramatic works as he indicates) to anything else written by him, but recycled with a cunning layer of paste to disassociate them from the poetry of any play, Shakespeare's thought or his words or turn of phrase. Some of the more obvious ones would include:

Hypozeugma

Richard II, II.ii.53-55	*Arte* 3.11
The lord Northumberland, his son young Henry Percy, The lords of Ross, Beaumont, and Willoughby, With their powerful *friends*, *are fled* to him.	My mates are wont to keep me company, And my neighbours, who dwelt near to my wall, *The friends* that swore they would not stick to die In my quarrel: they *are fled* from me all.

Anadiplosis

Richard III, V.v,.213-214	*Arte* 3.19
If you do fight in safeguard of your *wives*, Your *wives* shall welcome home the conquerors.	Comfort it is for man to have a wife, *Wife* chaste, and wise, and lowly all her life

Epizeuxis

A Midsummer Night's Dream, V.i.319ff

    Asleep, my love?
    What, dead my love ? ......
    These lily lips,
    This cherry nose
    These yellow cowslip cheeks,
    Are gone, are gone
    Lovers, make moan.

Arte 3.19

The chiefest staff of mine assured stay,
With no small grief, *is gone, is gone* away.

Prosonomasia 1

The Two Gentlemen of Verona, II.v.36-40

Speed. But, Launce, how sayest thou, that my master is become a notable *lover*?
Launce. I never knew him otherwise.
Speed. Than how?
Launce. A notable *lubber* as thou reportest him to be.

Arte 3.19

They be *lubbers* not *lovers* that so used to say.
From the allegedly lost drama *The Wooer*.

Prosonomasia 2

Richard III, I.ii.81-85

Gloucester. Fairer than tongue can name thee, let me have/Some patient leisure to excuse myself
Anne. Fouler than heart can think thee, thou canst make/No current *excuse* but to hang thyself.
Gloucester. By such despair I should *accuse* myself.

Arte: 3.19

Prove me, madam, ere you fall to reprove,
Meek minds should rather *excuse* than *accuse*.

Insultatio

Antony and Cleopatra, III.vii.61-62

O most noble emperor, do not fight by sea;
Trust not to rotten *planks*

Arte 3.19

Go now and give thy life unto the wind
Trusting unto a piece of bruckle [brittle] wood,
Four inches from thy death or seven good
The thickest *plank* for shipboard that we find.

Antimetabole

King John, II.i.500-501

Arte 3.19

....The shadow of your son/Becomes a sun, and makes your son a shadow.

We wish not peace to maintain cruel war
But we make war to maintain us in peace.

Puttenham uses as his (own) example " Ye have figure which takes a couple of words to play with in a verse, and by making them to change and shift one into others place; they do very prettily exchange and shift the sense.."

Rushton's remaining references, and there are more than 230 of them (see my caveat above), come from Puttenham's critical apparatus, which he attaches to each trope or figure:

Poets as the first priests, etc.

2 Henry VI, III.iii.19

O Thou *eternal mover of the heavens*

Henry V, II.ii.118

If that same *demon* that has gulled thee thus

Antony and Cleopatra, II.ii.17-20

That *demon* (that's thy spirit which keeps thee) is/ Noble, courageous, high, unmatchable, Where Caesar's is not: but near him, thy *angel* Becomes a fear, as being o'erpowered

Arte 1.3

Poets are of great antiquity. Then forasmuch as they were the first that entended to the observation of nature and her works and specially of the Celestial courses, by reason of the *continual motion of the heavens*, searching after the first mover, and from thence by degrees coming to know and consider of the substances separate and abstract, which we call devine intelligences or good *Angels (Demones)*, they were the first.........they came by instinct devine, and deep meditation.

Poets' Reputation, etc.

Julius Caesar, II.i.230-232

Thou hast no figures, nor no *fantasies*, Which *busy* care draws in the brains of men Therefore sleep'st so sound.

Arte 1.8

For as evil and vicious disposition of the brain hinders the sound judgment and discourse of man with *busy* and discordant *fantasies*....

Pastoral Poetry, etc.

I Henry VI, II.i.91-92

Gadshill, a thief: Give me thy hand: thou shall have a share in our *purchase*, For I am a true man....

Arte 1.18

All this I do agree unto, for no doubt the shepherd's life was the first example of honest fellowship, they trade the first art of lawful acquisition or purchase, for at those days robbery was a manner of *purchase*...

Epigrams or Posies

Romeo and Juliet, I.v..8

Good, then save me a piece of marchpane

Hamlet, III.ii.14

Is this a prologue, or a poesie of a ring?

Arte 1.30

There be also other like Epigram that were sent usually for new year gifts, or to be printed or put upon their banqueting dishes of sugar plate, or *march paines*... We call them *poesies*... or use them as devices in *rings* and arms about such courtly purposes.

Staff or Stanza

Love's Labour's Lost, IV.ii.104

Let me hear a staff, a stanza, a verse

Arte 2.2

Staff in our vulgar Poesie I know not why it should be called, unless it be that we understand it for a bearer of a song or ballad, not unlike the old weak body that is stayed up by his *staff*, and were not otherwise able to walk or stand upright. The Italians called it *Stanza*, as if we should say a resting place.

Proportion in figure

This is an unlikely piece of literary criticism, as Puttenham seeks to commend "form poetry" in the setting down of geometrically figured poems, and Rushton asks us to believe that Shakespeare considered such a practice for a moment, let alone seriously. Puttenham does, however, show in the example below the effect of Shakespeare's existing writings.

3 Henry VI, II.iii.48-51

Arte

Yet let us all together to our troops,
And give them leave to fly that will not *stay*
And call them *pillars* that will *stand* to us.

2 *Henry VI*, I.i.75

Brave peers of England, *pillars* of the state

Troilus and Cressida, IV.vii.94-95

I wonder how yonder city stands,
When we have her *base* and *pillar* by us

The *Pillar* is a figure among all the rest of the Geometrical most beautiful.....By this figure is signified *stay*, support, rest, state and magnificence; your ditty being reduced to the form of a *Pillar*.

Her Majesty resembled to the crowned *pillar*. Ye must read upward:

> Is bliss with immortality
> Her trimest top of all you see
> Garnish her crown
> Her just renown
> Chapter and head,
> Parts that maintain
> And woman head
> Her m aid en reign
> In te   gr   ity
> In hon our and
> With   ver i ty
> Her roundness stand
> Strengthen the state.
> With their increase
> With out   de bate
> Con cord and peace
> Of   her   sup port,
> They   be the base,
> With stead fastnesse
> Ver tue and grace
> Stay and comfort
> Of   Albion's   rest,
> The   sounde   Pillar
> And seene a farre,
> Is plain ly exp rest
> Tall, stately and strayt
> By this no ble pour trayt.
>   (2.12)

On three syllable feet

I Henry IV, III.i.29-31

And that would set my teeth nothing on edge
Nothing so much as mincing poetry
'Tis like the forc'd gait of a shuffling nag

Arte 2.16

I rather wish the continuance of our old manner of Poesy, scanning our verses by syllables rather than by feet, and using most commonly the Iambic and sometimes the Trochaic....and now and then a dactyl keeping precisely our sympathy or rime without any other *mincing* measures which an idle inventive head could easily devise.

Ornament

Merchant of Venice, III.ii.73-77

So may the outward shows be least themselves
The world is still deceiv'd with *ornament*.
In law, what plea so tainted and corrupt,
But, being season'd with a gracious voice,
Obscures the *show* of evil?....

Arte 3.3

This *ornament* is of two sorts, one to satisfy and delight the ear only by a goodly outward *show* set upon the matter with words

Epitheton

Love's Labour's Lost, I.ii.13-20

Armado. I spoke it, tender juvenal, as a congruent *epitheton* appertaining to thy young days, which we nominate tender.
Moth. And I, tough senior, as appertinent to your old time, which we may name tough.
Armado. Pretty and *apt*.
Moth. How mean you, sir? I pretty and my saying apt? Or I *apt*, and my saying pretty?

Arte 3.16

Your *Epitheton* or Qualifier, whereof we spoke before...... now he serves to alter and enforce the sense, we will say more........and conclude he must be *apt* and proper for the thing he is added to...

Metaphora

Julius Caesar, I.ii.300-302

This rudeness is sauce to his good wit,
Which gives him stomach to *digest his words*
With better appetite.

Arte 3.17

There is a kindle of wrestling of a single word from his own right significance, to another not so natural, yet of some affinity or convenience with it, as is to say, I cannot *digest your unkind words* for I cannot take them in good part.

Catachresis

I Henry VI, I.iii.14

Lean, raw-bomed *rascals*...

Arte 3.17

or as one should in reproach say to a poor man, thou *raskal* knave, where raskal is properly the hunter's term given to a young deer, *lean* and out of season, and not to people.

Atanaclasis

Antony and Cleopatra, V.ii.101-104

Arte 3.19

> Would I never
> O'ertake pursued success, but I do feel,
> By the *rebound* of yours, a grief that *smites*
> My very heart at root.

Ye have another figure which by his nature we may call *Rebound*, alluding to the tennis ball which being *smitten* by the racket *rebounds* back again

Climax.

Troilus and Cressida, I.iii.101ff

O, when degree is shaked,
Which is the *ladder* to all high degree
Then enterprise is sick.....
Then everything includes itself in powerful
Power into will, will into appetite;
And appetite, an universal wolf,
So doubly seconded with will and powerful
Must make perforce an universal prey..........
And this neglection of degree it is
That by a *pace* goes backward, with a purposes
It hath to climb. The general's disdained
One *step* below, he by the next by him ....

Arte 3.19

Ye have a figure which as well by his Greek or Latin originals, and also to the manner of a man's gate or going may be called the marching figure, for after the first *step* all the rest proceed, by double the space; and so in our speech one word proceeds double to the first that was spoken, and goeth as it were by strides or *paces*: it may as well be called the Climbing figure, for Climax is as much to say as a *ladder*.

Insultatio

The Comedy of Errors, II.ii.202-203

Luciana. If thou art changed to aught, 'tis to an ass.
Dromio of Syracuse. 'Tis true; she *rides* me and I long for grass.

Arte 3.19

Ye have another figure much like to Sarcasmus, or bitter taunt we spoke of before; and when it is with proud or insolent words, we do upbraid a man, or *ride* him, as we term it: for which cause the Latines also call it Insultatio.

Meiosis

The Winter's Tale, V.ii.161-163

and I'll swear to the prince, thou art *a tall fellow with thy hands*, and thou wilt not be drunk; but I know thou art no *tall fellow with thy hands* and that thou wilt be drunk....

Arte 3.19

We use it again to excuse a fault, and to make an offence to seem less than it is, by giving a term more favourable and of less vehemency than the troth requires, as to say of a great robbery, that it was but a pilfry matter; of an arrant ruffian that he is *a tall fellow of his hands*.

Pragmatographia

The Merry Wives of Windsor, IV.v.109-112

Arte 3.19

I was beaten myself into all colours of the rainbow: I was likely to be apprehended for the witch of Brentford: but that my admirable dexterity of wit *my counterfeiting the action* of an old woman, delivered me, the knave constable had set me I' the stocks, i' the common stocks, for a witch.

But if such description be made to represent the handling of any business, with the circumstances belonging thereunto, as in the manner of.......any other matter that lieth in feat and activity, we call it then the *Counterfeit Action,* pragmatographia.

Exargasia

Hamlet, V.ii.11-12

There is a divinity that shapes our ends, *Rough hew* them how *we will.*

Arte 3.20

Exargasia.... A term transferred from these polishers of marble or porphyrite, who after it is rough hewn, and reduced to that fashion *they will.....*

It is interesting that apparently Puttenham takes the *Hamlet* quotation, which much more likely refers to the laying of hedges than stone polishing, and links it to exargasia or polishing, which would not be likely to be in the original English writer's mind.

Barbarismus

Love's Labour's Lost, V.i..73-78

Costard...O, and the heavens were so pleas'd that thou wert but my bastard, what a joyful father wouldest thou make me! Go to, thou hast it *ad dunghill,* at the fingers' end, as they say.
Holofernes. O, I smell false Latin: dunghill for *unguem.*
Costard. Arts-man, perambulate, we will singuled from the *barbarous.* Do you not educate youths from the charge house on top of the mountain?

Arte 3.22

The foulest vice in language is to speak *barbarously....*so....when any of their [i.e., the Greeks' and Latins'] own natural words were sounded and pronounced with strange and ill-shaped accents, ... they said it was *barbarously* spoken. The Italians at this day by like arrogance called the Frenchman, Spaniard, Dutch, English, and all other bred behither their *mountains* Apennines Tramontani, as who would say '*barbarous*'

Cacozelia

Love's Labour's Lost, V.ii.402-409

Arte, 3.22

O never will I trust to *speeches* penn'd,
Nor to the motion of a school-boy's tongue;
No, never come in vizard to my friend;
Nor woo in rhyme, like a blind harper's song;
Taffeta *phrases*, silken terms precise,
Three-piled hyperboles, spruce *affection*
Figures pedantical: these summer flies
Have blown me full of maggot ostentation.

Hamlet, II.ii..447

nor no matter in the *phrase* that might indict the author of *affectation*.

Ye have another intollerable ill manner of *speech*, by which the Greeks' original we may call Fond *Affectation*. And is when we affect new words and *phrases* other than good speakers and writers in any language, or than custom, hath allowed; and is the common fault of young *scholars* not half well studied before they come from their universities and schools.

Tautologia

Love's Labour's Lost, IV.ii.55-56

will sometimes affect the *letter,* for it *argues facility*: 'The preyful princess pierced and prick'd a pretty pleasing pricket'

Arte, 3.22

Many of our English makers use it too much, yet we confess it doth not ill but prettily becomes the metre.... For such composition makes the metre *run away smoother*, and passes from the lips with more *facility* by iteration of a *letter* than by alteration.

Surplusage

Romeo and Juliet, III.ii.52

I saw the wound, I *saw it with mine eyes*

The Merry Wives of Windsor, I.i.136

He hears with *his ears*

Arte 3.22

Also the Poet or maker's speech becomes vicious and unpleasant by nothing more than using too much surplusage.... The first surplusage the Greeks call Pleonasmus,—I call him Too Full Speech—and is no great fault. As one should say, 'I heard it *with mine ears*, and *saw it with mine eyes*,' as if a man could hear with his heels, or see with his nose.

"Jet"

Twelfth Night, II.ii.29-30

Arte. 3.22

Contemplation makes a rare turkey-cock of him: how he *jets* under his advanced plumes!

Arden of Feversham, I.30

And bravely *jets* it in his silken gown....

Thomas of Woodstock, I.i.99-105

Tell me, kind Cheyney
How does thy master, our good brother Woodstock?
Plain Thomas, for by the rood so all men call him
For his plain dealing, and his simple clothing
Let others *jet* in silk and gold, says he
A coat of English frieze best pleaseth me.

All singularities or affected parts of a man's behaviour seem undecent, as for a man to march or *jet* in the street more stately

"Lion and Lamb"

Much Ado About Nothing, I.i.13-15

He hath borne himself beyond the promise of his age: doing in the figure of *a lamb*, the feats of *a lion*."

Othello, II.i.111-115

You are pictures sent out of doors,
Bells in our parlours, wild cats in your kitchens,
Saints in your injuries, devils being offended,
Players in your housewifery, and hussies in your beds.

Arte, 3.24

And touching a person, we may say it is comely for a man to be *a lamb* in the house and *a lion* in the field..... we limit the comely parts of a woman to consist of four points, that is to be a shrew in the kitchen, a saint in the Church, an angel at the board, and an ape in bed..... .

Indent (Contract)

I Henry VI, I.iii.86-87

Shall we buy Treason and *indent* with Fears,
When they have lost and forfeited themselves.

Arte, 3.24

Right in so negotiating with Princes we ought to seek their favour by humility and not by way of sternness, not to traffick with them by way of *indent* or condition, but frankly and by manner of submission to their wills, for princes may be led not driven.

Nature

The Winter's Tale, IV.iv..81ff

Arte, 3.24

Perdita....The fairest flowers of the *season*....
Are our *carnations* and streaked *gillivors*....Which some call nature's bastards.

Polixenes You see sweet maid, we marry....a gentler scion to the wildest stock...by bud of nobler race. This is an *art*....Which doth mend *nature* – change it rather; but....The *Art* itself is *nature*.

Perdita....So it is.

Polixenes. Then make your garden rich in *gillivors*/And do not call them bastards.

In some cases we say art is an aid and coadjutor to nature.... ......And the gardener by his *art* will not only make a herb or flower or fruit come forth in his own *season* without impediment but will also embellish the same in virtue, shape, odour and taste, that *nature* of itself would never have done: as to make the single *gillifloure* or marigold, or daisy, double, and the white rose, red, yellow or *carnation*.

Grammatical Criticism: the "falsifying" of accent to serve the cadence or the "wrenching" of words to help the rhyme

2 Henry IV, III.ii.278-279

He is not his art's *craft's master*: he does not do it right.

Arte, 1.9

it is a sign that such a maker is not copious [competent] in his own language, or (as you are wont to say) not half his *craft's master*.

Indirect Attribution

I *Henry VI*, 1.viii. 23-5

In memory of her, when she is dead....
Her ashes, in an urn more precious...
Than the rich-jewelled *coffer of Darius*.

Arte, 1.8

[Puttenham commends the recognition and generosity of princes towards poets (with possibility a plea to the Queen in respect of his own works)], "In what price the noble poems of Homer were held by Alexander the Great.......by day carried in the rich jewel coffer of Darius.

These examples are a small fraction of those available whereby Puttenham's quotations can be seen to be taken from works (and not just Shakespeare's) written and in circulation before Puttenham's publication date of 1589. Puttenham therefore provides vital pieces of evidence for the dating of works, and these rule out William Shakspere of Stratford-Upon-Avon as the author.

Endnotes

[1] All references herein to the *Arte* are to Frank Whigham & Wayne A. Rebhorn, eds., *The Art of English Poesy by George Puttenham: A Critical Edition* (Cornell U. P., 2007). The *Arte* is divided into three Books, each of which is further divided into chapters. Citations are given to Book and chapter, e.g., 3.19.

[2] W.L. Rushton, *Shakespeare and "The Arte of English Poesie"* (Henry Young and Sons, 1909). I owe Charles Willis my thanks for alerting me to this book (and supplying a copy).

[3] I note that Whigham and Rebhorn, while quoting from C.M. Willis, *Shakespeare and George Puttenham's The Arte of English Poesie* (2003) with its prominent references to Rushton's book, curiously do not seem to have read it, let alone acknowledge it or make use any great use of it: perhaps the fundamental "flaw" of Rushton's 's book (that the plays written after 1589 owe grammatical construction and ideas to *Arte*) was so obvious as to be dangerous to their schema. On their page 212 they quote Puttenham's instruction to his readers: "But chiefly in your courtly ditties take heed that you use not these manner of long polysyllables and especially that ye finish not your verse with them as *retribution, restitution, remuneration, recapitulation* and such like, for they smatch [taste of] more the school of common players than of any delicate poet lyric or elegiac." One authority suggests only two uses of "restitution" (by Gascoigne and Marlowe) can be found in plays before 1590, but Oxfordians will note four uses of the word (three in verse and one in prose dialogue) and eight uses of "remuneration" (only one in verse; the other seven are all in prose dialogue in *Love's Labour's Lost* alone). Perhaps other examples can be found in Oxford's earlier plays.

[4] According to most authorities, *The Arte* was substantially written by 1583, although not published until 1589 – ed.

[5] Whigham & Rebhorn, 52 ff.

[6] Id., 31ff.

[7] I have not been able to check seven or so further references to Gascoigne to see if Puttenham quotes accurately from them.

[8] Ennius, as translated by E.H. Warmington, *Remains of Old Latin* (Harvard U. P., 1935).

[9] Gager, hypertext edition by Dana F. Sutton, University of California, Irvine.

[10] Professor Martin Wiggins the co-author of the magisterial *British Drama 1533-1642: A Catalogue* readily acknowledged that this Puttenham-esque rendition clearly showed Puttenham's method of work. When I suggested that he applied the same approach to the "Shakespeare" examples below (to prove that the plays were written much too early for the 'orthodox' dating theories), he replied that he had no interest in any such "debate": "I am not going to be drawn into a fruitless discussion of that research [of the dating] at large." I suggested that if he disagreed and held to any 'orthodox' view, he would have to refute and destroy each and every one of the references which Rushton and I call in evidence.

[11] George Saintsbury, *A History of English Criticism* (Blackwood, 1922), 33-34.

[12] The majority of these dates are taken from Kevin Gilvary, ed., *Dating Shakespeare's Plays* (Parapress, 2011).

Edward de Vere: Translator of Johan Sturm's *A Ritch Storehouse or Treasurie for Nobilitie and Gentlemen*?[1]

Richard M. Waugaman, M.D.

Edward de Vere hid his authorship behind such pen names as William Shakespeare; Ignoto; Anomos; and E.K. Did he simply sponsor the publication of Bedingfield's translation into Latin of *Cardanus Comfort*, or did de Vere write the translation himself? We do not know yet. We do have evidence from the secretary of the Earl of Essex that Essex asked Fulke Greville to allow him to sign a document written by Essex as "F.G."[2] Essex's motives included a wish not to appear too self-congratulatory in this, well, self-congratulatory account of his role in the 1596 battle of Cadiz. So here is valuable evidence of another earl using a veiled allonym.

The 1570 English translation of Johann Sturm's Latin *A Ritch Storehouse or Treasurie for Nobilitye and Gentlemen* is a small, octavo edition of merely 96 pages. This was one of Sturm's few Latin works to be translated into the vernacular during the 16th century. The title page names the translator as "T.B.," and its dedicatory epistle is signed "Thomas Browne." But I will present multiple lines of evidence suggesting that Edward de Vere was its actual translator.

Colin Burrow, in his survey of Shakespeare's relationship with the Latin classics, speculates that this very book by Sturm "is just the kind of aspirational work which Shakespeare might have *read*" (26; emphasis added).[3] He surmises that "Shakespeare may have known *A Rich Storehouse* as early as the mid 1590s, since T.W. Baldwin notes an 'amusing parallel' between Holofernes' use of the word 'peregrinate' to describe an imported word and Sturm's treatise." Burrow adds that Donna B. Hamilton discusses the relationship of *The Tempest* with the same treatise (250 n. 8) .

Elsewhere, Burrow writes,

> A tiny clue in the text of *Troilus* may also indicate that Shakespeare had recently read and thought afresh about the theory and practice of literary imitation. Hector makes a famously anachronistic comment that his brothers have spoken like "young men, who Aristotle thought/Unfit to hear moral philosophy" (2.2.166-7). Aristotle (4th century BC) could not have been read by a Homeric hero who was fighting at Troy during the Bronze Age....Shakespeare's error could have come from a number of sources, but one possibility is Johann Sturm's *Nobilitas Literata* (1549), which was translated into English in 1570 as *A Rich Storehouse or Treasure for Nobilitye and Gentlemen*. This includes an extended discussion of how one author should imitate another, in the course of which Sturm declares that imitation is not a childish activity, but is indeed suitable only for grown-ups: "as Aristotle did exclude young boys from his *Ethics*: so I also remove from this artificial practice [of imitation] not only children and boys, but also those men which know not the precepts of rhetoric." That embeds Aristotle's remark in a rhetorical setting that fits the formal *disputatio* between Hector and Troilus in 2.2. Sturm was an unusually enthusiastic advocate of a kind of imitation that has been called "dissimulative," in which "an imitator must hide all similitude and likeness." (608)[4]

Translating Sturm may have provided de Vere with further encouragement for continuing his "dissimulative" practice of hiding his authorship of most of his literary works.

We do know something of de Vere's relationship with Johann Sturm (1507-1589). De Vere thought so highly of him that he went out of his way to visit him in Strasbourg during his 14-month trip to the Continent in 1575-76 (that is, some five years after the translation was published). De Vere and Sturm were part of a network of eminent inellectuals in England and on the Continent. Sturm's friends included John Calvin, Andreas Vesalius, and Guillaume Budé. His former student Petrus Ramus became a renowned logician. Queen Elizabeth's tutor Roger Ascham was so friendly with Sturm that he named a son Johannes Sturm Ascham, and he corresponded with Sturm for 18 years. The Queen herself also greatly admired Sturm's work. A 1590 edition of poems in Sturm's honor was dedicated to Queen Elizabeth.

Sturm wrote to Roger Ascham in 1551, praising the learning of some English noblemen. Spitz and Tinsley report that Ascham "was a devoted disciple of Sturm's educational and humanist writings."[5] Anderson notes that one of de Vere's servants said he "had a most high opinion" of Sturm. Sturm staunchly defended the French Protestants, harming himself financially through large loans to their cause. He was a liberal, tolerant humanist, whose efforts to build bridges among the Lutherans and Calvinists eventually led to his losing his academic position. He devoted much of his life and many of his writings to education. We might recall that Edward de Vere's grandfather founded a grammar school at Earls Colne in Essex, and that de Vere served as guardian of that school, appointing its schoolmaster.[6]

This article will present evidence that the 20-year-old de Vere admired Sturm's 1549 treatise on rhetoric so much that he translated it from Latin to English, hiding his role behind that of "T.B.," ostensibly Thomas Browne.[7] What do we know of Thomas Browne? There is no consensus as to his identity. We have not a single other work that he published. The brief *ODNB* article on him, by L.G. Kelly, has virtually no sources of information about him other than this 1570 translation. The article begins, "Brown, Thomas (*fl.* 1570), translator, was a member of Lincoln's Inn. He was either the Thomas Brown admitted on 13 October 1562, or Thomas Brown of London, admitted on 6 August 1565. The second of these could have been 'Thomas Browne of London', admitted to the Inner Temple in November 1575. He was not one of the myriad Thomas Browns in the university lists." I am skeptical of these inferences, given Marcy North's important work on the prominent role of anonymous Elizabethan authorship. Scholars who write articles about obscure Elizabethan authors for the *ODNB* need to consider the possibility that some of these authorial names are pseudonyms (or alloynms).

The 1570 translation is dedicated to the 13-year-old Philip Howard (1557-1595), who then had the honorable title of Earl of Surrey. Under the circumstances, dedicating a work to the son of Thomas Howard in 1570 was a bold act, possibly hinting at disloyalty to the Queen. The more reckless the act, the greater the likelihood that de Vere was its perpetrator. Philip Howard's father, Thomas Howard, Duke of Norfolk (1538-1572), was de Vere's first cousin, descended from their grandfather, the 15th Earl of Oxford, through Howard's mother, Frances de Vere. Lord Howard fell under suspicion of treason when he pursued possible marriage with Mary Stuart, Queen of Scots. This placed him in a faction that was directly opposed to de Vere's guardian and future father-in-law, William Cecil. Howard was placed in the Tower from October, 1569 to August, 1570, then under house arrest in Howard House, London. He was finally executed for treason in June, 1572. Philip Howard himself was to spend the last ten years of his own life in the Tower, also for treason.

How important was rhetoric to de Vere? It was central to his vision of writing, whether in his private letters; in his prose works (most notably, I believe, in *The Arte of English Poesie*)[8]; in his poetry; and in his plays. Quentin Skinner's *Forensic Shakespeare*[9] shows that "over and over again, Shakespeare's characters follow to the letter the instructions of the rhetorical handbooks….The hidden pattern within the plays, their close dependence on the ancient art of rhetoric, was perhaps intended for his eyes only" (from review by David Wootton, *TLS*, December 12, 2014, pp. 3-5). In my review of Skinner's book,[10] I wrote,

> One of the many reasons that I find Skinner's book so fascinating is that it dovetails with the likelihood that de Vere wrote the 1589 *Arte of English Poesie*. As Skinner points out, its third part deals extensively with rhetoric, especially figures of speech. By the

way, Angel Day's 1586 *The English Secretorie*, dedicated to de Vere, included marginal glosses highlighting rhetorical figures.[11] It is noteworthy that Day uses the word "coined" in the sense that de Vere seems to have coined it in 1570:[12] "Such odd coyned tearmes," referring to an example of a "preposterous and confused kind of writing." (39). Further, in 1592 Day seems to have been the second author, after de Vere in the *Arte*, to use the term "hendiadys" in English. In his 1592 edition, Day included a new section on rhetorical figures.

The hypothesis that de Vere wrote *The Arte of English Poesie* gains support from the connections between Quintilian and the Shakespeare canon, because the *Arte* twice mentions Quintilian by name. Recall that the *Arte* is only the sixth book in EEBO to cite Quintilian. In the second chapter of Book 3, its author recommends the use of figures of speech. In that context, he says "I have come to the Lord Keeper Sir Nicholas Bacon, & found him sitting in his gallery alone with the works of Quintilian before him, in deede he was a most eloquent man, and of rare learning and wisedome, as ever I knew England to breed" (224).[13] And, in chapter 9 of Book 3, the author says that "the learned orators and good grammarians among the Romans, as Cicero, Varro, Quintilian, and others, strained themselves to give the Greek words [for figures of speech] Latin names" (241). Further, according to editors Whigham and Rebhorn, the *Arte* uses some 70 of Quintilian's terms for figures of speech.

Skinner convincingly demonstrates that Shake-speare had a deep interest in and familiarity with rhetoric, even though past scholars overlooked his acquaintance with any books on that subject. Skinner shows that Shake-speare quotes from Cicero's rhetorical work *De inventione*; from *Rhetorica ad Herennium*; and that he cites Thomas Wilson's 1554 *Arte of Rhetorique*. Notably, Wilson received help with an earlier book from Sir Thomas Smith, Edward de Vere's later tutor. Skinner shows that past discussions of Shake-speare's rhetoric misleadingly place central emphasis on *elocutio* (including wordplay), whereas Shake-speare's real interest was primarily in *inventio*. The 1570 book's epistle to the reader states the "wish that the vulgar speech of commending might be kept until some worthy matters were *invented*..." (emphasis added).

Why has de Vere's central interest in rhetoric been downplayed in the past? Perhaps because of the misleading implications of the traditional authorship theory, that portray Shake-speare as a relatively unschooled, native genius. Even Oxfordians have not escaped from the influence of this misconception, perhaps making us loath to think of de Vere showing an intense interest in the rhetorical skills that underlay his works of literary genius. The image of an unschooled Shake-speare clashes with Skinner's description of Shake-speare working with treatises of rhetoric at the forefront of his mind, and possibly open on his desk. He contends that Shake-speare even draws attention to the role of artifice in his art.

If we accept Skinner's revised picture of Shake-speare—and I believe we should—it makes it all the more likely that Shake-speare is the author of the anonymous 1589 *Arte of English Poesie*, and of the 1570 translation of Sturm. Among the many ways that the Sturm translation influenced de Vere's later *Arte* is the fact that Sturm wrote his treatise to the Werter brothers in the second person, just as the anonymous author of the *Arte* addressed much of it to Queen Elizabeth in the second person. Both works emphasize that words can be misused to deceive. Both works use unusual drawings to schematize different structures in poetry.

David Wootton, in his review of Skinner, concludes that Shake-speare follows the rules of rhetoric "precisely because he was aware that that art could not deliver the proof that [courtroom] decisions of life and death required. There is something wrong with the rules themselves….Shakespeare's courtroom scenes show an author not enamoured of rhetoric, but frustrated by it" (5). Yet the recognition that rhetoric could be used to deceive is central to Sturm, as it is to the *Arte*. In the translator's epistle to the reader, he speaks disparagingly of "painted wordes and smooth Rhetoricke," in contrast with "good and precious" matter. So we might instead say that Shake-speare's courtroom scenes demonstrate just how deeply familiar with rhetoric he was, not that he idealized it as a foolproof way of ascertaining the truth. After all, the ancient stoics were controversial because they trained their students to win arguments, whether or not the truth was on their side.

Skinner emphasized that Shake-speare's primary interest in rhetoric is *inventio*. Coining new words is one well-known Shakespearean instance of *inventio*. *A Ritch Storehouse* coined, in fact, "to *coin* a word" in its introductory section, "To the friendly reader": "I of necessitie must either *coyne* newe wordes, the aunctient already being employed on lewde and peradventure wicked matters…" (1; emphasis added). Note the translator's justification for coining this use of the verb "to coin," and other words, as something he is compelled to do. This is 19 years before the first example of the verb "coin" in this sense given in the OED. For our purposes, it is significant that this later 1589 use is in an anonymous work I have previously attributed to de Vere, the *Arte of English Poesie*.

"Unfyled" is here newly coined in the dedicatory letter in the sense of "unpolished, rude." The OED erroneously states that Spenser coined that meaning of "unfiled" in his 1590 *Faerie Queene*. But it actually appeared 20 years earlier. The creative energy brimming in this 1570 work embodies the author's desire to make the English language suitable for great literature. He is saying, as it were, "anything Greek and Latin can do, English can do better!"

There are at least twelve other newly coined words in the short *A Ritch Storehouse*. The author introduces the coinage "concauses" [co-operating causes] by adding "or joined causes." "Sensentence" looks like a misprint, but it may have been de Vere's attempt to English the Latin "sententia," meaning opinion or maxim. "Sensentence" actually appears three more times in EEBO, though it failed to make the cut for the OED. "Turquif[y]ing" is a coined word that flopped, never to be used again. It meant "transforming"; as early as 1560, "turkish" could be a verb meaning "to transform." Transformation of ancient texts into new works that imitate them in a disguised way was central to the humanist literary project.

Another coinage that never got off the ground was "captaynecke." It is a quirky translation of "virumque" in the opening words of the *Aeneid*. The translator is here enacting the advice he gave two sentences earlier, that literary imitation should create in place of the original "a thing eyther as good or better" (40r). So he experimented with an English equivalent ("ecke," or "eke") for the Latin suffix "-que," both meaning "also." Virgil famously wrote "Arma virumque cano"; de Vere translates this, "of armes, and of a captaynecke I doe indite [meaning to write, to compose a tale]" (39v). "Peregrinity," borrowed from Latin and from Rabelais, means "foreignness." The translator indicates he is coining a word when he writes, "a certayne peregrinitie, *if I may so terme it*" (35r; emphasis added). The OED erroneously gives its first use as by G. Fletcher, in 1591. De Vere's younger sister Mary married Peregrine Bertie (1555-1601) in 1578. He lived in William Cecil's home as a teenager, so it is possible that de Vere had him in mind when he coined "peregrinity," especially because Bertie was named as an allusion to his Protestant parents' years spent living on the Continent during the reign of Queen Mary.

EEBO[14] gives *Ritch Storehouse* as the first use of "patavine" ("related to Padua"). "Counterchaunge" is also first used as the English word for the Greek rhetorical term "antimetabole" in this work. Its first use in EEBO is just three years earlier, in 1567, in the generic sense of "exchange of one thing for another." The OED incorrectly gives its first use as a term of rhetoric in the *Arte*. Naturally, it is significant that this translation of antimetabole appears in both the 1570 as well as the 1589 works that I attribute to de Vere.

Both EEBO and the OED give the 1585 T. Washington translation of a French book as the first instance of "defiguration," but it was apparently coined fifteen years earlier, in *A Ritch Storehouse*. Spitz and Tinsley translate a passage as "sketches... let our drawings be called...schematisms" (150). De Vere translates it as "figurative draughts, or if I might so terme them, *defigurations*" (24r; emphasis added). De Vere also introduced the word "aposchematisms" into the English language, transliterating the Greek word used by Sturm. This coinage did not catch on — it is the only instance of it in EEBO. "Schematism," but *not* "aposchematism," *is* in the OED. "Whuzzing [wind]" is the first of only two uses of "whuzzing" in EEBO; "whuzz" appears in the OED as a spelling variant of "whiz."

A Ritch Storehouse also coined new phrases, not just new words. For example, "envious emulation" is the first of 31 uses of this phrase in EEBO. A prominent Elizabethan meaning of "envious" was "malicious" in general. So the phrase plays on emulation as not only a desire to equal another, but also rivalry, and a dislike of those who are superior.

One theme in *A Ritch Storehouse* is secrecy and disguise. G.W. Pigman observes, "Of all the theorists of imitation Sturm is the most insistent on dissimulation" (11)[15] The word "hidden" occurs six times in this work; "hide" four times; "hider" once; "hyding" once; "secret" four times; "cover" in the sense of "conceal" four times; "covertly" once. Most of these words are in contexts that allude to the need to imitate the style of a great writer, while concealing this imitation—

> We must…follow these waies and rules that I have shewed: that nothing be done or placed without a cause: and *yet after such maner, that the common sorte may not perceive it*. For as it is to be wished that our speeche maye please all men, and as we ought speciallye to indevor to obtayne the same: so also we must take great heede, that Arte, and Imitation, and the similitude and likeness *be not espied*.
> (46r-v; emphasis added)

Court insiders knew of de Vere's literary activities, while "the common sort" were probably taken in by his use of anonymity, pseudonymity, and allonymity. Significantly, Sturm includes the Greek word κεκρυμμενον, or "hidden." De Vere uses a triple repetition to emphasize the importance of this word for him, translating it as, "that is as much as hidden, close, or secret" (35v). If I am correct in concluding that de Vere disguised his translation of this work, all these passages would have spoken to his early — as well as to his lifelong — authorial self-concealment. So this may be one of Sturm's more profound influences on de Vere's career.

As I have noted, this translation anticipates the anonymous 1589 *Arte of English Poesie*, which I consider to be de Vere's own extensive treatise on rhetoric. The word "figure" appears 10 times in *Ritch Storehouse*, and 87 times in the *Arte*, reflecting de Vere's close study of rhetorical figures. Sturm says of figuration, "the varietie of these bringeth delight & taketh away sasiety" (38r). "Sasiety" is the spelling here of "satiety." The former spelling occurs only one other time in EEBO, in 1579.

In the first three paragraphs of this work, "wit" is spelled three different ways: "wytte," "witte," and "wyt." Alan Nelson, a paleographer, has emphasized de Vere's pattern of spelling one word multiple ways, more than did his contemporaries. "Hand D" in the manuscript of *Sir Thomas More* is said to be that of Shakespeare. Hand D spells silence "scilens." De Vere similarly includes an "sc" in his spelling of "necescassarye" (sic).[16] *Ritch Storehouse* also misspells "unnecessary" as "unnessarie." Further, EEBO has no other instances of its quirky phrase "easiest and necessariest." It includes the word "apploying" for "applying"; this is the unique occurrence of the former spelling in EEBO.[17] The work includes "cowpling" for "coupling," "howres"[18] for "hours," and "pawse" for "pause."[19] De Vere usually preferred "owt" to "out" and "fowre" to "foure" in his letters, at a time when the former spellings had become unusual. It is helpful to recall that "w" stood for and was at the time sometimes printed with a double "v," and "v" and "u" were somewhat interchangeable. De Vere often doubled vowels at a time when most spelling had dropped one of them ("adoo" for "ado," etc.).

Hendiadys in *A Ritch Storehouse*

We know that de Vere favored the Virgilian rhetorical figure of hendiadys ("one through two"), or two related words connected by a conjunction (usually "and"). The figure was never described by classical authors, but was first described by Susenbrotus, in 1562. The 1589 *Arte of English Poesie* states, "Ye have yet another manner of speech when ye will seem to make two of one not thereunto constrained, which we therefor call the Figure of Twins, the Greeks *hendiadys*" (261). The 1592 edition of Angel Day's *The English Secretorie*, dedicated to de Vere, defines "hendiadis" as follows:

> when one thing of it selfe intire, is diversly laid open, as to say *On Iron and bit he champt*, for on the Iron bit he champt: And *part and proy* [prey] *we got*, for part of the proy: Also *by surge and sea we past*, for by surging sea wee past. This also is rather Poeticall then otherwise in use (89; Day's emphasis).

It would be fitting if de Vere was the first English author to describe hendiadys, and also the one who most employed it. Likening it to twins reminds us that Shakespeare's source for *The Comedy of Errors* included just one pair of twins, which de Vere doubled to two pairs of identical twins in his version of the play. A twin brother and a sister appear in *Twelfth Night*. The word "two" appears 574 times in Shakespeare;[20] "double" appears 82 times; "pair," 41 times; "twain" (two) 39 times. The basic metrical unit of de Vere's poetry was the two-syllable iamb, another instance of doubling. The Greek etymology of "hendiadys" as "one through two" is reflected in de Vere's poetry about love. Sonnet 36 begins, "Let me confess that we two must be twain ["two," or "a couple," but also "asunder, separate, estranged"],/ Although our undivided loves are one." "Let the bird of loudest lay," probably written about Queen Elizabeth's love for the Earl of Essex, after their deaths, includes the stanza, "So they lov'd, as love in twain/ Had the essence but in one;/ Two distincts, division none:/ Number[21] there in love was slain."

De Vere learned languages such as ancient Greek and Anglo-Saxon that still retained the "dual number" of nouns and verbs, that existed in proto-Indoeuropean. There are traces of this old form in modern words such as "both," "either," and phrases such as "you two." The two words in the dual number were related, which may have provided another source of de Vere's interest in hendiadys.[22]

Hendiadys may also reflect de Vere's pivotal image of mirrors and mirroring.[23] Hamlet was speaking of the entirety of de Vere's literary work when he said the purpose of art is to hold a mirror up to nature. Early modern mirrors did not reflect the exact likeness of today's mirror; in that sense, one word in hendiadys roughly — but not precisely — mirrors its twin. In addition, a foundational, implicit word pair for Renaissance humanists such as Sturm and de Vere was "now and then"— that is, the fundamental fact that the present can be informed and enriched by a deeper understanding of the classical past and its literature. Like other humanists, de Vere deliberately avoided simple imitation of classical models. Renaissance humanists consistently transformed[24] these classical models into their own creations. Their sense of time differed from that of their medieval predecessors, who felt they were essentially living in the same historical era as the ancient Romans and Greeks.

George T. Wright helped draw attention to the fact that Shake-speare used this figure of hendiadys more than 300 times.[25] Examples that have entered common use include "sound and fury," "slings and arrows," and "lean and hungry." Wright excludes from his use of the term what he derisively calls Shakespeare's "ceremonious parading of synonyms," that is, two closely related words, "without any significant increment, usually for an effect of expansion or elevation" (174). If we follow Wright in his derogation of insufficiently complex word pairs, we will deprive ourselves of taking the full measure of de Vere's lifelong fascination with word pairs, and the growth and development that his use of them underwent in his writing career. They tell us something important about his mind and spirit. One thing reminded him of another, and he linked them with a conjunction. One word alone often did not suffice, and in pairing it with a second, he drew a line that gestured toward meanings and connotations that went beyond mere words.

Wright does observe that, from the beginning, paired words are used "to give a feeling of elevation or complexity" (173), a description that is apt for *Ritch Storehouse*. What Wright considers true hendiadys, in its best examples, "make[s] us feel...that some structural situation we had become ready for...has jumped and become a different structural situation..." (175). One is reminded of the many jolting syntactical pivots in the *Sonnets*. In the present article, I do not presume to ascertain and judge what is an acceptable "figure of twins," and what is a "mere parading of synonyms." I believe we can better study and appreciate the development of de Vere's use of hendiadys by casting a wider net than does Wright. Doing so also allows us to see just how many word pairs de Vere coined and invented in this early work. Later writers paid tribute to many of them by borrowing them, in some cases dozens of times.

Wright observes that "Shakespeare's examples are dazzlingly various; the *developing* playwright appears to have taken this odd figure to his bosom and to have made it entirely his own" (169; emphasis added). We have a misleadingly limited picture and understanding of Shakespeare's development if we remain unaware of his earlier work, that has not previously been attributed to the same author.

Wright finds that Shakespeare's hendiadys "is always somewhat mysterious and elusive" (176). Wright speculates that "It may at times betoken [Shakespeare's] teeming mind" (173). At other times, he senses that it suggests "an oddly empty, discordant, and disconnected feeling...normal unions are disassembled" (175). Hendiadys "serves to remind us how uncertain and treacherous language...can be" (176) as it expresses "deceptive linking" (178). Wright is brilliant in perceiving the way de Vere increasingly used hendiadys to construct the extreme and enigmatic complexity of his writing—"hendiadys, far from explaining mysteries, establishes them...hendiadys resists logical analysis" (169), and it serves "at once to deny and to extend the adequacy of linguistic forms to convey our experience" (183). As Wright notes, the usual conjunction in hendiadys is "and," but in de Vere's use, it thwarts our expectation that we will be given a clear parallelism, which is "among our major instruments for ordering the world we live in" (169). Wright says Shake-speare's hendiadys can be "estranging" (173), and that it "usually elevates the discourse and blurs its logical lines, and this combination of grandeur and confusion is in keeping with the tragic or weighty action of the major plays" (171); "hendiadys is often characterized...by a kind of syntactical complexity that seems fathomable only by an intuitional understanding of the way words interweave their meanings" (171).

The psychoanalyst James Grotstein offered a startlingly similar observation about the way his own analyst Wilfred Bion made interpretations to him: he decided they were deliberately obscure, the better to evade his defenses, and thus speak directly to Grotstein's unconscious mind. So, here is another example of de Vere anticipating the discoveries of psychoanalysis by four centuries. Further, we might compare the verbal doubling of hendiadys with our binocular vision, which allows us to perceive the three-dimensional world in greater depth; so does hendiadys help us penetrate beneath the surface of language and its meanings, while our conscious mind is mesmerized by the shimmering tensions between the paired words. Cognitive psychology has expanded our understanding of memory, by distinguishing between two major memory systems—implicit and explicit. They are served by different neuroanatomical structures. At one level, language activates the explicit, more conscious memory system. But good creative writers use words to evoke our less conscious and less verbal feelings, linked with implicit memory. De Vere was a master of this use of complex language to appeal to both parts of our minds. Hendiadys assisted him in doing so.

One of the several categories of hendiadys is the use of the second word to amplify the first. *Amplificatio* is a central rhetorical device, enacted in miniature form in hendiadys. The Psalms characteristically use repetition for intensification. They profoundly influenced de Vere, and probably contributed to his use of hendiadys for amplification and intensification. In addition, Wright discovers that Shakespeare sometimes uses the device for "an interweaving, indeed sometimes a muddling, of meanings, a deliberate violation of clear sense that is in perfect keeping with Shakespeare's exploration...of 'things supernatural and causeless'" (173).

One thinks of Richard II's extraordinary prison soliloquy, when he wonders how he can possibly compare his prison cell to the wide world, alone as he is. He famously concludes that "My brain I'll prove the female to my soul,/ My soul the father; and *these two* beget/ A generation of still breeding thoughts,/ And these same thoughts people this little world" (V.v.6-9; emphasis added). Four lines later, he says that the "better sort" of thoughts "do set the word itself/ Against the word" (V.v.13-14). Literally, the sometimes seemingly contradictory words of the Bible. More broadly, though, the generative potential of "word against word" reminds us of de Vere's continual use of the figure of hendiadys, throughout some forty years of his literary career.[26] This generative genius of hendiadys forms close connections with the mind, and brain, of the reader and audience of de Vere's work, so that we ourselves become the "female" to de Vere's soul. It is known, for example, that listening to Shakespeare's poetry activates more parts of the brain than does listening to other poets. An ambiguous stimulus, whether a visual inkblot or its verbal equivalent, is most effective in drawing out the unconscious contents of our own mind, which we project onto that uncertain prompt. De Vere is ever elusive and complex, and he seduces us into a collaborative partnership with his language, as we "hammer out" how we will people our minds with the still-breeding thoughts that de Vere engenders in us.

Wright is disappointed that Shakespeare scholars have shown so little interest in Shakespeare's style, especially "those stylistic devices that make for elusiveness...Hendiadys is too confusing, too disorderly...Critics...often take little interest in the figurative devices that seem merely decorative" (172). If these critics realized that "Shakespeare" also wrote the *Arte of English Poesie*, and translated *A Ritch Storehouse*, they would have more reasons to re-examine Shakespeare's use of rhetoric.

Hendiadys is characteristic of the Latin poetry that had such a profound literary influence on de Vere. The 1570 translation is chock full of hendiadys, starting with its very title. "A Ritch *Storehouse or Treasurie*[27] for *Nobilitye and Gentlemen*" translates Sturm's title, "Ad Werteros Fratres, Nobilitas Literata." So, from the title on, de Vere doubles Sturm's more terse original, with de Vere's Mercutio-like effervescence and exuberance. Centuries before Hemingway and the restricting influence of his spare style, de Vere delighted in his expansive use of the English language. The dedicatory epistle is titled, "To the Right Honorable, vertuous, and my singuler good lord, Lord Philip Howard Erle of Surrey, all *felicitie and happiness*."[28] A third hendiadys, and we still have not gotten beyond titles (in both senses)!

The body of the dedicatory letter includes some seventeen further instances of hendiadys (six of them in the first sentence, and the other eleven in the letter's second and final sentence): "zeal and desire" [a commonplace] "service and duty" [5 earlier uses in EEBO], "more *excellent and precious* than *long or tedious*" [11 earlier uses], "infinite and exceeding" [one or two earlier uses], "reading and study" [8 earlier uses], "golden and honorable" [*unique use* until 1633], "noble and high" [9 earlier uses], "evil and unskillful" [*unique use*], "good and praiseworthy"[29] [*unique use* before 1600], "precious and goodly" [2 earlier uses], "pain and travail" [a commonplace, which occurs in the plural in de Vere's Ovid, line 910 of Book One], "pleasure and pastime" [a commonplace], "good and ample" [the *first* of 24 uses], "fruit and commodity" [a commonplace], "tedious or troublesome,"[30] and "rude and unfiled"[31] [the *first* of two uses in EEBO]. The last pair listed introduces a new meaning of "unfiled" as "not reduced or smoothed by filing; unpolished, *rude*," and does so twenty years before the first use of this meaning listed in the OED (in Spenser's *Faerie Queene*). De Vere may sometimes use hendiadys to suggest the meaning of his newly coined words.

Some of these pairs hint at a contrast between subjective and more objective states — "my *payne and traveyle* to be but *pleasure and pastime*." Subjective pain turns to pleasure; travail (which could mean a literary work at the time) turns to recreation, if and when the dedicatee finishes reading this work. I have quoted two examples of "paired" hendiadys, where the first and second words of the first pair contrast with the first and second words of the second pair, respectively.

"Evil and unskillful" is intriguing. At first glance, it seems to pair "wicked" with "inexpert," which jars a bit, especially in the context of the author's description of his own translation. But one OED definition of "evil," going back as early as 1530, is in fact "unskillful," in which case we would have exact synonyms. Here, there is ambiguity as to which meanings of "evil" are active. Just a few lines earlier, de Vere described the dedicatee as "vertuous," twice. "My evil...handling" also contrasts with the dedicatee's "good and praiseworthy desire," mentioned later in the same sentence. So this example illustrates the sort of disorienting complexity that Wright finds in Shakespearean hendiadys. Also intriguingly, de Vere's uncle Arthur Golding (or de Vere himself?) used the phrase "savage and unskillfull" in his 1565 translation of Caesar's *Martial Exploits in Gaul*, just five years before the present work.

De Vere's introductory "To the friendly reader" (which follows the dedicatory epistle) also overflows with hendiadys. The fourth sentence alone has five such word pairs: "But our time (alas) is so inclined, and as it were naturally bent to bestow upon *barren*[32] *and unhonest* fruites,[33] *precious and golden*[34] names, that neythere can *vertuous and prayseworthy*[35] workes enjoye their *due and deserved* [36]tytles, being *forestauled and defrauded* by the evill, neythere good deedes possesse their owne, and worthy termes being prevented by the meane."

Wright's subjective criteria might not deem all of these doublings to be true examples of hendiadys. On the other hand, Wright felt that more complex use of hendiadys grew over time out of Shakespeare's earlier "parading of synonyms." And we must remind ourselves that de Vere was about twenty years old when he translated the work at hand.

Naturally, the dedicatory letter was de Vere's own, not a translation from Sturm. But in comparing de Vere's translation of Sturm with that of Spitz and Tinsley, we can see de Vere's addition of hendiadys. There are several examples of word pairs on every page. For example, where the latter write simply "the *practice* of learned men," de Vere expands this to "the *use and custome* of the learned." Where our recent translators say of the Werter brothers that they have "a great *similarity* in *talent*," de Vere expands both nouns into "twins": "a great *agreement and similitude* in *disposition and wytte*." The former refer to the "*diligence* of your teacher"; de Vere, to "the *indevor and example* of your teacher." Where they say "a special *degree* of happiness," he writes "the chiefest *step and degree* of felicitie." They write "temperance in desires"; he puts it "*temperaunce and an honest measure* in delightes." Instead of "I shall prescribe," de Vere says "I wyll *appoynt and prescribe*." When they simply say "*bipartite*," de Vere writes "*bypartite and double*." Where they use "*collected*," de Vere writes "*gather and dispose*."

Later in the translation, there are countless more word pairs. Here, I omit the many examples that were commonplaces at the time. Instead, I focus on those that were first coined in *A Ritch Storehouse*. For example, the noun pair "use and practice" is the first of hundreds of uses in EEBO.[37] "Painful [i.e., painstaking] and industrious" is the first of 108 uses.[38] Significantly, the second use was in Angel Day's 1586 *The English Secretary*, dedicated to his employer, Edward de Vere.[39] "Store and varietie" is the first of 71 uses. "*Store* and choice," by the way, was the second of 15 uses. I mention it here because it was first used in the translation of Ovid's *Metamorphoses* that many of us attribute to de Vere himself. "Acceptable and welcome" is the first of 65 uses.

"Servile or slavish" is the first of 57;[40] "servile *and* slavish" was not used until 1572. "Slavish" suggests an intensification of "servile," as with the contrast between slave and servant. "Manners and inclinations" is the first of 53 uses;[41] it seems to suggest a contrast between learned "manners" and natural "inclinations." "Rules and bounds" is the first of 30. "Learned and politic" is the first of 23 uses,[42] including Robert Green in his 1592 *Repentance*. "Noble and commendable" is the first of 22 uses.[43] "Name and commendation,"[44] and "pawse [pause] or staye" are the first of 14 uses ["pause *and* stay" first appears in 1578]. "End and form" is the first of 13 uses.[45] "Art and language" is the first of 9. "Things and matter" is the first of nine uses; "using and handling" and "things and matter" the first of eight uses; "purpose and reason,"[46] "gardien [I assume "garden" was a misprint] or keeper," and "assay and attempt" are the first of six; "wisely and commendably,"[47] "adventures and travails [which also meant "travels"]," and "unapt and foolish"[48] are the first of four; "elocution or utterance,"[49] and "nature and comlinesse"[50] are the first of three; "*writing* and utterance," the first of two; as are "handling and *writing*," "comparing and applying" "addition and ablation," "devising and *writing*,"[51] "gather and dispose," and "letters and voyces." "Praiseworthy and earnest," "virtue and fealty [feudal fidelity toward one's lord],"[52] "endeavour and example," "abate nor faint," "gravity and fullness,"[53] "gravity and beautification," "oration or work," "comelinesse and delectation," "handle and polish," "plentiful and neat [elegant]," "bipartite and double," and "arte and similitude" do not appear elsewhere in EEBO. Significantly, most of these unique word pairs describes ideal rhetoric, inspiring de Vere's "inventio."

Earl Showerman has drawn attention to the influence of the Greek tragedians on de Vere. *A Ritch Storehouse* advises, "a maker of Tragidies [must] take Euripides, or Sophocles to be his pattern." In general, Sturm stresses the importance for any writer to emulate the good models of prior writers. This emphasis may have been one reason de Vere decided to "English" this very work—taking it as a model for a discussion of rhetoric.

In 1569 appeared a poem subscribed "A.G.," which I have also attributed to de Vere.[54] How does the pattern of hendiadys in that poem compare with *A Ritch Storehouse*, published merely a year later? It has a few examples, in the latter portion of the poem—"just and trew" [a commonplace]; "faithfulness and right" [unusual]; "great and long" [a commonplace]; and "weale and welfare" [first EEBO use is in 1600]. The first and third pair modify the word "accounts," as it is a commendatory poem on bookkeeping. De Vere's "Young Gentleman" poem includes "range and seeke" [the unique use recorded in EEBO until 1672]; and "carcke and care" [a commonplace].

In conclusion, I have presented evidence that Edward de Vere was probably the translator of the 1570 work, *A Ritch Storehouse or Treasurie for Nobilitie and Gentlemen*, written in Latin by Johann Sturm. It is an important precursor of the anonymous 1589 *Arte of English Poesie,* which I have attributed to de Vere. It shows the deep interest in rhetoric in general, and *inventio* in particular, that is also reflected in the works of Shake-speare. I devote special emphasis to the parallel fascination in the 1570 translation with the figure of hendiadys—"one through two"—that also characterizes the works of Shake-speare. The study of de Vere's previously unattributed early literary work deepens our understanding of his development as the world's greatest writer.

Endnotes

[1] I am grateful to Colin Burrow for his helpful suggestions for this article.

[2] See Susan Doran, *Elizabeth I and Her Circle*, Oxford: Oxford University Press, 2015, 179.

[3] *Shakespeare and Classical Antiquity*. Oxford: Oxford University Press, 2013.

[4] Colin Burrow, Chap. 27, Shakespeare. In Patrick Cheney and Philip Hardie (eds.), *The Oxford History of Classical Reception in English Literature*. Vol. 2 (1558-1660). Donna B. Hamilton, *Virgil and the Tempest: Politics of Imitation*, (Columbus, OH: Ohio State University Press) also discusses Sturm in connection with Shakespeare (11-18).

[5] Lewis W. Spitz and Barbara Sher Tinsley, *Johann Sturm on Education*. St. Louis: Concordia, 1995.

p. 374 note 64.

[6] Cf. Robin Fox, *Shakespeare's Education: Schools, Lawsuits, Theater and the Tudor Miracle*. Bucholz, Germany: Laugwitz Verlag, 2012.

[7] In their valuable edition of Sturm, Spitz and Tinsley refer to the translator merely as "T.B.," and do not speculate as to his identity. They call his translation "charming" (133), and they quote several lines of it.

[8] For extensive explanations for this attribution, please see Richard M. Waugaman, "*The Arte of English Poesie:* The Case for Edward de Vere's Authorship." *Brief Chronicles: The Interdisciplinary Journal of the Shakespeare Fellowship* 2:121-141 (2010); and Response to letter from Mike Hyde, *Brief Chronicles: The Interdisciplinary Journal of the Shakespeare Fellowship* 2:260-266 (2010).

[9] Oxford: Oxford University Press, 2014.

[10] *The Oxfordian* 18:175-182 (2016).

[11] See Robert Sean Brazil, *Angel Day: The English Secretary and Edward de Vere, Seventeenth Earl of Oxford*. Seattle, WA: Cortical Output, 2013.

[12] In his English translation of Johann Sturm's *A Ritch Storehouse*.

[13] Edited by Frank Whigham and Wayne A. Rebhorn. Ithaca: Cornell University Press, 2007.

[14] Early English Books Online.

[15] G.W. Pigman, "Versions of Imitation in the Renaissance." *Renaissance Quarterly* 33:1-32, 1980. I am grateful to Colin Burrow for bringing Pigman's article to my attention.

[16] Nelson calls this particular spelling "wildly egregious" (65). (Tut, tut, Shakespeare!)

[17] "Apploy'd" was used once, in 1643.

[18] "Howre" is found twice in de Vere's letters.

[19] The ever helpful Nelson writes that "Many [spelling] variants [in de Vere's letters] result from the substitution of 'w' for 'u' (64)." E.g., cowld, showld, and wowld.

[20] Sometimes, in a long series, such as "Between *two* hawks, which flies the higher pitch;/ Between *two* dogs, which hath the deeper mouth;? Between *two* blades, which bears the better temper;/ Between *two* horses, which doth bear him best;/ Between *two* girls, which hath the merriest eye" (*1 Henry VI*, II.iv.11-15).

[21] De Vere did not consider one to be a number.

[22] Ancient Hebrew also has the dual number. For example, the dual form of the verb, rather than the plural, is used when speaking of a person's two legs (Rabbi Joshua Habermann, personal communication, July 2, 2016).

[23] I am grateful to Elisabeth P. Waugaman for this observation.

[24] Cf. de Vere coining the word "turquify" as meaning "transform," as described above.

[25] See "Hendiadys and *Hamlet*." PMLA 96(2):168-193, 1981. I am most grateful to Colin Burrow for directing me to this classic article, and for his suggestions on the work of Sturm.

[26] In a future work, I will show abundant and original examples of hendiadys in the translation of the first four books of Ovid's *Metamorphoses* in 1565, and I will show why I believe de Vere was the translator.

[27] The second of 34 instances of this word pair in EEBO.

[28] The third of 275 instances in EEBO.

[29] Cf. "good and virtuous" in *Macbeth* IV.iii.23; "good and loyal" in the same play, IV.iii.97; "good and gracious" in *Timon* I.i.68; "good and galant" in *Tempest* V.i.269.

[30] The first of 22 uses, but "tedious *and* troublesome" was a commonplace. Still, an instance of de Vere fashioning something new out of old material.

[31] Cf. "rude and shallow" in *Henry V* I.i.57; "rude and wildly" in *Comedy of Errors* V.i.90; "rude and merciless" in *2 Henry VI* IV.iv.33; "rude and savage" in *LLL* IV.iii.233; and "rude and bold" in *MV* II.ii.174.

[32] Later, he writes "barren and void," the third of 27 uses in EEBO.

[33] Unique in EEBO. There are no instances of the related "barren and dishonest."

Shakespeare coined more than 300 words beginning "un-." Cf. "barren and bereft" in *Richard II* III.iii.86.

[34] First of 18 uses in EEBO.

[35] First of three uses in EEBO.

[36] Third of 145 uses in EEBO. Cf. "due and just" in *Pericles* V.iii.98; "due and wary" in *MM* IV.i.37; "due and forfeit" in *MV* IV.i.38.

[37] Cf. "use and counsel" in Shakespeare's *1 Henry IV* I.iii.20; "use and liberty" in *MM* I.iv.66; "use and wearing" in *Timon* V.i.157; and "use and fair advantage" in *TGV* II.iv.63. Likewise, "art and practise" in *MM* I.i.12; "device and practise" in *HVIII* I.i.238; "baits and practise" in *Coriolanus* IV.i.35.

[38] Cf. "dern [concealed, solitary] and painful" in *Pericles* III, Prologue, 15.

[39] It is possible that some of the works dedicated to de Vere were actually written by him—another use of an allonym.

[40] Cf. "slavish weeds and servile thoughts" in *Titus*, II.i.18.

[41] Cf. "manners and beauty" in *Othello* II.i.249; cf. "state and inclination" in *RII*, III.ii.195.

[42] Cf. "learned and well-beloved" in *HVIII* II.iv.256; "learned and valiant" in *TN* I.v.241; cf. "politic and safe" in *King Lear* I.iv.323.

[43] Cf. "noble and natural" in *Cymbeline* III.v.160; "noble and renowned" in *MM* III.i.232-233; "noble and well-warranted" in *MM* V.i.277; "noble and true-hearted" in *King Lear* I.ii.121; "noble and approved" in *Othello* I.iii.87; "noble and chaste" in *I Henry IV* I.ii.28. In each case, another favorable adjective highlights and intensifies the positive connotation of "noble."

[44] Cf. "name and fame" in *2 Henry IV* II.iv.70; "name and quality" in IV.i.90 of the same play; "name and birth" in *Cymbeline* I.i.32; "name and power" in *2 Henry VI* I.iv.26; "name and credit" in *Shrew* IV.ii.112; "name and estimation" in *I Henry IV* V.i.99. As with "noble," "name" leads to positive associations for de Vere.

[45] Cf. "manner and form" in *LLL* I.i.201, 204; "degree and form" in *Henry V* IV.i.242; "shapes and forms" in *T&C* V.iii.13.

[46] Cf. "judgment and reason" in *TN* III.ii.12.

[47] Cf. "wisely and truly" in *JC* III.iii.15-16.

[48] Cf. "old and foolish" in *Lear* IV.vii.97; "gross and foolish" in *WT* III.ii.214; "foul and foolish" in *Othello* I.i.154 and 155 (i.e., repeated in these two lines, not enjambed).

[49] Cf. "voice and utterance" in *JC* III.i.281.

[50] Cf. "Nature and Fortune" in *KJ* III.i.52

[51] Note that three of these pairs including the word *writing*.

[52] Cf. the nearly identical hendiadys "virtue and obedience" in *Shrew* V.ii.130, and also in *King Lear* II.i.122. Cf. also "virtue and nobility" in *Titus* I.i.93;

[53] Cf. "gravity and learning" in *Henry VIII* III.i.82 and in *MWW* III.i.51; "gravity and patience" in the latter play, III.i.48; "gravity and stillness" in *Othello* II.iii.190.

[54] "'A New 1569 Poem by Arthur Golding,' Re-attributed to Edward de Vere." *Shakespeare Oxford Society Newsletter* 49(1):9-10 (2013).

Engaging Academia:
Some Thoughts

James A. Warren

Literary scholars will eventually conclude that Edward de Vere, Earl of Oxford, wrote the literary works traditionally attributed to William Shakespeare. Once that happens, they will bring academia's tremendous resources to bear on exploring and documenting not only de Vere's authorship of Shakespeare's works, but also the broader issue of authorship in the Elizabethan era. Oxfordians can take steps to help make that day arrive sooner rather than later.

Oxfordians will be most effective in engaging Stratfordians on behalf of de Vere's authorship of Shakespeare's works if they identify the distinct activities involved in that effort and combine them into a formal game plan. Such a plan might include the following five steps:

- **Defining Goals:** What specifically do Oxfordians want to accomplish through their engagement with orthodox scholars or freelance Stratfordians?

- **Identifying Interlocutors:** Who specifically should Oxfordians interact with to reach their goals? Which segments of those they engage are most important for each goal?

- **Determining Interlocutors' Actions:** What specific actions do Oxfordians want their interlocutors to undertake?

- **Selecting Methods:** What are the most effective ways for Oxfordians to reach and engage each segment of their target audience?

- **Drafting Messages:** What should Oxfordians say to convince their interlocutors to take the actions they want them to take?

When carrying out these activities, Oxfordians might benefit by keeping in mind James Q. Wilson's distinction between inputs, outputs, and outcomes.[1] Inputs are resources such as dollars and staff time invested in carrying out the game plan. Outputs are what is done with those resources: the number of speeches given, editorials placed in newspapers, comments posted on blogs and so on. Outputs are often regarded as accomplishments in themselves, but they are not what is most important. Rather, Oxfordians should focus on outcomes, on what has changed as a result of their actions. Outcomes are such things as the number of people who have changed their views about the legitimacy of the Shakespeare authorship question (SAQ) or who have accepted Edward de Vere's authorship.

In designing their game plan, Oxfordians could also benefit from thinking like entrepreneurs rather than following traditional budgeting procedures. In most organizations, staffs consider the most effective ways to use available funds to reach their organization's goals. Entrepreneurial thinking, however, requires a different process, one with funding levels determined at the end rather than the beginning of the process. Guided by entrepreneurial thinking, Oxfordians should first identify their goals, then determine which activities are necessary to reach them, calculate what those activities would cost, and finally go out and get the money needed to fund them. Fundraising would thus be critical to the success of the game plan.

Oxfordians should always remember that their aim is not to do the best they can with the funds available. It's not to make a good effort or to be able to say that they tried hard, but rather to achieve widespread acceptance of de Vere's authorship. Success, not the effort or resources put into the activities that comprise the game plan, is what matters. But Oxfordians should not be satisfied with merely changing Stratfordians' personal beliefs. That is only half the battle. The other half—the critical half addressed in this paper—is that of persuading literary scholars to act on the basis of their belief in Oxford's authorship even in the face of institutional and peer pressure against doing so.

The Ultimate Goal

Of course the ultimate goal of the Oxfordian movement is full acceptance by academia—and everybody else—of Edward de Vere's authorship of Shakespeare's works. However, as professor William Leahy of Brunel University concludes, "the conversion of academics [to acceptance of de Vere's authorship] is not going to happen in current circumstances" (Leahy 7).

Given that reality, it will be necessary for Oxfordians to identify and pursue certain subgoals in order to create circumstances more conducive to consideration of de Vere's authorship. The nature of the most important subgoals will become clear as key interlocutors are identified, so it is to that task that we now turn.

Identifying Key Interlocutors

The key institutions that must be engaged are university literature departments and a few other independent organizations such as the Folger Shakespeare Library. These institutions should be Oxfordians' primary targets for engagement because they are the institutions that others turn to for guidance on the Shakespeare authorship question. If the scholarly community becomes convinced of de Vere's authorship, all others will follow as a matter of course.

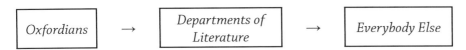

And yet, the academic community of literary scholars—academia, in short—will be the hardest nut to crack. It's the group least open to consideration of de Vere's authorship of Shakespeare's works.

"Everybody Else," generally speaking, is more open to considering the authorship question than are most professors of literature. A few examples should suffice to establish that openness outside of academia. PBS demonstrated its interest in the issue by broadcasting a documentary on the authorship question titled "The Shakespeare Mystery" on *Frontline* in April 1989, and interest in the subject by the broader media was shown by the editorials that appeared in more than a dozen newspapers across the United States and Canada the week of that broadcast. Those editorials were not the result of a campaign carried out by Oxfordians, but instead arose spontaneously because of interest in the subject.

Another sign of interest outside academia is Michael H. Hart's book *The 100: A Ranking of the Most Influential Persons in History: Revised and Updated for the Nineties*. After carefully examining the arguments on both sides of the question, Hart concluded that "the weight of the evidence is heavily against the Stratford man and in favor of de Vere." Hart accordingly changed Entry No. 31 from Shakespeare to de Vere is the second edition of the book in 1992.

Yet another example is that of James F. Broderick's and Darren W. Miller's book *Web of Conspiracy: A Guide to Conspiracy Theory Sites on the Internet*. Broderick explained that "What I discovered is that most [conspiracy theories] do not hold up under scrutiny. The more one digs, the shakier and less credible they become. The Authorship Question was different. The more I dug, the more credible it seemed, until I became fully convinced of its validity. What I had set out expecting to debunk turned out to be the most compelling, fact-based 'conspiracy' I had ever researched."

These examples all arose independently, without any encouragement from Oxfordian organizations. The openness to consideration of the authorship issue—and even of de Vere's authorship—by Everybody Else is a factor that Oxfordians could use in their efforts to engage academia. That being the case, perhaps the diagram shown above should be redrawn to show that Oxfordians could engage departments of literature directly as well as indirectly though the activities of

Everybody Else, as shown in the following diagram.

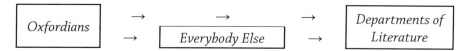

Everybody Else also includes academic departments other than departments of literature. History departments that examine the Elizabethan and Stuart eras could produce information supportive of de Vere's authorship. So too could psychology departments that study the nature of genius and creativity. Oxfordians, then, do not lack potential allies either inside or outside of academia in their engagement of literary scholars.

The departments of literature that form Oxfordians' key target audiences are not monolithic. Some scholars are more receptive than others to consideration of the authorship question. Literature professors' commitments to authorship by the man from Stratford ranges from those who strongly defend his authorship (let's call them Militant Stratfordians) to those who don't have strong feelings about the authorship issue but who go along with traditional beliefs (let's call them Ordinary Stratfordians) to those who secretly have doubts strong enough to consider the authorship question worthy of academic study (let's call them Secret Doubters). Literature professors could also be categorized by the stage they are at in their careers and categorized as Senior Professors, Rank and File Professors, or Assistant Professors. Combining these two ways of distinguishing between literary scholars results in the nine types shown in the following chart.

	Militant Stratfordians	*Ordinary Stratfordians*	*Secret Doubters*
Senior Professors	A	D	G
Rank and File Professors	B	E	H
Assistant professors	C	F	I

Militant Stratfordians (categories A, B, C) are a small minority of all academics. They should not be Oxfordians' primary target for engagement because they are fierce defenders of Shakspere's authorship and are hostile to any attempt even to discuss the authorship issue. William Leahy calls them "the militant minority," and notes that

> [Although they] are very well versed in the issues . . . [they] resist any talk of Shakespeare not being the author of all of the works attributed to him. Such academics are set in their ways, convinced of their case and can, for the most part, counter fact with fact and evidence with evidence. They are often

> very aggressive and dismissive in their views and seek not only to win the argument but to humiliate the opponent. (Leahy 7)

Most Stratfordians in academia (categories D, E, and F) either believe that the man from Stratford was the author and/or have not investigated the issue for themselves. Leahy describes this group as those academics

> who do not feel they need to take the time to research the authorship issue because they do not have to and do not have time to. This is, I feel, the majority. But, when prompted, they have their views....on the Authorship Question, founded in received opinions and questionable evidence....They are currently dismissive of the Question, but not necessarily for all time.
> (Leahy 7)

This is the group that must be won over to the Oxfordian paradigm if it is to become accepted by academia. In engaging this group, Oxfordians do not need to act alone. They have potential allies in the third group of academics, the Secret Doubters (categories G, H, I). Secret Doubters are Stratfordians in their public stance but who already have doubts that the man from Stratford wrote Shakespeare's works, and might even already believe that Edward de Vere was the real author. They have not made their beliefs known because of political pressure against doing so.

Secret Doubters are more numerous than they might appear. A *New York Times* survey in April 2007 showed that seventeen percent of literature professors see reason to doubt Shakspere's authorship (*New York Times*, 22 April 2007). That percentage might actually have been higher at the time, given the reluctance of Secret Doubters to make their views known, even anonymously; it could be much higher now, given the high profile public events such as the movie *Anonymous* that have taken place since.

Oxfordians face two related issues when it comes to Secret Doubters. The first is identifying who they are. Assistant Professors (categories C, F, I) are a good place to look for them. As is widely recognized, younger members of any community are more open to alterative views simply because they do not have as long or as extensive a history of support for a community's views as their more senior colleagues.

The second issue is that of motivating Secret Doubters to act on the basis of their true beliefs. If they could be persuaded to do so, they would form a third line in Oxfordians' effort to engage Non-Doubting Scholars, one well placed inside departments of literature. One line of engagement comes directly from Oxfordians. A second is through Everybody Else outside of literature departments. A third is through former Secret Doubters within departments of literature, as shown in the following diagram.

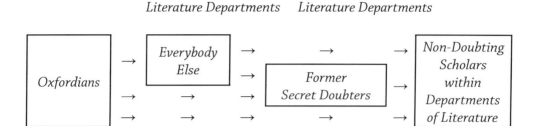

This analysis has revealed three tasks for Oxfordians:
- Engaging Non-Doubting Scholars directly;
- Encouraging Secret Doubters to publicly state their doubts and to begin engaging Non-Doubting Scholars;
- Engaging Everybody Else, who could in turn influence Secret Doubters and Non-Doubting Scholars.

Persuading Non-Doubting Academics to Examine the Authorship Issue

So far, our analysis has revealed (1) that Non-Doubting Scholars within departments of literature are the key group to be engaged, (2) that most of them are not yet ready to consider the idea of de Vere's authorship of Shakespeare's works, and (3) that it will be necessary for Oxfordians to aim at subgoals to make progress toward their ultimate goal of academia's acceptance of de Vere's authorship. With that in mind, we can now consider which specific subgoals would best create an environment in which scholars would be receptive to engagement on the idea of de Vere's authorship.

William Leahy concludes that recognition of the weakness of the Stratfordian claim is a precondition to academia's consideration of the wider question of who the real author might have been. As he explains,

> [F]or the positing of alternative authors to be academically acceptable, the field of knowledge in this area needs to change. . . . Only when . . . academia begins to accept that the case for Shakespeare of Stratford is weak, or at least weaker than they realized, will the field open up to other, wider possibilities. That, it seems to me, is what those involved in the Authorship Question need to do before anything else: alter the rules before starting to play a new game. (Leahy 81)

The Shakespeare Authorship Coalition reached a similar conclusion. As its Chairman and CEO John Shahan writes,

> The threshold question in the authorship controversy is whether
> there is room for doubt about the traditional author from Stratford.
> If not, then there is no authorship issue. . . . Answering this question
> is a necessary first step toward the ultimate goal of identifying and
> gaining recognition for the true author. (Shahan and Waugh i)

That is a reasonable conclusion. Gaining recognition of the weakness of the evidence in support of Shakspere's authorship is a necessary first step leading toward recognition of the authorship question as a legitimate subject for academic study and then on to the conclusion that de Vere wrote Shakespeare's works.

But what is meant by "a legitimate subject for academic study"? On this point we can turn for guidance to Stanley Fish, Dean Emeritus at the College of Liberal Arts and Sciences, University of Illinois, Chicago. Academic study, he explains, is the study of subjects in a disinterested manner rather than the promotion of any specific conclusions from that study. In academic study, Fish writes, subjects

> should be discussed in academic terms; that is, they should be the objects of analysis, comparison, historical placement, etc.; the arguments put forward in relation to them should be dissected and assessed *as* arguments and not as preliminaries to action on the part of those doing the assessing. The action one takes (or should take) at the conclusion of an academic discussion is the action of tendering an *academic* verdict as in "that argument makes sense," "there's a hole in the reasoning here," "the author does (or does not) realize her intention," "in this debate, X has the better of Y," "the case is still not proven." These and similar judgments are judgments on craftsmanship and coherence—they respond to questions like "is it well made?" and "does it hang together?" (Fish 25-26)

Because academic study involves examining evidence rather than reaching predetermined conclusions, Oxfordians should perhaps push only for the goal of academic study of the authorship question. To go beyond that point—to push academia to accept de Vere's authorship—would be just as inappropriate as pushing for any other nonacademic goal.

A case could be made that pushing academia to accept de Vere's authorship would not only be inappropriate but also unnecessary. Paradoxically, Oxfordians do not need to aim at conversion of literary scholars to belief in de Vere's authorship for them to be converted to it. They will convert themselves if the conditions are right. Oxfordians need only aim to create the right conditions.

The key condition is recognition within academia that the Shakespeare authorship question is a legitimate one for academic study. Because de Vere was the author of the works attributed to Shakespeare, any serious objective examination of the authorship question by intelligent people who care about the subject will eventually result in acceptance of his authorship. Therefore, if Oxfordians could just get the question established for consideration on a level playing field, they will win. Getting the more general authorship subject inside the gates of academia would be the Trojan Horse that would eventually result in academia's acceptance of de Vere's authorship.

The goal of academic study of the authorship question, therefore, is not just a stepping stone to the ultimate goal, but the single most important step of all. The three-step process just identified is shown in the following diagram.

Subgoal 1: →	**Subgoal 2:** →	**Ultimate goal**
Academia recognizes the weakness of the Stratfordian claim	Academia accepts legitimacy of the SAQ	Academia accepts de Vere as author of Shakespeare's works

But the situation is not as simple as that. Another factor remains to be considered within this scenario—the existence within the field of literary studies of a methodology unfavorable to examination of the authorship question. The reigning methodology considers the study of literature to be a subfield within Cultural Studies, where works of literature are examined as mere data to be mined for information about the society in which their authors lived and wrote. In this methodology, what the author unintentionally or unconsciously embedded in his works is at least as important as what he consciously and intentionally included. The result is a focusing of attention away from the author, a development with obvious negative implications for examination of the relationship between an author and his works. This "death of the author" mentality denies the validity of the strongest evidence challenging authorship by the man from Stratford—the lack of correspondences between his life and works—and denies the value of the strongest evidence in support of de Vere's authorship—the scores of linkages between events and people important in his life and events and characters in Shakespeare's plays and poems.[2]

Changing the methodology that prevails within literary studies to one more conducive to the study of literature as works of art important in themselves and as works written by specific individuals for specific reasons is beyond the scope of this paper. It is, however, a goal bound up so tightly with the authorship question that it might not be possible to make much progress in either area without also making progress in both. The so-called "death of the author" mentality must be replaced by the "resurrection of the author" if the authorship issue is to find a home in academia.

We have thus identified four goals: the ultimate goal of full acceptance of de Vere's authorship, and three supporting goals that would make attaining the ultimate goal more likely, as shown in the following diagram.

Subgoal 2a:
Academia accepts the legitimacy of the SAQ

Subgoal 1:
Academia recognizes the weakness of the

↕

Ultimate goal
Academia accepts de Vere's authorship of Shakespeare's works

Subgoal 2b:
Academia adopts a methodology more appropriate for the study of literature

Persuading Secret Doubters to Become Public Doubters

Oxfordians face a different challenge when it comes to engagement with Secret Doubters. Whereas Non-Doubting Scholars have to be convinced to examine the weakness of the Stratfordian case, Secret Doubters only need be persuaded to act on the basis of beliefs they already hold in the face of institutional and peer pressure not to do so.

Few actions Oxfordians could take could have benefits as far reaching as persuading Secret Doubters to become Public Doubters. Once out of the closet, so to speak, they could alert their students to the importance of the authorship issue, and perhaps even organize courses specifically on that topic. They could engage their colleagues on the issue, and perhaps even organize conferences focused on it. And because they are already in academia, they would be well placed to push academic publications to accept papers on the issue.

But there are no free lunches. They are Secret Doubters for a reason, and the difficulty of convincing them to go public with their doubts should not be underestimated. The pressure on them to keep their doubts to themselves is intense and unrelenting. As Charlton Ogburn, Jr., recognized,

> There would seem . . . to be no mystery in the maintenance of academic uniformity. No young instructor in a Department of English, even if his early educational conditioning does not preclude his examining objectively that which he has been taught to scoff at as the badge of his professionalism, will find his career advanced if he threatens to expose the tenets of his elders as nonsense. . . . Once he has his professorship he is hardly likely to repudiate the steps by which he attained it and certainly he is not going to read himself

> out of his profession and bring down on his head the obloquy of his fellows, vicious as we have seen such can be. (Ogburn 162)

More recently, Roger Stritmatter also described the pressures that exist within academia for adherence to the "party line,"

> There is, of course, a price to be paid [for admission into academia].... the initiate must solemnly promise not only to forgo dalliance in the field of unauthorized ideas, but to zealously defend, as a matter of honor and sanity, the jurisdiction of the paradigm into which he has been initiated. A reluctance to do so marks him, at best, as an outsider or a misfit: unqualified for employment, tenure, or professional respect.   (Stritmatter 38)

So this is the nut that Oxfordians face: professors are not free to conduct unbiased academic investigations into the Shakespeare authorship question even if they want to. Secret Doubters find themselves pushed in one direction and pulled in another—pushed by Militant Stratfordians to hide or renounce their doubts on one hand, and pulled by their desire to investigate the authorship question on the other. The problem is that the pressure from Militant Stratfordians far outweighs their desire to engage in academic investigation of the authorship question.

If Secret Doubters do not feel free to act on the basis of their beliefs because of pressure from one side, then perhaps one strategy for Oxfordians is to bring pressure from the opposite direction. Once the pressure from the two sides is equal in intensity, Secret Doubters will be able to act on a level playing field. They would then be free to express their beliefs and to pursue unbiased academic study of the issue.

In seeking to pressure Secret Doubters, Oxfordians face two issues even after Doubters have been identified: identifying a source of pressure that could be brought to bear on them, and understanding the process through which that pressure could be applied. Let's consider the process first.

A model comes from the field of diplomacy—not the feel-good diplomacy associated with photos of smiling diplomats shaking hands, but the tough diplomacy Teddy Roosevelt had in mind when he talked of speaking softly and carrying a big stick. The key to this type of diplomacy is (1) explaining the reality of the situation to those with whom we are engaged but who do not yet realize the nature of that reality, (2) highlighting the harm they will suffer if they do not act in accordance with it and the benefits that will flow to them if they do, and (3) getting out of the way so that they can make their own decision about what to do based on their new understanding of the situation.

An example of how this might work comes from none other than Edward de Vere, speaking through the voice of Henry V. Henry, we can recall from the play, faced a situation similar to that faced by Oxfordians today. He wanted the leaders of the town of Harfleur to open the town's gates so that his army could enter, just as Oxfordians want literature departments to open their curricula and publications to discussion of the authorship question.

How did Henry proceed? By the set of actions just outlined. After the town leaders rebuffed his request, Henry explained to them aspects of the reality of the situation they had not fully realized. He then highlighted the benefits of acting in accordance with those realities and the harm the town would suffer if it didn't. And then he sat back to wait for the town leaders to discuss the situation among themselves. In the end, they decided to open the gates.

The reality, Henry had explained, is that the English are implacable. One way or another we are coming in, he said. It's up to you to decide whether to let us in peacefully or have the town destroyed as we force our way in. Henry did not just convey that reality in pleasant terms, but used vivid and forceful language to drive home to them the harm that the town would suffer if his army had to force its way in.

Here is how he phrased that reality in *Henry V*:

> . . . the fleshed soldier, rough and hard of heart,
> In liberty of bloody hand shall range
> With conscience wide as hell, mowing like grass
>
> Your fresh fair virgins and your flow'ring infants. . . .
> What is't to me, when you yourselves are cause,
> If your pure maidens fall into the hand
> Of hot and forcing violation?
> What rein can hold licentious wickedness
> When down the hill he holds his fierce career?
> We may as bootless spend our vain command
> Upon th' enragèd soldiers in their spoil
> As send precepts to the leviathan
>
> To come ashore.
>   Therefore, you men of Harfleur,
> Take pity of your town and of your people
> Whiles yet my soldiers are in my command,
> Whiles yet the cool and temperate wind of grace
> O'erblows the filthy and contagious clouds
>
> Of heady murder, spoil, and villainy.
> . . .
> What say you? Will you yield, and this avoid?
> Or, guilty in defense, be thus destroyed?
>   (*Henry V*, 3.3.11-43)

In modern English, Henry was saying that the reality is that the English are coming into your town. We can do this the easy way or the hard way. The easy way is for you to open the gates. If not, I will be forced to unleash my soldiers, and we all know what soldiers have traditionally been like during and just after the heat of battle. They will be out of my control, just as they will be out of yours. They will take the spoils of war, and we all know what that means. As Henry plainly said, what is it to me if your pure maidens are violated and your flow'ring infants cut down, when you yourselves are the cause because you did not open the gates.

Of course, Oxfordians are not going to sack departments of literature if they don't open their curricula and publications to discussion of the authorship question. So, what form of pressure can Oxfordians bring to bear on Secret Doubters to convince them to come out of the closet? What reality of the situation have Doubters overlooked?

The pressure that Oxfordians can bring comes from the reality of the groundswell of public interest in the authorship question. Oxfordians must demonstrate that the groundswell of interest has been building for decades outside of academia, and that it now forms a drumbeat of interest that academia ignores at its peril. The following talking points might bring that reality home to them:

- The reality is that many major media publications have recognized the legitimacy and importance of the authorship question, including *The Atlantic*, *Harper's*, *The Smithsonian*, *The Wall Street Journal*, *The New York Times*, and *The Washington Post*.

- The reality is that a December 2014 *Newsweek* article favorable to de Vere's authorship sparked more than 1,700 comments on its blog in less than one month.

- The reality is that five U.S. Supreme Court Justices have expressed doubts about Shakspere's authorship and that three law journals have organized symposia on the authorship question and devoted entire issues to it.

- The reality is that many of the greatest literary minds in American and English letters in the past 150 years have doubted Shakspere's authorship, including Walt Whitman, Mark Twain, Henry James, and Anne Rice.

- The reality is that many of the greatest actors of the past hundred years have doubted Shakspere's authorship, including Leslie Howard, Charlie Chaplin, Orson Welles, Sir John Gielgud, Michael York, Sir Derek Jacobi, Jeremy Irons and Mark Rylance.

- The reality is that scores of diplomats, politicians and other public figures have publicly doubted his authorship, including Frederick Nietzsche, Sigmund Freud, Clifton Fadiman, Mortimer J. Adler and David McCullough. The same is true for Paul Nitze, Benjamin Disraeli, Otto von Bismarck, Charles de Gaulle, Helen Keller, Malcolm X and Clare Boothe Luce.

- The reality is that academia has already lost the issue. As Professor Alan Nelson concluded in 1999, "Establishment Shakespeareans . . . are losing the public debate over the 'authorship question'" (Paster).

Then, having established the reality of the groundswell of interest in the subject outside of academia to those who had not been aware of it, Oxfordians must highlight the benefits that will accrue to Secret Doubters and their departments by acting in accordance with that reality and the harm they will suffer if they don't. Oxfordians should seek to increase Doubters' anxiety by making their remarks up front and personal because psychologists tell us that losses are 2½ times as painful as gains are pleasurable. The following are a few talking points that incorporate those factors.

- Recognition of de Vere's authorship is coming. Why not join the vanguard now and be recognized as a leader?

- If you don't—if you abdicate your responsibility to examine an important literary question in an academic manner—how will you explain your failure to those outside academia? How will you respond to charges that academia tried to block progress on this important issue?

- Once Edward de Vere is recognized as Shakespeare, others outside academia—the media, for instance—will be given the credit that rightly should have gone to departments of literature. How will you handle the shame of your own department's failure to investigate such an important issue?

- Don't you have even normal human curiosity about why so many prominent and accomplished people today and over the past century have doubts about Will? Why have you, a professional in this field, not investigated to see why so many people consider the authorship question to be one of such interest and importance?

- Stratfordians routinely make statements that they know to be false, such as claiming that several plays had been written after Edward de Vere's death in 1604, while knowing full well that nobody knows for sure when any of the plays were written. Only their publication dates are known. Why do you continue to belong to a group that honors those engaging in such shoddy practices?

- Well-known Stratfordian Stanley Wells described those who doubt Shakspere's authorship as suffering from "a psychological aberration" attributable to "snobbery . . . ignorance; poor sense of logic; refusal . . . to accept evidence; folly, the desire for publicity; and even . . . certifiable madness."[3] Do you think such comments accurately describe five Supreme Court justices? If not, why do you remain part of a group that honors men who make such comments?

Enter Thomas Kuhn, Paradigm Shifts, and Moments of Crisis

The strategy for engagement with academia outlined so far sounds reasonable.

And yet, Thomas Kuhn, in *The Structure of Scientific Revolutions*, brings information to the table indicating that such a strategy is unlikely to succeed. The reason, he explains, is that scientific communities *never* move from one paradigm to another simply because of weaknesses in the original paradigm. As he writes, "No process yet disclosed by the historical study of scientific development at all resembles the methodological stereotype of falsification by direct comparison with nature" (Kuhn, 77).

Rather, Kuhn concludes, intellectual communities move from one paradigm to another *only* when a point of crisis is reached, and that point of crisis is *always* generated by the introduction of a new paradigm that explains anomalies that the old paradigm couldn't. "Once it has achieved the status of paradigm, a scientific theory is declared invalid only if an alternate candidate is available to take its place" (Kuhn 77). As he explains further,

> The act of judgment that leads scientists to reject a previously accepted theory is always based upon more than a comparison of that theory with the world. The decision to reject one paradigm is always simultaneously the decision to accept another, and the judgment leading to that decision involves the comparison of both paradigms with nature and with each other.
>
> (Kuhn 78)

If Kuhn is correct and if his findings can legitimately be applied to the change in paradigms that Oxfordians want to see take place within departments of literature, then academia will not abandon the dominant Stratfordian paradigm merely because the evidence in support of it appears to be weak. The paradigm shift will take place only when Stratfordians are confronted by the Oxfordian paradigm and recognize that it can explain anomalies that the Stratfordian paradigm cannot. It will come only when Stratfordians are forced into an examination of the Oxfordian paradigm.

In Kuhn's model, scientific communities usually operate within an existing set of beliefs and practices that he calls a paradigm, a set of "universally recognized scientific achievements that for a time provide model problems and solutions to a community of practitioners" (Kuhn, xliii). Once established, paradigms "define the legitimate problems and methods of a research field for succeeding generations of practitioners" (Kuhn 10). Paradigms are effective in defining a community's activities because they combine two essential characteristics. "Their achievement was sufficiently unprecedented to attract an enduring group of adherents away from competing modes of scientific activity," and they are "[s]imultaneously . . . sufficiently open-ended to leave all sorts of problems for the redefined group of practitioners to resolve" (Kuhn 10-11).

"Normal science" is the term Kuhn uses to describe the work of solving those problems, which he calls puzzles. In this phase, individual scientists are challenged by "the conviction that, if only he is skillful enough, he will succeed in solving a puzzle that no one before has solved or solved so well" (Kuhn 38). In this phase, "Failure to achieve a solution discredits only the scientist and not the theory" (Kuhn 80).

But sometimes, Kuhn explains, problems or puzzles arise that resist solution. These can be set aside for a time while other problems are dealt with, but eventually further attempts must be made to solve them. If the problems continue to resist explanation even after becoming the focus of much attention within the community, they come to be regarded as anomalies, which begin to discredit not the scientist but the paradigm itself.

Scientists will resist recognizing that a puzzle has become an anomaly because anomalies are unsettling. They are a sign "that an existing paradigm has ceased to function adequately in the exploration of an aspect of nature to which that paradigm itself had previously led the way" (Kuhn, 92-93). Because such a realization would be disruptive of the community's work, defenders "will devise numerous articulations and *ad hoc* modifications of their theory in order to eliminate any apparent conflict" (Kuhn, 78).

Eventually, if the anomalies are severe enough, they result is a growing-sense-of-crisis phase that is greatly disconcerting to its members because the community itself is defined by its commitment to the existing paradigm. If that paradigm falls, the community falls with it. It is for that reason that the growing-sense-of-crisis phase can last indefinitely; it explains why members won't abandon the paradigm even as evidence in support of it weakens. The moment of crisis won't come unless and until a new paradigm that explains the anomalies is introduced—and is not just introduced, but is practically forced on the community by those few who see its value in explaining the anomalies.

Applying this model to Shakespeare studies within academia, the Stratfordians' paradigm is obviously that of authorship by William Shakspere of Stratford-upon-Avon. Their "normal science" is seeking to understand Shakespeare's works better through study of Elizabethan and Jacobean societies and through the study of the nature of poetry and drama. Seeking to understand the works better by drawing connections between the works and the author doesn't have much place in their scholarly activities because of the "death of the author" mentality and because of the paucity of connections that can be drawn between the works and the man they believe is the author.

Many Stratfordians are now in the growing-sense-of-crisis phase as a result of anomalies they cannot explain. The two most important of them are (1) the growing recognition of the disconnect between the dearth of information about Shakspere's education and literary experiences and the wealth of information about his business activities on one hand, and the qualities and bodies of knowledge and variety of experiences reflected in the literary works on the other; and (2) the frequency of references in the works to events in Elizabeth's court and government that occurred fifteen years earlier than when they believe the plays to have been written. By refusing to focus too closely on these issues, Stratfordians enable themselves to continue to believe that the Stratfordian paradigm, though perhaps frayed here and there, is fundamentally sound.

We should expect Stratfordians to seek to avoid acknowledgement of the seriousness of the Oxfordian paradigm for as long as possible. As uncomfortable as the growing-sense-of-crisis phase might be, the moment of crisis would be even more disruptive. We should expect them to try to muddle through by ignoring the anomalies or providing *ad hoc* explanations for them, and by ignoring the groundswell of interest in the authorship question outside of academia.

The task for Oxfordians is clear: they must continually highlight the weakness of the evidence supporting Shakspere's authorship so that problems are seen for what they are: not mere puzzles that have not yet been worked out, but anomalies so severe that the inability to explain them challenges the entire Stratfordian paradigm.

But if Kuhn's model is correct, Oxfordians must do two additional things.

First, Oxfordians must ratchet up the emotional pressure on Stratfordians. Oxfordians must do all they can to increase Stratfordians' nagging feeling that something is not right. Intellectual recognition that serious anomalies exist may be accompanied by uncomfortable emotion. Second, Oxfordians cannot let the growing-sense-of-crisis state continue indefinitely. They can and should take the additional step of bringing things to a head by forcefully pushing for more openness towards the Oxfordian paradigm. It is up to them to bring the situation to a boil because they are the ones who want to see this change happen.

Oxfordians should not push for a move to the halfway point of objective consideration of the authorship question, because doing so would not generate the crisis needed to move Stratfordians to the new paradigm. Literary scholars themselves would not be able to stop at the point of a neutral academic consideration of the authorship question. The emotional energy—the vexation—that has been bottling up inside them will not allow them to stop with a neutral "I don't know, let's examine this further" attitude. The emotional pressure will continue to back up until the shock of the realization of the existence of a new paradigm that explains the vexing anomalies pushes them into the paradigm shift. The new paradigm will be fiercely resisted until the moment when it is accepted. There can be no middle ground.

Even apart from paradigm shifts in the scientific world, it is unusual to find people who are satisfied with "I don't know" as an answer to life's major questions. In the religious aspects of life, there are very few agnostics. Even those who have doubts about some aspects of their religion remain nominal members of their church, synagogue or mosque. It is even rarer to find an institution or intellectual community that would make "I don't know" its guiding idea. Intellectual communities are united by their guiding belief and shared activity in accordance with it. In short, by a paradigm. Take away the paradigm and the unity of the group ceases to exist. So, it is all or nothing: The Shakspere paradigm or the Oxfordian paradigm. There is no legitimate stopping point between the two.

In a way, Oxfordians are fortunate that the authorship question is a winner-take-all situation. This is not a scenario similar to the shift from Sir Isaac Newton's physics to that of Albert Einstein's, in which Newton's laws are still valid in everyday conditions, where the velocities of bodies being examined are far below the speed of light. Rather, this situation is similar to the shift from the Ptolemaic earth-centric system to that of the Copernican heliocentric system. Both could not be right.

This stark situation may be unfortunate for the goal of academic study of the authorship question, but it is, almost paradoxically, fortunate for pushing the Oxfordian paradigm. If a clash between two theories is needed for a paradigm shift to occur, then it is perhaps beneficial that the two paradigms clash so completely. A direct conflict between two theories can generate far higher pressure than that of theories less directly opposed to each other—and high pressure is what is needed here. The situation is similar to that of two continental plates being pushed against each other by forces deep within the earth. Sometimes the two plates can slide against each other and the movement of each is relatively easy. But sometimes they are stuck and cannot slide. In those cases, the pressure builds until the plates finally jerk free. The result is an earthquake in which their movement is far faster and more forceful than if they had simply slid by each other.

By positing the Stratfordian and Oxfordian paradigms in a head-to-head contest, we are witnessing two plates pushing directly against each other. The longer the pressure builds through the growing-sense-of-crisis phase, the greater the resulting force will be at the moment of crisis. It is the emotional energy of that crisis that Oxfordians must harness to move Stratfordians across the divide, safely into the Oxfordian paradigm.

Oxfordians, then, face a choice between two conflicting strategies. One seeks to demonstrate the weakness of the evidence in support of Shakspere's authorship and to engage academia on behalf of academic study of the authorship question only, because doing so is all that is necessary to bring about acceptance of de Vere's authorship. The second says to do the first, but also to go for the jugular, to push hard for Oxford's authorship because doing so is the only way to get Stratfordians across the abyss. The conflict between the two strategies is shown in the following diagram.

Strategy 1:
Push ONLY for academia's
acceptance of the legitimacy
of the Shakespeare authorship question

vs.

Strategy 2:
Push for academia's acceptance
of the legitimacy of the Shakespeare
authorship question AND for
acceptance of the Oxfordian paradigm

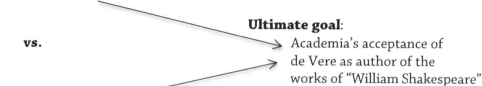

Ultimate goal:
Academia's acceptance of
de Vere as author of the
works of "William Shakespeare"

To increase the tension Stratfordians feel and to create the conditions in which the moment of crisis can be triggered, Oxfordians need clear and persuasive materials documenting just how weak the evidence in support of Shakspere's authorship is. To that end it is hard to imagine a publication more effective than the Shakespeare Authorship Coalition's book *Shakespeare Beyond Doubt? Exposing an Industry in Denial*. Oxfordians might consider organizing a fundraising effort geared toward the goal of getting a copy of that book into the hands of every Shakespearean scholar in the English speaking world.

Oxfordians can't stop there. They must also have clear and persuasive materials comparing the two theories to each other and to the "state of nature" that Kuhn talked about. Although consideration of such materials is beyond the scope of this paper, the Appendix contains an outline of types of information that could be used in preparing more detailed documents and talking points. Of particular importance is the summary in the Appendix showing that for the 105 pieces of evidence considered, Shakspere receives 103 "No's" (indicating absence of evidence in support of that piece of evidence) and de Vere receives 90 "Yeses" (indicating existence of such evidence).

Getting Stratfordians Across the Abyss

Oxfordians face one final task, that of guiding Stratfordians across the abyss separating the Stratfordian and Oxfordian paradigms. Having pushed Stratfordians for so long, the moment of crisis will be the time for Oxfordians to move from pushing to pulling, from vexing to soothing, from pointing out flaws in the old paradigm to describing the benefits of the new one for Stratfordians and their institutions.

To bring them across the abyss, Oxfordians should emphasize two points: (1) the psychic and emotional benefits of the move to the Oxfordian paradigm, and (2) the practical benefits of the move.

Oxfordians must show Stratfordians that accepting the new paradigm will provide relief from the emotional tension they have experienced throughout the increasing-sense-of-crisis phase and during the moment of crisis itself. They can do that, in part, by showing how the new paradigm solves the anomalies that have plagued Stratfordians and that led to their crisis.

Oxfordians must also reassure Stratfordians that they value Shakespeare's works as literary treasures just as Stratfordians do. They engage in the same effort to understand the works and how they came to be written, but with the understanding that they had been written by Edward de Vere. They must demonstrate that the Oxfordian community, strong and growing, would welcome Stratfordians with open arms, that they value their critical research skills and scholarly approach to Shakespeare studies, and that much of traditional Shakespearean research would remain valid within the new paradigm.

Oxfordians must also show Stratfordians that joining the Oxfordian camp would have professional advantages for them by creating significant new opportunities for research and publishing. They could highlight the intellectual challenge of opening up a new literary field for academic study, and ask Stratfordians if such challenges weren't the reason they entered academia in the first place.

Oxfordians could also make the point that the harm to Stratfordians' good names by making the shift would not be as severe as they might imagine. On the contrary, many of their colleagues already secretly have doubts about Shakspere's authorship—many more than they might imagine—and would admire their courage in taking a stand in favor of de Vere's authorship.

Finally, Oxfordians should show that they understand how difficult it is to jettison lifelong beliefs in Shakspere's authorship. After all, all Oxfordians were Stratfordians at one time. They can call Stratfordians' attention to Esther Singleton's moving article describing how difficult it was for her to accept de Vere's authorship—and how elated she felt at finding that obscure passages in the plays, reread with knowledge of de Vere's authorship and biography, had become "so clear, so plain, so reasonable, and so delightful" (Singleton 9-10).

Given all of these talking points, it might seem contradictory to say that Oxfordians cannot convince Stratfordians of the validity of de Vere's authorship; they must do that for themselves. And it might seem paradoxical to say that Stratfordians cannot convince themselves, either. Paradigm shifts do not occur within individual minds through logic or reasoning, but through insight—and insights cannot be commanded to occur. As Kuhn explains, "the issue of paradigm choice can never be unequivocally settled by logic and experiment alone . . . It cannot be made logically or even probabilistically compelling for those who refuse to step into the circle" (Kuhn, 94, 95). Rather, "because it is a transition between incommensurables, the transition between competing paradigms cannot be made a step at a time, forced by logic and neutral experience. Like the gestalt switch, it must occur all at once (though not necessarily in an instant) or not at all" (Kuhn 149).

Oxfordians' most important task, then, is that of creating the conditions in which Stratfordians can transform their own beliefs. They will become convinced of the validity of the Oxfordian paradigm (or not) at different rates, in response to different types of evidence. Some will never be convinced. That's okay. Oxfordians will have reached their goal if a predominant number of scholars accept his authorship.

As more in academia recognize de Vere's authorship, battles will break out within literature departments. Neither side will entirely understand how the other thinks. Stratfordians, of course, will not understand the new converts to the Oxfordian paradigm. What is surprising is that the new Oxfordians will not understand how any of their colleagues could fail to see what they now see.

Those who move to the new paradigm will have experienced a true revolution in how they see their own field. Even Shakespeare's literary works, as familiar as they are, will seem different. The shift is not merely that of replacing one author with another, but that of changing the central fact through which all other facts are interpreted. As Kuhn notes,

> The transition from a paradigm in crisis to a new one . . . is a reconstruction of the field from new fundamentals, a reconstruction that changes some of the field's most elementary theoretical generalizations as well as many of its paradigm methods and applications. . . . when the transition is complete, the profession will have changed its view of the field, its methods, and its goals.
>
> (Kuhn 85)

Once that happens—once academia shifts to the Oxfordian paradigm—we can expect to see a period of extraordinary discovery as academia's tremendous resources become focused on the authorship issue, just as astronomers discovered more than twenty new minor planets and asteroids in the fifty years after Herschel's modification of Copernicus's paradigm told them what to look for and where to look (Kuhn 116).

Resolution of the Two Conflicting Goals

It remains now only to try to reconcile Oxfordians' two conflicting strategies as much as possible. Pushing awareness of the weakness of the Stratfordian claim to authorship in a non-confrontational manner is certainly necessary to prepare the ground. But, as Kuhn's conclusions about the nature of paradigm shift seem to indicate, it won't be sufficient. It will also be necessary for Oxfordians to push hard for recognition of de Vere's authorship because paradigm shifts occur only when a crisis occurs, and crises are always triggered by the conflict between two rival paradigms.

Is there a way to reconcile these two conflicting approaches?

Yes, at least partially. Having pushed the new Oxfordian paradigm, Oxfordians do not need to see it enacted in academia to be sure of success. Having brought the issue to the crisis point by pressing for the Oxfordian paradigm,

Oxfordians should be satisfied if newly-minted Oxfordians within academia, mindful of the opinions of their colleagues, decide to adopt the face-saving step of introducing authorship studies rather than de Vere studies into their curricula. Acceptance of the legitimacy of the authorship question is all that needs to happen, even though that cannot be the goal that Oxfordians push for. They must push for both in order for the first to occur.

To conclude, much work must be done by Oxfordians to create the conditions conducive to bringing their Stratfordian colleagues across the abyss to the Oxfordian paradigm. Creating those conditions will require much advance preparation and careful thought. This paper has laid out some factors that Oxfordians should consider as they design their game plan for engagement with Stratfordians to secure rightful recognition of Edward de Vere as the man behind the pen name William Shakespeare.

APPENDIX: DOCUMENTING THE CLASH BETWEEN THE SHAKSPERE AND OXFORDIAN PARADIGMS

Applicable to William Shakspere?	Criteria	Applicable to Edward de Vere?
J. Thomas Looney's characteristics of the author[1]		
General Characteristics		
No	**A matured man of recognized genius**	Yes. Oxford was praised as best the best of the court poets and as being the best for comedy and tragedy.
No	**Apparently eccentric and mysterious**	Yes. Several contemporaries commented on his eccentricity.
No	**Of intense sensibility—a man apart**	Yes.
No	**Unconventional**	Yes. He was praised as "the most singular man" in England.
No	**Not adequately appreciated**	Yes. Puttenham raises this very point when identifying Oxford as the best of the court poets whose works are not widely known.
No	**Of pronounced and known literary tastes**	Yes. Oxford sponsored many literary publications; many works praised his literary sensibilities.
No	**An enthusiast in the world of drama**	Yes. Oxford was praised as being the best for comedy and tragedy.
No	**A lyric poet of recognized talent**	Yes. Many of his poems still exist.

No	Of superior education—classical—the habitual associate of educated people	Yes. See list of writers he knew below.
Special characteristics		
No	A man with feudal connections	Yes. He was the Earl of Oxford.
No	A member of the higher aristocracy	Yes. He was the Earl of Oxford.
No	Connected with Lancastrian supporters	Yes. His ancestors supported the Lancastrian cause.
No	An enthusiast for Italy	Yes. He stayed there for an extended visit and was regarded as the most "Italianate gentleman" of his generation.
No	A follower of sport (including falconry)	Yes. Falconry and other sports were common activities of men in Oxford's position.
No	A lover of music	Yes. He was praised as being a better performer than most professional musicians.
No	Loose and improvident in money matters	Yes. He sold or was forced to sell most of his estates.
?	Doubtful and somewhat conflicting in his attitude to women	Yes. See Oxford's poems.
Yes	Of probably Catholic leanings, but touched with skepticism	Yes.
Diana Price's list of a literary paper trail (modified)[2]		
No	Evidence of Education	Yes – Private tutors, Thomas Smith, Oxford University, Cambridge University.

No	**Record of correspondence, esp. concerning literary matters**	Yes, letters to and from the Cecils.
No	**Evidence of having written literary works**	Yes – many references to him as a poet and dramatist.
No	**Evidence of a direct relationship with a patron**	**
No	**Extant original manuscript**	No
No	**Handwritten inscriptions, receipts, letters, etc. touching on literary matters**	Yes, in the Geneva Bible, many handwritten letters.
No	**Commendatory verses, epistles, or epigrams received or contributed**	Yes. More than 30 works were dedicated to him; he wrote many such verses for others.
No	**Misc. records referred to personally as a writer**	Yes, many.
No	**Evidence of books owned, written, borrowed, or given**	Yes, many.
No	**Notice at death as a writer**	No overt references; many indirect references.
Ramon Jiménez's ten witnesses who would have known Shakspere but did not comment on any literary activities by him[3]		
No	**William Camden, historian**	**
No[4]	**Michael Drayton, poet and dramatist**	**
No	**Thomas Greene, Stratford Town Clerk and writer**	**
No	**John Hall, doctor and son-in-law**	**
No	**James Cooke, surgeon**	**
No	**Sir Fulke Greville, Lord Brooke, Recorder of Stratford; poet and dramatist**	**
No	**Edward Pudsey, avid theatergoer**	**

No	**Queen Henrietta Maria, amateur playwright who visited Stratford**	**
No	**Philip Henslowe, theatrical entrepreneur**	**
No	**Edward Allyn, most distinguished actor of Elizabethan era**	**
Katherine Chiljan's list of plays written too early for Shakspere, born in 1564, to have been the author[5]		
No	*Romeo and Juliet* (1562)	Yes
No	*The Taming of the Shrew* (1578)	Yes
No	*Measure for Measure* (1578)	Yes
No	*The Merchant of Venice* (1579)	Yes
No	*Timon of Athens* (1579)	Yes
No	*Antony and Cleopatra* (1579)	Yes
No	*King John* (1579)	Yes
No	*Twelfth Night* (1579)	Yes
No	*Much Ado About Nothing* (1579)	Yes
No	*Henry IV, Part 2* (1579)	Yes
No	*Cymbeline* (1583)	Yes
No	*Henry VI, Part 1* (1587)	Yes
No	*Richard III* (1587)	Yes
No	*Julius Caesar* (1587)	Yes
No	*The Merry Wives of Windsor* (1587)	Yes
No	*Troilus and Cressida* (1588)	Yes
No	*Richard II* (1588)	Yes
No	*King Lear* (1588)	Yes
No	*Richard III* (1588)	Yes
No	*Titus Andronicus* (1588)	Yes
No	*Hamlet* (1588)	Yes
Links to important people that appear in disguised form in the plays		

No	**Queen Elizabeth (many)**	Yes. De Vere was Lord Great Chamberlain in her court.
No	**Lord Burghley (Polonius)**	Yes. Burghley was his guardian and father-in-law.
No	**Robert Cecil (Richard III)**	Yes. Cecil was Oxford's brother-in-law.
No	**Earl of Southampton (Sonnets)**	Yes. Both were wards raised by Burghley and later were fellow members of court.
Links to other writers		
No	**George Baker**	Yes. Dedication to Oxford in *Practice of the New and Old Physic*, and in *Oleum Magistrale*.
No	**Thomas Bedingfield**	Yes. Dedication to Oxford in *Cardanus' Comfort*.
No	**John Brooke**	Yes. Dedication to Oxford in *The Staffe of Christian Faith*.
No	**Angel Day**	Yes. He served as Oxford's secretary. Dedication to Oxford in *The English Secretary*.
No	**Edmund Elviden**	Yes. Dedication to Oxford in *Peisistratus and Catanea*.
No	**John Farmer**	Yes. Dedication to Oxford in *Plainsong* and in *English Madrigals*.
No	**Arthur Golding**	Yes. Dedication to Oxford in *The Histories of Trogus Pompeius* and *The Psalms of David*.
?	**Robert Greene**	Yes. Dedication to Oxford in *Card of Fancy*.

No	**Gabriel Harvey**	Yes, went to school with Oxford.
No	**John Hester**	Yes. Dedication to Oxford in *Phioravanti's Discourse on Surgery*.
?	**Ben Jonson**	?
No	**Henry Lok**	Yes. Dedication to Oxford in *Ecclesiastes*.
No	**John Lyly**	Yes. Dedication to Oxford in *Euphues and His England*. Served as Oxford's secretary.
No	**Christopher Marlowe**	?
No	**Anthony Munday**	Yes. Dedication to Oxford in *The Mirror of Mutability*, and in *Palmerin d'Olivia, Parts I and II*, and in *Primaleon of Greece*.
No	**Thomas Nashe**	Yes. Dedication to Oxford in *Strange News*.
No	**Edmund Spenser**	Yes. Dedication to Oxford in *The Faerie Queene*.
No	**Thomas Stocker**	Yes. Dedication to Oxford in *Diverse Sermons of Calvin*.
No	**Thomas Twyne**	Yes. Dedication to Oxford in *The Breviary of Britain*.
No	**Thomas Underdowne**	Yes. Dedication to Oxford in *An Aethopian History*.
No	**Thomas Watson**	Yes. Dedication to Oxford in *Hekatompathia*.
	Substantive knowledge and experience	
No	**Education**	Yes. Private tutors and universities.

No	**Law**	Yes. Attended law school.
No	**Medicine**	Yes. Studied with Smith.
No	**Classical mythology**	Yes. William Golding, translator of Ovid's *Metamorphoses* was Oxford's uncle, and Oxford's tutor at the time the translation was done.
No	**Aristocratic sports**	Yes. Two-time champion at jousting.
No	**Science**	Yes. Smith.
No	**Philosophy**	Yes. Smith.
No	**Greek drama**	Yes. Smith.
No	**Heraldry**	Yes. His own.
No	**Military**	Yes. Campaigns in Scotland (1570), the Netherlands (1585), and against the Armada (1588).
No	**Fluency in several languages**	Yes. From tutors, travels, letter written in French.
No	**Travel to Italy**	Yes. Travels there in 1575-76, including all of the cities in which scenes were set in Italy in Shakespeare's plays.
No	**Shakspere at court**	**
	Works that most influenced Shakespeare	
No	**Ovid's *Metamorphoses***	Yes. It was translated by Oxford's uncle when Oxford was tutored by him.
No	***The Geneva Bible***	Yes. Oxford's annotated copy is in the Folger Library.
No	**Chaucer's *Canterbury Tales***	Yes.
No	**Plutarch's *Lives***	Yes.

	Psychologists' understanding of genius, creativity	
No	Development of genius through early exposure to many subjects	Yes: His father's acting troupe, tutoring by Thomas Smith, education at Burghley's house.
No	10,000 hours of intense involvement needed to acquire basic competence in any field	He was praised as the best for comedy and tragedy, and was known to have produced theatrical productions at court.
No	Highly connected with others creating in the same field	Yes. See above.
No	Authors write about what they know about.	Yes.
	Totals	
William Shakspere		**Edward de Vere**
Yes – 1 Maybe - 3 No – 101		Yes – 89 Maybe - 4 No – 1 N/A – 11

Endnotes

[1] John Thomas Looney, 1920. See especially pages 109-133.

[2] Diana Price, pages 310-313.

[3] Ramon Jiménez, pp. 74-85.

[4] Actually Drayton does refer posthumously to Shakespeare as his familiar in his 1627 *The Bataile of Agincourt,* p. 206. See Waugh and Stritmatter, forthcoming.

[5] Katherine Chiljan. See especially pages 343-381.

Works Cited

Broderick, James F. and Darren W. Miller. *Web of Conspiracy: A Guide to Conspiracy Theory Sites on the Internet.* Medford, NJ: Information Today (2011).

Chiljan, Katherine V. *Shakespeare Suppressed: The Uncensored Truth about Shakespeare and His Works.* San Francisco: Faire Editions (2011).

Fish, Stanley. *Save the World On Your Own Time.* New York: Oxford University Press (2008).

Gore-Langton, Robert. "The Campaign to Prove Shakespeare Didn't Exist," *Newsweek*, 29 December 2014, accessed at http://www.newsweek.com/2014/12/26/campaign-prove-shakespeare-didn't-exist-293243.htm

Hart, Michael H. *The 100: A Ranking of the Most Influential Persons in History, Revised and Updated for the Nineties.* New York: Citadel Press (1992).

Jiménez, Ramon. "Shakespeare in Stratford and London: Ten Eyewitnesses Who Saw Nothing," in *Report My Cause Aright: The Shakespeare Oxford Society Fiftieth Anniversary Anthology, 1957-2007.* The Shakespeare Oxford Society (2007). 74-85.

Kuhn, Thomas S. *The Structure of Scientific Revolutions, 50th Anniversary Edition*, with an Introductory Essay by Ian Hacking. Chicago: University of Chicago Press (2012).

Leahy, William. "'Two Households, Both Alike In Dignity:' the Authorship Question and Academia," in *The De Vere Society Newsletter* (February 2007), 4-11.

Looney, J. Thomas. *"Shakespeare" Identified.* London: Cecil Palmer (1920).

—. "The Earl of Oxford as 'Shakespeare: New Evidence." *The Golden Hind* 1.1 (October 1922), 23-30.

New York Times. "Did He or Didn't He? That Is The Question" [survey of professors of Shakespeare] April 22, 2007.

Ogburn, Charlton Jr. *The Mysterious William Shakespeare*. McLean, VA: EPM Publications, Inc. (1992).

Paster, Gail Kern. "From the Editor." *Shakespeare Quarterly* 50.3 (Fall 1999), iii-iv.

Price, Diana. *Shakespeare's Unorthodox Biography: New Evidence of an Authorship Problem*. First paperback edition. Shakespeare-authorship.com, (2012).

Shahan, John M. and Alexander Waugh, editors. *Shakespeare Beyond Doubt? Exposing an Industry in Denial*. Tamarac, FL: Llumina Press (2013).

Simonton, Dean Keith. *Origins of Genius: Darwinian Perspectives on Creativity*. New York: Oxford University Press, (1999).

Singleton, Esther. "Was Edward de Vere Shakespeare? *Shakespeare Fellowship Newsletter* (American Branch). 1.4 (June/July 1940), 9-10.

Stritmatter, Roger A. "What's in a Name? Everything, Apparently . . .," *Rocky Mountain E-Review of Languages and Literature* 60.2 (2006), 37-49.

Warren, James A. "Oxfordian Theory, Continental Drift and the Importance of Methodology." *The Oxfordian* 17 (September 2015).

Waugh, Alexander, and Roger Stritmatter. *The New Shakespeare Allusion Book*. Forthcoming, 2017.

Letters

Dear Editor,

    I am writing in response to James Warren's article "The Use of State Power to Hide Edward de Vere's Authorship of the Works Attributed to 'William Shake-speare'" (*Brief Chronicles* VI [2015], 59-81).

    Warren's thesis is that "Those who controlled state power used it not only to destroy evidence of the Earl of Oxford's literary activities, but also to airbrush him from much of the historical record," and that "the only explanation weighty enough to account for the use of state power for that extraordinary purpose was Oxford's bodily involvement in the succession issue in some way—as described in the so-called Prince Tudor or Tudor Heir theories — an involvement that could have affected Queen Elizabeth's reputation and provided a possible challenge to the legitimacy of King James's reign."

    I find much to agree with in the article, but I cannot agree that the so-called "Prince Tudor" theory is the only possible explanation "weighty enough" to account for the use of State power to destroy the records of Oxford's authorship, or to "airbrush him from much of the historical record," as proposed. The article seeks to narrow the possibilities to that one alternative, and in my view it does not succeed. Rather, I think it succeeds only in making itself a classic example of the fallacy of limited alternatives. It doesn't even succeed in making a case that the Prince Tudor theory is one of the viable alternatives.

    Warren offers no direct evidence that state power *was* used to destroy records relating to Oxford, but he makes a strong circumstantial case that someone must have done so, and I am largely in agreement. It should be mentioned, though, that we have no idea how many records we are talking about, whether Oxford himself, or others, avoided putting anything in writing about his activities in the first place, or whether Oxford himself may have participated in, or supported, the destruction of any such evidence. We do know, as Warren points out, that he wrote in the Sonnets that he neither wanted, nor expected, to be remembered. So it doesn't sound like something imposed posthumously without his knowledge.

In arguing for the role of state power, Warren refers to "the large number of documents that resulted from Oxford's authorship of Shake-speare's works and his role in the creation of the public theater," but he never establishes that this is necessarily so. Oxford may have been so skilled at concealing his activities that he did not produce many documents. We know he worked through secretaries, such as John Lyly, who ran a company of boy actors for Oxford. There was a norm against noblemen being involved in such activities, so perhaps he gave instructions to others and did not get involved directly. At least one prominent Oxfordian believes that Oxford kept his authorship of the works secret from virtually everyone, and that no state power was involved, but in my view this is extremely unlikely.

My main disagreement is with the claim that the so-called "Prince Tudor" theory is the only possible explanation "weighty enough" to account for the hypothesized use of state power. Warren claims that removing Oxford from the record was necessary to establish and preserve King James I on the throne, but he never explains exactly why. In referring to "Prince Tudor/Tudor Heir theories," he implies that a secret Royal Bastard would have been eligible to assert a claim to the throne upon Elizabeth's death. I believe Thomas Regnier's article "Did Tudor Succession Law Permit Royal Bastards to Inherit the Crown?" (*Brief Chronicles IV*, 2012-13) demonstrates that a Royal Bastard could *not* inherit the throne.

Warren says of Oxford that "his existence threatened the purity of Queen Elizabeth's reputation and the legitimacy of King James' reign." How did the legitimacy of James's reign depend on Elizabeth's reputation? Elizabeth had executed James's mother, Mary, Queen of Scots, and James hated her for it. That is offered as a reason for his favorable treatment of Southampton and others who participated in the Essex Rebellion. If Southampton were a secret Tudor Royal Bastard, it would have been in James's interest to expose him as such to discredit Elizabeth, thereby enhancing his legitimacy as the King of England.

Monarchs don't often befriend potential rivals, as James did with Southampton. Rather, they typically have them killed, as the Tudors often did with those whom they perceived as potential threats to their rule. The fact that James befriended Southampton suggests that he did not regard him as a son of Elizabeth. If the objective was "to eliminate any potential challenges to King James's reign by direct descendants of Queen Elizabeth," and Southampton was a son of Oxford and Elizabeth, the logical thing to do was to knock off Southampton. Airbrushing Oxford out of the record did not eliminate the potential threat.

Warren gives no criteria for deciding what would be a "weighty enough" reason to warrant the use of state power to purge the record, so his view that only a PT-based explanation will suffice is subjective. In my view it is sufficient that (1) the plays were propaganda, intended to legitimize the Tudor regime and unite the country, (2) theaters and acting companies were part of the state-sponsored spy network, (3) the plays were political and it would have been embarrassing if it became known who wrote them, and (4) the powerful Cecils, in particular, would have wanted to conceal that Oxford had written them both for reasons of state (per 1-3) and because they disliked him and viewed him as an embarrassment.

In addition to the Cecils, Queen Elizabeth also had her own reasons to want to sanitize the records—something Warren never mentions. Elizabeth, not Lord Burghley (as is often claimed), was Oxford's legal guardian, owned his wardship, and exploited his earldom to benefit her favorite, Robert Dudley. Nina Green's article "The Fall of the House of Oxford" (*Brief Chronicles I*, 2009) documents in great detail that the Queen treated Oxford very badly and was chiefly responsible for his financial downfall. As the person most responsible for him, she had good reason to be concerned what the record showed. If she wanted it cleaned up, that would clearly be a "weighty enough" reason for the Cecils to see to it.

And there's something else Warren never mentions. In addition to saying in the Sonnets that he neither wanted, nor expected, his name to be remembered, Oxford said repeatedly that he was in some sort of disgrace, beyond recovery. He never explains exactly why, but his evident disgrace and outcast status is another possible explanation. I do not see that either of the so-called "Prince Tudor" theories would account for it. For that to be the case it would have to be widely known among his peers; but then it is hard to imagine why he would be in disgrace and not Queen Elizabeth. There must be something else.

Both John Hamill and Alexander Waugh have proposed credible explanations, based on the Sonnets, either of which could account for Oxford's outcast state and for the Cecils' wish to purge the records. Either of them seems to me to be "weighty enough," especially in the context of all the other reasons. Either theory strikes me as more plausible than the PT scenario that Warren claims is the only option. Oxfordians should not be railroaded into accepting the so-called "PT Theory" based on nothing more.

One minor point: Warren writes that Oxford "published two lengthy poems in 1593 and 1594 under the name William Shake-speare." No, it was spelled "Shakespeare" beneath the dedications to both *Venus and Adonis* and *Lucrece*. If we are going to criticize James Shapiro for incorrectly stating that the name was hyphenated when it first appeared, as we should, then we should get it right ourselves. I'm not a fan of hyphenating the name throughout articles, since it was hyphenated only 45% of the time on the works. Here's an example where the practice results in saying something that's incorrect.

John M. Shahan

Dear Editor,

    I am pleased that John Shahan found "much to agree with" in my article, including the idea that state power must have been used to hide Oxford's authorship of Shakespeare's works. Our views differ principally over the reasons why state power was used. As he explained, his "main disagreement is with the claim that the so-called 'Prince Tudor' theory is the only explanation 'weighty enough' to account for the hypothesized use of state power."

    Shahan believes that other explanations for the use of state power are more credible, and cited those proposed by John Hamill and Alexander Waugh. Although Shahan does not state what their ideas are or attempt to establish their validity, it should be noted that their explanations consist primarily of personal reasons for the use of state power. That is, those who controlled it used it to accomplish personal goals such as protecting their reputations.

    Like Shahan, I believe that the steps taken to hide Oxford's authorship began for personal reasons, a point I made in my article. Those holding state power believed that the connection between the literary works and the court had to be cut to assuage the feelings and protect the interests of those portrayed and ridiculed in them, and that the best way to do that was by cutting the connection between the works and Oxford.

    Then the Essex Rebellion changed everything.

    At the time of the Rebellion, the most pressing political issue was the question of who would succeed the 67-year old Elizabeth. The existence of a blood heir to the queen—the essence of the Prince Tudor theory—posed an enormous threat to James's ambitions. Southampton, if he was a direct descendant of the queen, would have had priority in succession over all non-direct descendants, including James, who was Elizabeth's half-nephew.

    Southampton's being sentenced to death for his role in the Rebellion gave Cecil and James the opening they needed to clear the path for James's succession. Southampton's life had been saved by someone, and the cornerstone of how that was done could only have been a deal. Although the details of the deal are not known precisely, the logic of the situation leads to the conclusion that Southampton's life was spared in return for his renouncing any claim to the throne and for Oxford's agreeing to bury his claim to authorship of "Shakespeare's" works.

    As a result of the deal, state power began to be used for two additional purposes: hiding Oxford's authorship not just from the current generation but also from future generations, and effacing Oxford himself from much of the historical record. It is at that point that Hamill's and Waugh's explanations begin to fall short.

They do not address the change in the purposes for which state power was used. The so-called Prince Tudor theory directly addresses that change, and that is why it is the only explanation I am aware of that is emotionally weighty enough to explain the new uses of state power. This is, perhaps, a subjective judgment—but subjective does not mean arbitrary. In the absence of direct evidence, a subjective weighing of the evidence that does exist, combined with an understanding of the circumstances in which events took place, is the most that can be hoped for.

Shahan tries to counter the significance of Southampton's being a blood descendant of the queen, if that was the case, by citing an article by Thomas Regnier as evidence that a Royal Bastard could not inherit the throne. Regnier's article notes that the 1571 change in the law only provided for allowing "discussion" of the queen's "natural issue," but did not in fact change the laws in place prohibiting a Royal Bastard from inheriting the throne. But laws could be changed to meet the political needs of the moment, a point Regnier recognized when he quoted Boris to the effect that "Succession was 'determined by politics more than law.'" That was indeed the case with Elizabeth Tudor, who became queen even though Parliament had twice declared her a bastard ineligible for succession.

Shahan also appears to misunderstand another important point. He states that James hated Elizabeth for having executed his mother, Mary, Queen of Scots, and that "If Southampton were a secret Tudor Royal Bastard, it would have been in James's interest to expose him to discredit Elizabeth." Well, no. Shahan's reasoning is faulty. James' top goal was to become king. Nothing could be allowed to get in the way of the attainment of that goal, not even his desire to exact revenge on Elizabeth by destroying her reputation as the Virgin Queen by outing Southampton as her son. Doing so would have opened up a can of worms with the potential to complicate the succession, and would have upset the deal that had already been brokered.

And there is another point where Shahan's reasoning does not seem quite right. He states that "Monarchs don't often befriend potential rivals, as James did with Southampton. Rather, they typically have them killed . . . The fact that James befriended Southampton suggests that he did not regard him as a son of Elizabeth. If the objective was 'to eliminate any potential challenges to King James' reign by direct descendants of Queen Elizabeth,' and [if] Southampton was a son of Oxford and Elizabeth, [then] the logical thing to do was to knock off Southampton."

Again, no. Shahan doesn't appear to recognize the likelihood that James's immediate goal after becoming king would have been to strengthen the legitimacy of his reign. He could not simply have had Southampton murdered because those of royal blood, if that was the case with Southampton, were not ordinary political rivals. They had to be handled carefully. That is why Elizabeth treated Mary so gingerly and held her for almost twenty years before executing her for treason. And besides, there was no reason to murder Southampton because the deal had already neutralized him. That deal had changed the reality of things for everyone, and everyone had to live with it whether they liked it or not. For James to renege on the deal would immediately have placed him at risk, and he had to know that. It is also significant that Southampton was never allowed to gain any genuine political power during James' reign.

We now come to a particularly important point. Shahan writes "And there's something else Warren never mentions. In addition to saying in the *Sonnets* that he neither wanted, nor expected, his name to be remembered, Oxford said repeatedly that he was in some sort of disgrace, beyond recovery. He [Oxford] never explains exactly why, but his evident disgrace and outcast status is another possible explanation. I do not see that either of the so-called 'Prince Tudor' theories would account for it. For that to be the case it would have to be widely known among his peers; but then it is hard to imagine why he would be in disgrace and not Queen Elizabeth. There must be something else."

Yes, there was something else causing disgrace and shame: Oxford's involvement in treason. He was not only probably the father of a man condemned to death for treason, but also probably involved to some degree in events surrounding the Essex Rebellion. Paul Hammer's *Shakespeare Quarterly* article ("Shakespeare's Richard II: The Play of 7 February 1601 and the Essex Rising," Vol. 59/1, Spring 2008) has settled the point about it being Shakespeare's *Richard II* that was performed on the eve of the Rebellion. It would not have been possible for that play to have been performed at that politically sensitive moment without Oxford's knowledge and authorization.

It is interesting that Shahan and I both hold the important yet still controversial belief that Shakespeare's *Sonnets* were not mere literary devices but instead portray the author's thoughts about important events in his life. It is because of what the *Sonnets* reveal about Southampton's parentage as explained by Hank Whittemore in *The Monument* that (1) the *Sonnets'* original sequence apparently was suppressed upon publication, continuing underground until the early eighteenth century; (2) the 1623 Folio failed to include the poems or sonnets or the dedications to Southampton or any mention of this single person whom Oxford had publicly linked to "Shakespeare"; and (3) the 1640 edition by John Benson, who was Ben Jonson's posthumous publisher, destroyed the original work as a coherent sequence. All this adds to the argument that Southampton is the central figure in the explanation for the expunging of Oxford.

Shahan has, through the work of the Shakespeare Authorship Coalition that he founded, done as much as anyone alive today to increase awareness of the weakness of the evidence supporting Shakspere's authorship of Shakespeare's works. But his understanding of the reasons for the use of state power to hide Oxford's authorship is not quite as fully developed as his understanding of the weakness of the Stratfordian claim.

James A. Warren

Designed at The Snail's Head
Press.
Baltimore, MD.
Where the design meets the mind.

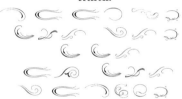

On our cover, "Danse de figures grotesques" (c. 1520) is by the Augsburg engraver Daniel Hopfer (1470-1536), who is widely believed to be the first artist to use etching in printmaking. Originally an armorer and goldsmith, Hopfer translated the techniques used in etching metal to apply them to print. In 1590 he was, Wikipedia reports, named as the inventor of etching in an imperial patent bestowed on his grandson Georg, who had carried on a family tradition then in its third generation. Albrecht Durer's "Peasant Couple Dancing" (c. 1514) carries the tune on p. i, and Sebald Beham's "The Wedding Procession" (overleaf) concludes the volume.

Made in the USA
Columbia, SC
08 October 2020